The Order of God

The Order of God

Renewing the Doctrine of God
for the Twenty-First-Century Christians

Aaron Yom

WIPF & STOCK · Eugene, Oregon

THE ORDER OF GOD
Renewing the Doctrine of God for Twenty-First-Century Christians

Copyright © 2018 Author Name. All rights reserved. Except for brief quotations in critical publications or reviews, no part of this book may be reproduced in any manner without prior written permission from the publisher. Write: Permissions, Wipf and Stock Publishers, 199 W. 8th Ave., Suite 3, Eugene, OR 97401.

Wipf & Stock
An Imprint of Wipf and Stock Publishers
199 W. 8th Ave., Suite 3
Eugene, OR 97401

www.wipfandstock.com

PAPERBACK ISBN: 978-1-5326-5789-4
HARDCOVER ISBN: 978-1-5326-5790-0
EBOOK ISBN: 978-1-5326-5791-7

Manufactured in the U.S.A. 10/11/18

I dedicate this book to Dr. Peter Gräbe.

Contents

Preface   ix
Abbreviations   xi

Introduction   1

Chapter 1
Setting the Stage: From Nature's Order to God's Order   6

Chapter 2
The Prius of God's Ontological Order   42

Chapter 3
God's Order of Communication and Its Relationship to the Unthematic Dimension of Human Existence   81

Chapter 4
God's Order of Pathos   116

Epilogue   157

Bibliography   165

Preface

I HAD PLANNED TO write a book on Christology, fleshing out the details of the God-man nature of Jesus Christ based on the principle of identity and duality. After working on the project for a few years, I realized that the principle of identity and duality stems from the doctrine of the Trinity, and I had no choice but to back paddle and revisit some of the methodological and pneumatological aspects of the doctrine of God. So, I ended up writing two books, one for the doctrine of the God and another Christology. The former is titled *The Order of God* and the latter *God in Our Likeness*. I am hoping to publish the second book shortly after this one.

I wrote this book to clarify and define the order of God such as God's ontological order and his unthematic dimension of communication, as well as its cognate themes, such as the order of nature and the order of salvation. In doing so, I was hoping to recover the neglected order of God by critically examining old paradigms as well as new theological developments. The book builds on the earlier work of contemporary scholars such as Karl Barth, Thomas Torrance, Karl Rahner, David Coffey, Stanley Grenz, Jürgen Moltmann, and Clark Pinnock, as well as patristic and medieval scholars, like Augustine and Aquinas, but it takes the themes of systematic theology further, coordinating and refining previous conclusions, especially from a pneumatological perspective.

What I have in mind is a theological exposure to the dangers of arguing from the order of nature without understanding the proper order of God's ontology as some of the interlocutors in this book have done. Thus, I have organized the book around the main thesis—i.e., there exists a unique form of God's order that cannot simply be read off from the order of nature or the order of culture.

I hope that my theological analysis that unpacks God's own logic, principles, and ontological status can help the readers and students navigate through the rough waters of contemporary theology. As I am reminded by

Prof. Clark Pinnock, Christian theology is in a state of great confusion, and inadvertently, it has created a great labyrinthian maze that defies tracking. I pray that this book can be a useful theological roadmap for those bold travelers exploring the world of theology today.

Abbreviations

JAAR Journal of the American Academy of Religion

TS Theological Studies

PT Philosophy and Theology

JECS Journal of Early Christian Studies

IJST International Journal of Systematic Theology

SJT Scottish Journal of Theology

NZSTR Neue Zeitschrift für Systematische Theologie und Religionsphilosophie

PRS Perspectives in Religious Studies

AJTP American Journal of Theology and Philosophy

NIV New International Version

Introduction

THIS STUDY IS ABOUT the pursuit of God's order. Searching for God's order is not new. Christians have been searching for God's order for centuries. One of the earliest attempts to define God's order is the formulation of the trinitarian order of God. In the patristic period, much ink was spilled to outline the trinitarian relationship of God. How can the three distinct persons of the Godhead be one? Are three persons of the Godhead equal in power and authority? What is the precise order of the trinitarian relationship? The patristic writers were preoccupied with these questions and more like them. Although the Bible gave them the necessary language to speak about the trinitarian order like the baptismal formula (Matt 28:19) or the principle of Spirit baptism (Acts 2:32), early Christian writers had to rely on Hellenic philosophy to address these questions. The difficulty of unpacking God's order could not have been accomplished by merely reading the biblical order about how the believers were baptized. They had to dig deeper into the realm of philosophy through which they could articulate the specifics of God's order such as the order of his being and the order of his communication. Conveniently, these ideas of God's order were already available through Platonic philosophy. So, the patristic writers such as Origen, Tertullian, the Cappadocian Fathers, and Augustine freely engaged different aspects of Platonism to unpack the true nature of God's order.

As time progressed, the pursuit of God's order became more and more rational and systematic. Perhaps this tendency is also of Hellenic thinking. In the ancient Greco-Roman world, the general tenor of philosophy is that the pattern of nature reveals the order of our own existence as well as God,[1] so that the attainment of order became the source of not only the life of well-being and intelligence, but also the understanding of the true nature of

1. Jaegar, *Padeia*, xiii–xxviii.

God. Christians gradually accepted this belief and began to organize their thoughts and actions in a systematic and well-ordered way, by which they could configure God's order more clearly and distinctively. This is evident in the early part of the medieval period. For instance, the medieval Victorines, like Hugh of St. Victor, were drenched in the world of order and beauty.[2] They saw that the exterior life of nature had profound impact on the inner spiritual life that communes with God. Especially for Hugh of St. Victor, it was imperative to pursue all knowledge based on the life of spiritual discipline. Knowledge and spirituality could never be separated for him. Likewise, the emphasis on well-disciplined spiritual life coupled with rational illumination became the major theme of Christian scholars until the advent of modernism.

Modernism is normally associated with the "Copernican Revolution." The Copernican Revolution signifies the discovery of a new center of our world. In ancient society, the center of the universe was Earth. However, with new scientific discoveries, the old Ptolemaic view of geocentricism was overthrown, and as a result, the heliocentric model of Copernicus took its place. We now know that the Earth is not the center of the universe, let alone our solar system. Similarly, an epistemological revolution gained full force at this time. Thanks to Kant, the order of being was supplanted by the order of the knower. This modern reconstructionism is often referred to as the Kantian Revolution.[3] Kant's contribution was huge in this regard, though he was not the only person to suggest that our knowledge depends on our own subjective grid. After Kant, a new center was located. It is none other than the subject that superseded the object. In the wake of modernism, nothing bypasses the subject. It is the subject that became the ordering center. With it came the responsibility to re-order not only ourselves but also God.

In the premodern era, the order that people saw in nature, or in themselves, was believed to be the reflection of God's orderliness. In this view, all orders were accepted as given. They were the objects of faithful reception. This meant that Christians had to understand God before they could understand themselves, and for this reason, they continued to seek after God's laws, principles, and logic. So, in the pre-modern period it is safe to say that they were God-dependent. However, the opposite is true for the modern period. In the modern world, rather than finding the center in God, people

---

2. Coolman, *Hugh of St. Victor*, 3–10.
3. Berry, "The Kantian Revolution," 43–53.

INTRODUCTION

found the center in themselves. The old theocentric order was displaced and the new order of self-sufficient manhood took the center stage.[4]

In the self-sufficient world, the subject is the reigning champion. Whether we see the world through the well-ordered reason or the well-ordered feeling, the subject determines the rules and the rest of the categories in this world, including God, had to abide by its rules. Such a dramatic change indeed deserves to be called a revolution. It has brought an historic change in the way we view the world. The world is no longer dependent on God. Rather, the predominant idea of modernism is that the world operates based on its own inner purpose. It functions according to its own rules and regulations without the need for divine intervention. Consequently, the chief achievement of the Enlightenment is the severing of the laws of nature from the order of God. For instance, modern scholars like Baruch Spinoza and Pierre-Simon Laplace systematically attacked supernatural things and surgically removed them out of nature, and in their place, they erected a self-perpetuating cosmos so that the natural laws and phenomena could be described in terms of the natural processes alone.

Theology followed suit. Theology in the modern period began to lay the patterns of God not by what God has revealed himself to be but by the order we seem fit for God. Even if revelation was recognized as the primary data for theology, nonetheless it was at the mercy of the interpreter who had the right to judge the value and usefulness of God's revelation. In many cases, in the court of biblical and theological interpreters, the central pillar of God's revelation, such as Jesus' resurrection, was dismissed or reinterpreted as a symbol for human existential situations.[5] Systematically, God's order was replaced by the order of nature and our own order of rationality. As a result, the miraculous and supernatural elements of theology gave way to the naturalistic and positivistic view of the world. This shift in theology eventually led to the point where God's order became unrecognizable, for it has turned into the order of nature.[6]

---

4. My assessment of modernism follows the work of Stanley Grenz and Roger Olson. According to Grenz and Olson, although pre-modernism or modernism is a complex intellectual movement that eludes any sweeping generalization, from a theological perspective, we can conclude that there was a shift from the theocentric focus to the anthropocentric emphasis. For more details, see Grenz and Olson, *20th-Century Theology*, 15–23.

5. Rudolph Bultmann's work is a good example. See Bultmann, *New Testament and Mythology*, 45–59.

6. Spinoza, *Theological-Political Treatise*, 81–96.

In the postmodern world, the situation has not improved much. Even with the renewed effort to recover religious language and symbols of the past, the postmodern emphasis is on what God does for us rather than who God is in himself. It is God's immanence that has become the locus of postmodern theology. The fallout from giving the privilege position to God's immanence is that, once again, God is intermingled with the process of nature in such a way that God's history is transformed into the history of nature or the history of culture. Even with the promotion of God's transcendence, a way back to God himself is not guaranteed, for the concept of "transcendence" is often fleshed out from our own philosophical perspective.

In this context, the aim of this study is to recover and renew the order of God.[7] This task cannot be accomplished simply by going back to the past and re-appropriating the theological contents of the premodern world. We have come too far. The pursuit of God's order must be done critically examining new theological developments as well as old paradigms. Moreover, because the old and new theologies carry their own shortcomings, we simply cannot borrow the old for the sake of remodeling the new, and vice versa. We need to rigorously assess the viability of both the old and the new. For this purpose, I draw upon a holistic pneumatological vision of God. The pneumatological vision of God provides for this study its substance as well as presupposition, for it crosses the paths of the old and new theological programs without marginalizing one at the expense of the other. In so doing, I look for the lost pieces of God's order so that God is clearly distinguished from the order of nature all the while locating the area of consonance between the two.

Consequently, I argue throughout the book that there exists a unique system of God's order that cannot simply be read off from the order of nature, although we may rely on natural analogy to discern God's order. To move beyond the postmodern impasse, I show that the proper understanding of God's order must be worked out from the vantage point of God's own logic, principles, and ontological status. My primary aim is to identify the

---

7. I acknowledge some pioneering works in this field of study, though their focus is different than mine. Keith Ward's *The Christian Idea of God*, Vern S. Poythress' *Logic: A God-Centered Approach to the Foundation of Western Thought*, Alister E. McGrath's *The Order of Things*, Stephen T. Davis' *Logic and the Nature of God*, Ronald H. Nash's *The Concept of God*, and lastly but most importantly, Thomas F. Torrance's *Divine and Contingent Order*.

key features of God's own logic, principles, and ontological status in this book. For this task, I divide the book into four related chapters.

In the first chapter, I discuss the relationship between God's order and the order of nature to set the stage for re-appropriating the order of God. Without seeing the asymmetrical relationship between God's order and created order, we cannot take the next step in identifying the salient features of God's order. Also, in this chapter, despite the difference between God's order and nature's order, contra Karl Barth, I point out the commensurability between the two systems, and based on this discussion, I provide the epistemic justification for reading God's order from nature rationally and analogically.

I plunge into the heart of the matter in the second chapter and fully unpack God's ontological order. In fact, I argue for the *prius* of God's ontological order. My intention here is to show that God's order moves from God's ontology to God's economy-for-us though our knowledge of God is reliant upon God's revealed economy in this world. In this way, we can clearly identify God's addenda—e.g., the things that he has taken upon himself in his mingling with us, which do not belong to God himself intrinsically.

In the third chapter, I analyze God's order of communication to apply what we have discussed thus far. Based on my critical analysis of David Coffey, Karl Rahner, and Stanley Grenz, I come up with my own view of God's order of self-communication. I name it a "dual core theory." This theory recognizes God's order of communication that starts from the unthematic dimension of our being to the conscious action that cooperates with God. It also highlights God's unthematic communication that involves God's offer of grace that counters our sinful nature.

In the final chapter, I tie the loose ends and drive home my point, highlighting the importance of reading God's order on its own terms as I discuss the order of God's pathos. Here, I unveil the errors of reading indiscriminately God's order from God's involvement with the world. My goal in this chapter is to rethink the order of God's pathos and claim that we can preserve God's own logic, and at the same time, talk about God's pain and suffering for us. For this reason, I counter Jürgen Moltmann and Clark Pinnock, arguing that they have dismissed God's ontological order for the sake of keeping God's order of passibility.

Chapter 1

Setting the Stage: From Nature's Order to God's Order

CAN WE DISCERN GOD'S order from nature? If so, how should we approach God's order from nature? Should we adopt a formalist, realist, historical, or transcendental approach? These are the questions I will be addressing in this chapter. My claim is that nature as God's creation reveals the order of God though analogically and implicitly. So, for me, the starting point of the theological discussion of God's order must begin with nature. This does not mean that I am arguing for a Spinozian uniformity principle of order. Spinoza equated the immutable laws of nature to God's immutable order of his being.[1] For him, God's order was nature's order, and vice versa. This is an explicit endorsement of pantheism. We cannot commit the same error by confusing nature's order and God's order as a non-divided whole. What we need to understand is that nature's order is not God's order.

Likewise, we cannot run the same scenario of reducing God's order to nature's order, like Ernst Troeltsch's principle of analogy.[2] Troeltsch had argued for the homogeneity of history, and with this principle, he demonstrated that there is no such thing as supernatural causality. His argument goes like this: because the miracle of resurrection is not taking place today, it did not take place in the past. Troeltsch's claim is based on naturalistic history, in which the mechanism of nature is the measuring rod for all other events in history, including divine history. So, like many naturalistic scholars, he simply dismissed the order of God's miracle.

1. Spinoza, *Theological-Political Treatise*, 81–83.
2. For more details, see Echol, *Ernst Troeltsch*, 62–66.

As a corrective to these approaches, and at the same time, to find a way to God from nature without undervaluing God's ontological order, I demonstrate in this chapter that God's order in nature is distinguishable and yet consonant with nature's order. To accomplish this task, I begin with the discussion of natural theology, or more specifically, with a question, "is natural theology possible?" Karl Barth did not think so, and I disagree with him, though I understand why natural theology can be deleterious to Christianity. So, I critically review Barth's disclaim of natural theology and argue that, to a certain extent, natural analogues can be functionally useful to point out God's order from nature. In fact, I show that natural theology is the basic building block for discerning God's order "for us," which is a necessary ingredient for discerning God's order in himself. I also claim that natural order is the propitious ground upon which God's order of salvation is manifested.

What follows then is a three-step presentation. The first part deals with Barth's dismissal of natural theology. I highlight his key arguments against natural theology. Based on the first analysis, the second part concentrates on the shortcomings of Barth's arguments. Here, I try to show that Barth's view of nature is too narrow and misleading. Lastly, I present my own view of the principle of analogy that cautiously acknowledges nature's order as a viable option for conceptualizing God's order "for us."

Is Natural Theology Possible?

As I have said before, to discuss about the possibility of natural theology, we need to dialogue with Barth, who has put forth a unique argument against natural theology. My interaction with Barth identifies the key features of natural theology, and at the same time, its shortcomings so that I can clarify the usefulness of natural theology in unveiling God's order. Of course, I do not accept Barth's strong denial of natural theology wholeheartedly, but nonetheless, I take his criticism seriously, for we have been reading too much of nature into God. Like Barth, I see this trend to be the greatest ill of modern theology. As a way to correct modern theological deficiencies, I turn to Barth's celebrated criticism against natural theology.

Barth's Misapprehensions

Barth's theological scope is wide and broad. In addition, his theology is known to invoke controversy and dispute, which are too numerous to number. For this reason, Barth's analysis on natural theology is kept within a specific premise here, relying on primarily selected writings from *Church Dogmatics*, where he provides workable data for us to think about the ontological order of God. This analysis for sure is not the last word describing what Barth was trying to say about natural theology, but nonetheless, it is an honest attempt to clarify and take advantage of Barth's work, all the while critically engaging his thought from a pneumatological perspective.

Reading Barth's *Church Dogmatics*, we can undoubtedly encounter his persistent argument against natural theology. In almost every corner of his theological presentation, the voice against natural theology is easily heard. Actually, it balances well with his christocentric paradigm. While the christocentric vision takes the central spot as the positive development of his theology, an attempt to defy all forms of natural theology is equally forceful as a negative form of his theology. So, Barth's Christology as the positive reinforcement of Christian theology is balanced with the negative side of his theology, namely, his aversion toward natural theology. In this respect, although Barth's negation of natural theology has been reviewed from many different perspectives, I prefer to work with a comparative approach, playing it off against Barth's Christology. What better way is there than to compare two extreme poles of Barth's theology? Let me begin with a christological analysis.

As Marc Cortez notes, Barth is rightfully called a christocentric theologian.[3] If we compare Barth's theology to a wheel, Jesus Christ is the hub and the remaining theological categories are the spokes that are attached to it. Even if we say that Barth's chief theological category is revelation, it too is driven by Christology, for he believes that God reveals himself in and through Jesus Christ. In my judgment, this is a telltale sign that Barth has fallen into a theological particularism. For Barth, Jesus Christ differentiates us from the rest. Jesus Christ makes us unique. It is where we find our theological niche. We cannot blame Barth for taking this stance, since the Bible itself attests to the particularity of Christian faith. John 14:6 specifically denotes that Jesus "is the way and the truth and the life," and "no one comes to the Father except through [him]." All is good, but Barth has taken

---

3. Cortez, *Embodied Souls, Ensouled Bodies*, 17.

this particularism to its limit and created a theological expanse that is excessively filled with christocentrism. I list a few examples.

First, Barth differentiates what is unreal from what is real based on his christocentric focus. For instance, Barth's anthropology is unique in the sense that our existence is not defined by the study of biology but the study of Jesus Christ. For Barth, the study of evolutionary biology only details the *phenomena* of human beings. It does not explain the *essence* of humanity.[4] Like Kant's differentiation of phenomena and noumena, Barth's christological viewpoint makes the difference between the phenomena of humanity and the essence of human beings. However, what we need to note is that Barth's theological move turns the post-Kantian paradigm on its head. In the post-Kantian era, especially for those who have associated with phenomenology, the world of phenomena has been understood as real and the rest such as metaphysics and theology were cast in the dungeon of irrelevance. Taking a starkly different turn, Barth states otherwise. It is our dependence on phenomena that leads to philosophical and theological abstractions. The concreteness and essence of human nature is disclosed only through Jesus Christ.

Essentially, Barth is making a theological statement, bypassing a scientific description of humanity. He does not believe that theological issues can be resolved by the interjection of science.[5] For him, human nature is fully revealed only when we understand that we are under the bondage of sin. What is sin? Again, Barth's definition is simple. It is christocentric. Sin is unbelief. It is a rejection of Jesus Christ. He writes, "Man's sin is unbelief in the God who was 'in Christ reconciling the world to himself,' who in Him elected and loved man from all eternity, who in Him created him, whose word to man from and to all eternity was and will be Jesus Christ."[6] What this means for Barth is that, if we remove Jesus Christ out of the anthropological equation, all that remains is sin. The final telos of sinful humanity is non-existence, or nothingness. In other words, without Christ, we lose our existence, because our existence can only be confirmed and sustained by God through Jesus Christ. Sin in this sense is "impossible pos-

---

4. Barth notes that evolutionary biology "can offer us only modest, i.e., limited, conditioned and relative certainty, and definitely not the certainty which life demands of us as human beings." Cited from Hunsinger, "Barth on What It Means to Be Human," 145.

5. Barth notes, "That there can be no scientific problems, objections or aids in relation to what Holy Scripture and the Christian Church understand by the divine work of creation." Barth, *Church Dogmatics* 3/1, xi.

6. Barth, *Church Dogmatics* 4/1, 415.

sibility." There are two sides to this order. On the one hand, our existence is meaningless because of sinfulness, and on the other hand, our existence cannot be meaningless because of Jesus Christ.

As a second example of Barth's christological unconventionalism, I mention his emphasis on a clear and unbridgeable gap between true and abstract history. For him, true history is salvation history. To be more explicit, Barth points to the history that was decisively enacted by Jesus Christ. For this reason, he regards non-christological history as meaningless. It is meaningless because history is arbitrarily determined by "human pre-decisions, and human affirmation of this or that historical possibility."[7] What he wants to say is that, if we allow human decisions to determine the real essence of history, "there is no encounter with God decisively intervening from outside or above, and demanding faith as man's final decision to obey."[8] So, as Rodney Holder affirms, Barth does not allow non-christological historical studies to prove or disprove biblical claims. According to Barth, no historical evidence will suffice to prove the christological event such as Jesus' resurrection. In the end, he cordons off salvation history from the encroachment of historical science. Why is he so harsh against the intrusion of science?

We can go back to Barth's undervaluing of the phenomena aspect of science. For him, science is the study of human activities seen from a human perspective. So, in Barth's point of view, it is an abstract and arbitrary form of explanation. It does not answer what is real. Where can we find the answer to what is real? He points to Jesus Christ. Barth asserts that "Jesus Christ is the Word by which the knowledge of creation is mediated to us because He is the Word by which God has fulfilled creation."[9] Thus, if science is to be true to the essence of things, it must study it from a faith perspective. Without faith in Jesus Christ, we cannot know what is real, at least, from Barth's point of view.

My brief interlude regarding Barth's reaction against science here is to accentuate his incessant effort to promote Christology as the real and true science as opposed to an abstraction and arbitrariness of human science. What I detect from Barth's writings is that he has been troubled by modern scholars who indiscreetly removed miraculous elements from theology,

---

7. Barth, "Lessing," 248.
8. Barth, "Lessing," 248.
9. Barth, *Church Dogmatics* 3/1, 28.

replacing and reinterpreting them in the light of scientific rationalism.[10] Barth's acerbic criticism against theological liberalism, which embraced modernism with unrelenting zeal, is a natural outcome of his rejection of science. If science has no place for divine miracles, what other alternative is there? It is obvious for Barth that Jesus Christ is either put aside or turned into something that is not him.

Lastly, Barth's christological particularism is all the more reinforced by his refutation of transcendentalism. Barth's reaction against spiritualism is a good example. He writes,

> But if by devotion we mean an exercise in the cultivation of the soul or spirit, i.e., the attempt to intensify and deepen ourselves, to purify and cleanse ourselves inwardly, to attain clarify and self-control, and finally to set ourselves on a good footing and in agreement with the deity by this preparation, then it is high time we realized that not merely have we not even begun to pray or prepared ourselves for prayer, but that we actually turned away from what is commanded us as prayer.[11]

Barth is reacting negatively against spiritual practices that may elevate human spirituality to a divine-like status. For him, this is nothing but a futile attempt on our part to transcend the limits of our being, which in Barth's view, is impossible. Whether the transcendental channel may be our morality, self-negation, or being open to greater things, they can never serve as the true Archimedean point of reference. In this regard, George Hunsinger writes,

> What spirituality and virtue both seem to have in common, in other words, is that they both in one way or another understand salvation to have a constitutive, innate, and therefore independent basis within us (whether it be reflected by way of spiritual preparation or spiritual acquisition), apart from the miracle of grace which, both ontically and noetically, takes us beyond our innate capacities.[12]

Hunsinger's assessment is quite revealing of Barth's attitude toward the idea of self-transcendence, that is, Barth's uncompromising claim that

---

10. For a list of Christian scholars who adhere to so-called the scientific method (e.g., the historical-critical method driven by naturalistic outlook) in interpreting the Bible, see Matera, "New Testament Theology," 1–21.

11. Barth, *Church Dogmatics 3/4*, 97.

12. Hunsinger, *How to Read Karl Barth*, 140.

we cannot move beyond our limitations without Christ. For Barth, we can only move out of our sphere by the in-breaking of grace. So, there is only the disruption of grace, which Barth often calls it a miracle. It is a miracle since nothing in this world can transpire the Christ-event. God had to come to us and reveal himself in and through Jesus Christ. Otherwise, we would have never known God's work of salvation and his love that never fails.

From this assessment, it is clear that Barth rejects any attempt for us to build theology based on the knowledge of nature or ourselves. It is because, for Barth, without God's self-revelation in and through Jesus Christ as attested by the Bible, we will not be able to discern anything about God. According to Barth, "natural theology is the doctrine of a union of man with God existing outside God's revelation in Jesus Christ."[13] In other words, natural theology is an attempt to see things without God, or more drastically, it is a reflection of our own image. So, Barth's assessment of natural theology is closely linked to Ludwig Feuerbach's assessment of religion, namely, a conception of God as the projection of our own image. In fact, Barth's position is more extreme since he claims that our natural path leads to nothingness—e.g., there is nothing substantial for us to know without Christ. All knowledge minus Christ means no knowledge at all. As far as Barth is concerned, Christ-less knowledge leads to a meaningless abstraction without any regard for what is real. Reality is affirmed and confirmed only in Jesus Christ. This is Barth's acknowledgement of the impossibility of natural theology.

From a christological point of view, Barth's aversion toward natural theology is understandable. Even with a quick survey of the modern era, we can see that the miracles of Jesus Christ had been undermined by theological liberalism propelled by multiple factors such as Hegelian idealism, Heideggerian existentialism, post-Kantian phenomenology, and scientific naturalism, such as the theory of evolution. Barth's rejection of natural theology was intended to regain the lost force of Christology and counter scientific reductionism, which was overwhelming the theological arena. This is well attested by Barth's remark. "Even if we only lend our little finger to natural theology, there necessarily follows the denial of the revelation of God in Jesus Christ."[14] However, in my opinion, Barth has swung his theological pendulum too wide to the side of Christology. Although Barth is right to say that we cannot know God without Christ, it does not give him

---

13. Barth, *Church Dogmatics* 2/1, 163.
14. Barth, *Church Dogmatics* 2/1, 173.

the license to do away with the knowledge of nature, which is so essential in the way we discern God's order. Consequently, I cannot accept Barth's rationale for completely rejecting natural theology. In his argument for the impossibility of natural theology, he has missed the usefulness of natural theology. Thus, at this point, I address Barth's concerns and show the inadequacies of his argument.

Countering Barth's Claim

Contra Barth, I find natural theology to be a valuable source for today's theology. Although it cannot sustain theology on its own, nonetheless I believe that it can function as a handmaid to revealed theology. As a supplement to what God has revealed to us in and through Jesus Christ, our study of nature, as an intellectual discipline in its own right, could potentially lead us to the knowledge of not only God's creative order but also God's ordering of his inner life. What I am proposing is to see that there are both continuity and discontinuity between natural knowledge and revealed knowledge. Following Barth, if we wholeheartedly dismiss natural knowledge at the expense of christological faith, only focusing on the dissonance between the two, we would lose not only the vast spectrum of human historical events, but also the considerable amount of data built up by modern scientific discoveries. This is one of the reasons why Robert C. Neville rejects Barth's theological paradigm as the basis for his own theology of nature.[15] For him, Barth's theology became unnecessarily isolated from the world and lost the relevance "to culture and to the religious dimensions of individual's investments in culture."[16]

Although I do not think that Barth's theology is entirely irrelevant to our scientific culture, my complaint against Barth is that he has neglected the usefulness of natural theology. Granted that natural theology falls short of the glory of God and perhaps veils the true nature of God due to the limitation of nature and the "fallible man"[17] always missing the mark, I still

---

15. Neville, "Naturalism and Supernaturalism," 77–84. Of course, Neville is not alone. Barth's christocentric particularism has pushed Christian scholars away from neo-Orthodoxy to its opposite direction. To name a few, we have Wolfhart Pannenberg, Jürgen Moltmann, and Karl Rahner. They all attempted to make revelation relevant to our culture as they take into consideration our understanding of nature as the viable data for constructing theology proper.

16. Neville, "Naturalism and Supernaturalism," 79.

17. Ricoeur, *Fallible Man*, 1–6. Ricoeur unpacks philosophically the "pathétique" of

believe that nature reveals God because creation is where God's grace indwells. This is my thesis. I am firmly convicted that nature, like humanity, has been endowed with God's order, that is, the order of intelligibility and grace. John Calvin affirmed it. McGrath writes in this regard, "Calvin is arguing that anyone, by intelligent and rational reflection upon the created order, should be able to arrive at the idea of God . . . The created order is a 'theater' (I.v.5) or a 'mirror' (I.v.II) for the displaying of the divine presence, nature, and attributes."[18] Calvin recognized that despite our fallenness a *sensus divinitatis* is still alive and well, not because we have this innate capability as a pre-condition of man, but because of God's unceasing outpouring of grace. Pneumatologically, this is attested by the Spirit being poured out upon all flesh (Acts 2:17) and renewing the face of the earth (Ps 104:30).

With this in mind, I counter Barth's claim of the impossibility of natural theology and show that natural theology is potentially useful only if we cautiously tame it in the service of clarifying and reinforcing the redemptive-transformative activities of God. For this purpose, I cover three main areas of Barth's rationale for rejecting natural theology, which has been highlighted in the previous analysis: the dichotomy of what is formal and what is real, the problem of history, and the problem of transcendence. I omit his discussion of sin because I will cover this topic in detail later in chapter 3.

Barth's Dichotomy of What Is Formal and What Is Real

I start with Barth's problematic dichotomization of what is formal and what is real. Barth's dismissive attitude toward what is formal for the sake of preserving what is real is problematic to both theology and science. There are two issues connected to this claim: the utility of the formal system and the description of realism. I cover each of these two topics respectively, as I dialogue with a Barthian scholar, Thomas F. Torrance. Like Barth, Torrance treats natural theology as a formal aspect of theology, whereas revealed theology the true and real aspect of theology. Although I do not agree with either Barth or Torrance on this point,[19] Torrance nonetheless is helpful

---

human nature. How can we disagree with his claim that "man is by nature fragile and liable to err"?

18. McGrath, *A Scientific Theology*, 274.

19. Strictly speaking, we cannot say that natural theology is a formal theological system. As Torrance has pointed out, every science has its own ontological status. Each

here because he has found a way to respect the utilitarian side of the formal system all the while avoiding the dangers of natural theology.

Concerning the utility of the formal system, Torrance asserts that it has a heuristic potency despite its abstract qualities. He highlights this point by referring to mathematics. He explains, "[The formal system] appears to have an aesthetic and speculative value in itself, for the sheer beauty of internal consistency which it idealizes, like that of pure mathematics, can apparently enhance scientific vision and guide speculation."[20] Immediately, we can see here that Torrance is recognizing the value of a formal system like pure mathematics, which is operated based on a coherent system of "abstract" logic. He knows that without it science cannot see the "big picture" and discover general rules and principles that undergird the natural processes—Torrance has in mind Einstein's theory of relativity.

Going further, Torrance notes that a formal system of thought has the potential to make our ideas "clear and precise" all the while functioning as a guide for empirical determination. He states that

> the particular value of modern logic is that in a computer-like way it enables us to formulate very complex statements and to perform feats of elaborate and sophisticated deduction which we would not be capable of otherwise, just as the casting of scientific results into a mathematical notation may not only give them consistency, making them precise and clear, but, as it were, do some difficult thinking for us by unfolding the implications of our scientific work beyond what we could determine with our empirical statements alone.[21]

This is Torrance's way of acknowledging the value of theoretical ponderings. In science, theory-making activities and hypothetical calculations play a crucial retroductive role, and Torrance knows this because he is a well-informed scientist as well as a working theologian.[22] If this is true, is

---

science deals with its own reality. Henceforth, natural analogy we glean from the study of different sciences cannot simply be an abstraction. Rather, we have to recognize that natural science has an ontological value of its own as it refers to the reality of nature. However, we should at the same time realize that natural theology can turn into a meaningless abstraction if it simply reduces the miraculous and supernatural elements in the Bible to what is natural.

20. Torrance, *Theological Science*, 250.
21. Torrance, *Theological Science*, 250.
22. Albert Einstein's theory-making process is a good example. At the initial stage of Einstein's study, he could not afford to duplicate his theory in a real-world laboratory

Torrance ignoring Barth's warning and siding with abstract science? He is not.

Like Barth, Torrance is aware of the danger of working with abstract systems of thought. The danger is noted this way. "Once we start freely generating formal possibilities in total disregard of our intuitive or empirical contact with the world of actuality we are bound not only to develop artificial patterns of thought that are incompatible with the real world but to give rise to serious discrepancies bringing our thought into conflict with it."[23] Certainly, Torrance is cautious of the use of scientific abstractions; however, he nonetheless accepts it as a complementary tool that can help us think clearly and holistically as long as we tied it down to the reality in question. Torrance likens it to a semantic use of language.[24] Language is conceptually detached from the world as we use it in a meta-linguistic way, and only when we trace its referential source can we see that it is tied to a reality. If it is not, then the language has lost its referential value and the meaning of language is marginalized.

Concerning the identification of realism, Torrance adheres to a broader form of realism than Barth. For Barth, only Jesus Christ and what is relevant to the Christ-event are considered real. The rest remains in the world of abstractions or phenomena. However, for Torrance, natural sciences do really deal with reality. In fact, since formal logic and real events work in tandem in the development of scientific theories, Torrance locates a similar realism at play between theology and science—McGrath calls it "critical realism."[25] He thinks that there is "a scientific way of acting and

---

setting, so he chased after the physical properties such as light and ether through thought experiments. He published his theory backed by mathematical and scientific-theoretical manipulations in 1915. It was never the result of his "lab" work. His theory was tested years after the publication. So, Einstein's theory of relativity had been detached from the world in the beginning stage of a theory-making activity but reattached to it later as it was verified by the actual process of nature. For more details on the Einstein's thought experiments, see Weinstein, *Einstein's Pathway*, 112–202. There is a controversy as to the nature of Einstein's so called "thought experiments." For a more precise scientific language, some scholars prefer to call them "conjectures" since Einstein did not simply imagine things in his head but made a well-informed intellectual inference about his theory from studying the natural phenomena. So I would use a more nuanced term "conjecture" in a formal scientific discussion, but for our purpose, the term "thought experiment" serves us well.

23. Torrance, *Theological Science*, 251.

24. Torrance, *Theological Science*, 261–2.

25. McGrath, *Scientific Theology*, 204–40.

thinking which is to be pursued in every field of learning and discovery."[26] What is this universal science? Torrance writes,

> This is the way of acting and thinking that is no more and no less than the rigorous extension of our basic rationality, as we seek to act toward things in ways appropriate to their natures, to understand them through letting them shine in their own light, and to reduce our thinking of them into orderly forms on the presumption of their inherent intelligibility.[27]

This implies that all scientific activities including theology are "essentially open and flexible through fidelity to the manifold character of reality and is therefore universally applicable, but as such it is the antithesis of the paranoiac rigidity manifest in every form of 'scientism.'"[28] Scientism here refers to scientific naturalism or naturalistic reductionism that rejects the inclusion of theology as a form of science it its own right.

What we can see here is then Torrance's way of appreciating scientific realism. Unlike Barth, he accepts fellow scientists working in their own field of study such as natural sciences as colleagues doing the approximately the same thing as theologians, namely, finding the patterns of reality that the reality itself is disclosing to us. He calls this "*scientia generalis,*" which is differentiated from "*scientia specialis,*" the former denoting the commonness of science such as critical realism that Torrance is promoting, and the latter the uniqueness of each science which is incommensurable due to the different "objects" of each science. For instance, theologians are looking for particularly the intelligibility of God whereas natural scientists the intelligibility of nature with no regard for the intelligibility of God. Torrance's basic argument is that, if we are performing the same type of scientific exercises and locating the intelligibility of nature or God, despite the difference between theology and science, the two orders must be correlatable. This is precisely what Torrance states:

> When we look at scientific activity in this way it should not surprise us that the development of theological thought and the development of natural science have influenced each other especially in regard to questions of method, not only because theological and natural science are pursued side by side within our common

---

26. Torrance, *Theological Science,* 106–7.
27. Torrance, *Theological Science,* 107.
28. Torrance, *Theological Science,* 107.

existence on earth but because of the scientific attitude which respect for their proper subject-matter begets in both.[29]

This means that realism of natural science plays a heuristic role for theology as it encourages to sustain a realist-oriented research program, seeking the intelligibility of nature or God. Therefore, following Torrance and contra Barth, we do not need to dismiss the formal system as a meaningless abstraction. We should, at least, recognize its utilitarian functionality.

Barth's Dismissal of Natural History

Next, we move to Barth's dismissal of natural history. Barth prefers salvation history over natural history and brushes off natural history as something that is inadequate to support salvation history. Wolfhart Pannenberg has put forth an extensive counterargument on this matter so I review his points here briefly. Although Pannenberg has argued specifically against Oscar Cullman on this point in his article "*Weltgeschichte und Heilsgeschichte*,"[30] since we are talking about the similar issue, even though Pannenberg is not criticizing Barth directly, it will serve our purpose of clarifying Barth's shortcomings.

In his review of Cullmann's idea of salvation history, Pannenberg identifies at least three problems of erecting theology on the foundation of salvation history. The first instance he presents is the narrowed view of history. If, as Cullmann has claimed, which applies equally to Barth's theology, salvation history is divorced from the rest of history because it is radically different from all other histories, we fall into a sort of historical dualism, creating an unbridgeable gap between salvation history and general history. In Pannenberg's mind, this is a pure idealization of history. In the real world, Pannenberg sees history as one unified flow of events. For him, even in theology, we should never work with the idea that there are two histories that are mutually exclusive. The two histories, perhaps divided into two separate spheres, one as salvation history (*Heilsgeschichte*), and the other as general history (*Weltgeschichte*),[31] cannot make sense for Pannenberg if we know that God works in creation holistically and universally. He rhetori-

---

29. Torrance, *Theological Science*, 107.

30. I am using the English translation of this article by Ed Miller. See Miller, "Salvation-History," 21–25.

31. In his systematic theology, Pannenberg uses *Universalgeschichte* in place of *Weltgeschichte*. But the idea is the same. See Pannenberg, *Systematic Theology*, 1:229.

cally exclaims, "Does God work only in this 'line' [of salvation history] and not also in the other events of history?"[32] This duality, insists Pannenberg, introduces an inconsistency in God. It negatively implies that God is inactive or passive in general history and active only in salvation history.

Indeed, it is wrong to view that God's work in creation is divided into different spheres. Even though we may admit, like Pannenberg, that "not all events of history are in the same way relevant for the question of salvation,"[33] because of the prevenient care of God, we cannot create a gap between salvation history and general history. We have to recognize that there is a continuity between what God does generally and salvifically, though the two may be distinguished with respect to God's redemptive work. According to Pannenberg, God works in creation to move and sustain the life of creaturely things for the sake of helping them reach their final telos, that is, the participation in God's life, which brings about the fulfillment of our being (e.g., our salvation). Thus, for Pannenberg, God's work in creation becomes the propitious stepping stone for nature to find its way to God's salvific work.

However, Barth does not see history this way. He emphasizes that God's redemptive work in the world is not a continuation from the general natural process, but an utterly new and disruptive event, which he often denoted with the word, "singularity."[34] Christ as the point of singularity surely is justifiable since the Word made flesh is a unique event that can only be brought upon by God. However, did not the Incarnation take place within the space and time continuum, as Barth admits? It did not take place outside of the spheres of our creation. Even if we say that the Christ-event is a disruptive, miraculous moment in history, it nonetheless is a part of history. Hence, as Pannenberg notes, we must see that there is continuity between salvation history and general history. In fact, we must say that there is only one history, namely, universal history. Salvation history then is just a subset of universal history.[35] It is one particular event amongst the constellation of general events. If our history is universal, which is guided by God's specific salvific intention, the study of history in other areas of sci-

---

32. Pannenberg, "Salvation-History," 24.

33. Pannenberg, "Salvation-History," 24.

34. E.g., Barth, *Church Dogmatics* 4/1, 120, 135, 339, 519, 269, 329, 701.

35. Perhaps, Barth is saying that salvation history is universal and creation history is particular. If this is true, he may be encroaching universalism, for which Barth is often criticized. For more details on this topic, see Roger E. Olson's "Was Karl Barth a Universalist? A New Look at an Old Question."

ences should not be neglected or dismissed as something that is completely irrelevant to salvation history.

But at this point, we are reminded by Barth that the modern historical-critical method, especially utilized by the early twentieth-century liberal scholars, is reductive.[36] As Barth notes, we have to recognize the fallacy of the previous historical-critical method that demythologizes the miraculous and supernatural elements of the Bible into something that is natural or anthropocentric. However, just because one tradition has misused "history," we do not have the right to cordon off salvation history from natural history. Going back to Pannenberg, he has pointed out that the study of natural history reveals that "contingency can be regarded as the fundamental character of every elementary event."[37] This means that the study of nature need not be reductionistic like the liberalistic understanding of history. Instead, history should be underwritten by the contingent event of creation, recreation, and renewal, which is closely aligned with God's redemptive plan. In this respect, we can say that God's creative act aligns with his redemptive act, or at least, a propitious ground upon which God's redemptive act pans out.

The second problematic area of limiting God's history as salvation history that Pannenberg points out is the demise of theological intellectualism. If we follow Barth's suggestion and say that "there can be no scientific problems, questions, objections or aids in relation to Holy Scripture and the Christian Church understand by the divine work of creation,"[38] Pannenberg cannot but assume that salvation history "involves a selection of events which depends too much on a 'decision of faith' and too little on properly conceived historiographical methods."[39] The Barthian trade-off per Pannenberg is that we give up the rigors of rational enterprises for the sake of a subjective decision of faith. He makes a similar comment about Barth's "theocentric turn." He writes, "In the early twentieth century, a theocentric turn occurred, espoused first by Erich Schaeder and then by

---

36. I can list a few examples here. H. S. Reimarus opted for a rationalist approach following the Cartesian tradition. He explained away the supernatural elements of the Bible in terms of what is natural. Also, F. C. Baur is well-known for removing the transcendental or "timeless" elements of the Bible. J. G. Herder looked at the Bible and found only man's constructive work devoid of any supernatural elements. For more details on the divine inspiration of the Bible, see Abraham, *Divine Revelation*, 58–111.

37. Pannenberg, *The Historicity of Nature*, 32.

38. Barth, *Church Dogmatics* 3/1, xi.

39. Miller, "Salvation-History," 22.

Karl Barth . . . But then the question is whether one can get to the theocentric position simply by way of personal decision, as Barth originally proposed."[40] As we can see, Pannenberg is skeptical about the subjective turn. According to Pannenberg, the main implication of turning to the personal decision of faith is that this type of theology tends to be "predetermined by the particular faith position of that confession and which is not open to public debate."[41] Pannenberg is arguing that theology has a public function. It should never be privatized. It must serve the public inasmuch as any other scientific disciplines, because it is rationally rigorous and critical like all other sciences. For Pannenberg, only via cross examinations involving other sciences can we progress and learn more about the true nature of reality. Thus, Pannenberg configures a privatized history of salvation deleterious to the theologian's critical quest for the true nature of the world and God. Being isolated with the rest of the world, salvation history would only be compartmentalized and closed off from the scrutiny of the rest of the world. For Pannenberg, this attitude only defies the purpose of seeking the true depth of God's work in creation. He simply refuses to accept a ghetto theology that shuns the extensive outreach program of God's work.

Does this mean that Barth was an irrationalist or fideist, as purported by Pannenberg? I do not think Pannenberg is right in this regard. As Hunsinger notes, Barth was not an irrationalist, fideist, or isolationist.[42] He took theological rational exercises seriously, for faith could not be just a passive or subjective acceptance. For Barth, Christian theology must be tested and tried through the rigors of academic investigation. Barth as much as Pannenberg, promoted faith seeking understanding, and for this reason, Barth checked the viability of all theological paradigms, cross-examining them through the lens of modern philosophy. During the years of his teaching, he was known to have engaged modern philosophers as well as theologians, pinpointing their strengths and weaknesses based on his intellectual acuity. No doubt that Barth carries a well-developed rational program to write his magnum opus, *Church Dogmatics*. Taking this into account, Torrance had identified the logical structure of Barth's writing resembling much like a science.[43]

---

40. Pannenberg, *The Historicity of Nature*, 4.
41. Pannenberg, *The Historicity of Nature*, 21.
42. Hunsinger, *How to Read Karl Barth*, 27–43.
43. Torrance, "Karl Barth," 1–9.

So, it may be too harsh to pass judgment on Barth and state that he has fallen into some sort of a subjective theological turn. The problem I see is not so much about his subjective turn but his particularism. As identified by Hunsinger, Barth tends to hold onto a specific frame of reference, which is christocentric through and through, and does not allow any other scientific studies to encroach it. One of the reasons is that, in Barth's theological paradigm, God and creation live in a wholly differentiated realm. He was very careful to keep them separated. It was anathema for Barth to have God mixed with or determined by the things of this world. I agree. We cannot let God be determined by secular science. It has to be decided primarily by God's self-revelation revealed through Jesus Christ and the historical narratives recorded in Holy Scripture. However, as Pannenberg notes, God is relevant in all aspects of life because he is the God of creation. If God is relevant to all spheres of life, we ought to allow natural analogy to expand our theological horizons and move away from privatized thinking to a more open and collegial discourse sitting down with non-theological friends.

If we accept that there is not only disruption between God and creation, but also continuity, we can move beyond a ghetto mindset and begin to develop what Ted Peters calls "holistic postmodernism."[44] Holistic postmodernism recognizes that there are many histories out there that vie for prominence, and at the same time, one history, the universal history of nature, which has the potential to weave the variegated threads of history into a single tapestry. What Barth needs is a unity-in-difference attitude. By engaging different disciplines and expanding our horizons by inclusively welcoming natural analogies, being also careful not to be like the old liberals, we can preserve salvation history. We do not need to give up the core of our faith as we move from general revelation to salvation history. Rather, we can explain and make our faith relevant to emerging generations as we include in our theology the multifaceted events of God's universal history.

Before I move to the next topic, a word about Pannenberg's natural theology is in order, since it is often misread as antithetical to God's specific work of salvation. Surely, Pannenberg interprets God's salvation differently than Barth. For him, the order of God's salvation is the order of God's creation, and vice versa. There is undeniable continuity between the two. For this reason, Pannenberg has been read off as a panentheist.[45] I do not think

---

44. Peters, *God—The World's Future*, 35.
45. E.g., Cooper, *Panentheism*, 259–81.

Pannenberg is a panentheist, but rather he is operating on an eschatological logic. For Pannenberg, God is all inclusive, not because he is immanent from the onset of creation, but as the one who rules over creation, he enters the history of creation from the end.[46] As Stanley Grenz and Roger Olson note, "this thesis implies that the idea of God, if it corresponds to an actual reality, must be able to illuminate not only human existence but also our experience of the world as a whole."[47] So, for Pannenberg, because God enters from the end, God embraces everything there was, is now, and will be. Nothing escapes God since the whole of cosmic history is recapitulated by God's future entering into the present that bears the mark of the past. Thus, in Pannenberg's eschatology, we see two streams of history existing side by side, that is, the continuing event of God's creation that extends from the past to the present, and the disruptive force of God's future fulfillment entering into the present. For this reason, we cannot say that there is no disruptive element in Pannenberg's theology.

Furthermore, because of Pannenberg's eschatology, he wants all theology to present a "coherent model of the world as God's creation."[48] What is this coherent model of theology? Pannenberg explains, "Such a systematic presentation [of Christian doctrines] must be not only consistent within itself and consonant with the biblical witness but also coherent with regard to all matters that have to be taken into account in such a presentation."[49] So, the task of theology is to fit the history of nature as well as our history of redemption into a unified history of God. They cannot be contradictory, in Pannenberg's eschatological scheme. At this point, we need to ask this question. Is Pannenberg removing the supernatural elements as he wants the history of our redemption to cohere to the natural events?

---

46. Pannenberg belongs to a group of scholars who value eschatology highly such as Jürgen Moltmann and Ted Peters, and recently Pentecostal scholars such as Frank Macchia. His theory of prolepsis is biblical as attested by C. H. Dodd. Dodd examining the New Testament narrative of the kingdom of God stated that Jesus did not speak about the kingdom of God as something that is to be progressed toward. Rather, he asserted that the kingdom of God as a future reality had already broken into the present. So it was Dodd's famous dictum that highlights the already-and-not-yet of eschatological logic. For more details see, Dodd, *The Parables of the Kingdom*, 34. Also see Dillistone, *C. H. Dodd*, 55–56.

47. Grenz and Olson, *20th-Century Theology*, 191.

48. Pannenberg, *An Introduction to Systematic Theology*, 10.

49. Pannenberg, *The Historicity of Nature*, 7.

Pannenberg does not discount the biblical miracles such as resurrection. He believes that resurrection is an actual historical event.[50] However, there is a catch. For Pannenberg, resurrection is a foretaste of what is to come. In other words, resurrection represents the inbreaking of the future into the present. The implication of this message is clear. God's miracle cannot be fully explained here and now. It falls under the category that we must defer to the future. We will not know its full reality until the end, since it has come from the future. Therefore, our understanding of miracles is provisional at best. For this reason, theology is never finished. It is in the process of ever becoming something new, all the while bearing the mark of what is old. For this reason, all theological statements are considered to be provisional and hypothetical. Pannenberg explains, "It [hypothesis] is a condition of taking an affirmation seriously that it is possible to raise question of whether the claim of the affirmation accords with reality. In all sciences, humility is required. Our affirmations are not by themselves infallible but may be questioned. Theology is no exception to this rule."[51] Thus, heeding to Pannenberg's coherence theory, we must strive to expand our theological horizon to cover both the natural and supernatural territories, checking and rechecking, interpreting and reinterpreting, and forming and reforming our theological programs against the vast array of natural and theological data.

Barth's Intolerance for Self-Transcendence

Lastly but most importantly, we come to Barth's problem of transcendence. Barth has little tolerance for any idea of self-transcendence. His intolerance for self-transcendence is a vital source for the critical re-assessment of not only today's religious but also philosophical claims of self-transcendence. For instance, religious self-transcendence may lead to a reductionistic natural idea of transcendence. As a religious naturalist Jerome Stones notes, such transcendence seeks "to understand our experiences of the sacred within a naturalistic framework."[52] By contrast, philosophical self-transcendence may dismiss the concept of God, and at the same time, seek

---

50. Pannenberg, *Jesus—God and Man*, 111–3. Also see Burhenn, "Pannenberg's Argument," 368–79.

51. Pannenberg, *The Historicity of Nature*, 8.

52. Stone, *Religious Naturalism Today*, 125.

to rise above the limits of mankind by the pure will to power, to borrow Nietzsche's language.[53]

There are prominent Christian scholars who also adhere to a sort of self-transcendent ideas. As an example, Paul Tillich's courage-to-be is "the power of being, a power transcending the nonbeing which is experienced in the anxiety of fate and death."[54] Tillich's self-transcendent courage-to-be leads to self-affirmation that "opens up levels of reality which are normally hidden."[55] Tillich is insinuating that the "hidden" level to which our self-transcendence should rise is God. He compares this experience to a mystical experience. He writes, "In a similar way all mystics draw their power of self-affirmation from the experience of the power of being-itself with which they are united."[56] In Tillich's theology, the being-itself symbolizes "God." So, in essence, Tillich is interpreting our relationship with God in terms of a self-transcendence. We come to God because we can push ourselves to the higher levels of hidden reality.

Reading these claims about the idea of self-transcendence, I have to give Barth credit for dismissing them. They are clearly the remnant of modern anthropocentric philosophy that Barth passionately disputed. Even though we give modern philosophy its due by acknowledging the need to work rigorously and move out of the rut that we have created, we can go so far with this. The history of our civilization well attests to our disorder, always falling short of transcending our problems. The reality of human transcendence is not utopia but dystopia.

Thus, I am troubled to see that Christian theology has indiscreetly adopted this notion of self-transcendence as if it belongs to the church, without heeding to the danger sign that Barth had forged for us all. What is the danger? As Barth would say, we may discard Christ and find no need of his salvific work when we mispresent salvation as our natural capacity to transcend the limits of our being. Indeed, Christ had to come, and he had to help us transcend the limits of our being, namely, to borrow Calvin's word, "total depravity." Indeed, we are sinful to the core and there is no "power" in us that can propel us to transcend the depravity that is deeply rooted in our being. Barth's attitude is the same. Sin, which is the desire to

---

53. Nietzsche, *The Will to Power*, 85–126.
54. Tillich, *The Courage to Be*, 155.
55. Tillich, *The Courage to Be*, 67.
56. Tillich, *The Courage to Be*, 157.

do away with Christ, is so rampant that we have no power to free ourselves from the pit of meaninglessness.

In this respect, there is no reason for us Christians to object Barth's disclaim of man's self-transcendence. Besides, Barth's objection to the modern idea of self-transcendence is up to code with the biblical concept of transcendence. In the Bible, God is transcendent (e.g., Isa 55:8–9; Acts 7:49). The biblical language that emphasizes God's sovereignty or his omnipotence proves this point. Consequently, God is the source of our transcendence (e.g., Luke 10:9; John 15:5; Phil 4:13). At the same time, we cannot self-transcend ourselves because of our sin. We cannot overcome sin on our own; only in Christ can we transcend this limit (Rom 3:23–25). The Bible is clear about the boundary conditions we have. We are limited and our limitations prevent us to "self-transcend." Paul paints a bleak picture of this condition in Romans 3:10–18. Barth's *Der Römerbrief* picks up on this attitude and boldly declares that there is no such thing as man's innate ability to self-transcend due to the inherent corruptibility of humanity.

However, this begs the question. If we cannot self-transcend and therefore cannot reach God on our own, why are there many different religions that purport to have reached the realm of the divine? Barth may claim that they are "a false idea about God."[57] Barth is essentially saying that all religions are false. What about Christianity? For Barth, Christianity is not a "religion," since it bears the mark of God's self-revelation in and through Jesus Christ. Even with this claim, I still see a problem.

The issue I have with Barth is that his claim does not truly address the nature of our "self-transcendence." My question to Barth is, can we learn anything positive from this so-called "false ideas about God?" Granted that all religions may have false ideas about God, nonetheless they are related to *an idea about God*. Hence, we have to give an account for this "*sensus divinitatis*," even though it may be corrupted or misleading. Why do we have this desire to be "self-transcendent"? Why do people, even non-Christians, seek God at all? Where does the will to transcend come from? While his opponents are ready to provide the public with explanations of their own, Barth's dismissive attitude does not answer these questions in depth. To fill this gap, I turn to David Coffey, who has proposed an innovating idea

---

57. Barth, *Church Dogmatics* 4/1, 186. He writes, "We have to be ready to be taught by Him that we have been too small and perverted in our thinking about Him within the framework of a false idea of God. It is not for us to speak of a contradiction and rift in the being of God, but to learn to correct our notions of the being of God, to reconstitute them in light of the fact that He does this."

explaining why we all are "transcendent." What is ingenious about his explanation of transcendence is that he remains faithful to the christocentric and pneumatological vision of the world, even though he is interacting with the scientific theory of evolution, which demonstrates that the ideas of self-transcendence can still be a useful source for understanding God's order of creation and redemption.

Why do we have this desire to transcend? Coffey finds the answer in the Spirit of Christ working *prior* to the first advent of Christ. His claim is unconventional, to say the least. The Spirit of Christ, traditionally, has been understood as the mission of the Son, sending to the world after his resurrection and ascension. No one has pursued the idea of the Spirit of Christ working prior to the Son's mission. How can it be? Did not Jesus say that he would send another comforter when he returns to the Father (Jn. 14:16)? Coffey thinks otherwise. He thinks that the Spirit of Christ has been working even before the birth of Jesus Christ. So, Coffey's investigation takes us to the history of pre-incarnation.

Coffey, breaking new grounds, traces the work of the Spirit of Christ not only in the life of Jesus Christ, but more importantly, in the cosmic process that leads to the conception and birth of Jesus Christ. Coffey terms the work of the Spirit of Christ *a priori* an "entelechy" of the Spirit. The word "entelechy" is defined as a "guiding principle of a process, which not only moves it forward to its telos or end, but as it operates actively seeks out this end."[58] The entelechy of the Spirit of Christ is employed by Coffey to accentuate the Spirit's work of seeking out Christ in and through the entire spectrum of the cosmic process. Does this theory have a biblical basis? Coffey believes that there is a biblical basis, and to justify his claim, he turns to the scriptural verse of 1 Peter 1:11.

For Coffey, 1 Peter 1:11 points to the fact that the Holy Spirit had a historical role to play as the Spirit of Christ even before the time of Christ. He disagrees with historical scholars such as J.N.D. Kelly who has hinted that the Spirit of Christ denoted in this verse is simply a pointer to the "pre-existent Christ."[59] Kelly hence rejects the Spirit of Christ in this context as having any historical relevance. By contrast, from a theological perspective and staying close to the exegesis of 1 Peter 1:11, as the prophets in the Old and New Testaments testified "in advance to the sufferings destined

---

58. David Coffey cites Peter Phan's definition of the entelechy of the Spirit. See Coffey, "The Spirit of Christ," 364.

59. Kelly, *A Commentary*, 58–60.

for Christ and the subsequent glory," Coffey denotes that the "Spirit of Christ" is the Holy Spirit who inspired and empowered the prophets of old "to descry in advance the essential features of Christ the savior."[60] This scriptural basis becomes a springboard for Coffey to explore the entelechy of the Spirit in the cosmic process itself. For an additional help in this matter, he turns to Pierre Teilhard de Chardin and Karl Rahner, which I will review respectively.

Teilhard is well known for his work in the area of interfacing theology and science in general, and Christology and evolution in particular. Coffey's interest pivots on Teilhard's implied spiritual entelechy, so we are going to pay attention to Teilhard's work in this area. In Coffey's view and rightly so, the lasting contribution of Teilhard to Christian theology is his belief that evolution and theology are mutually complementary, the former investigating the "without" (e.g., the material or measurable things), and the latter the "within" (e.g., the immaterial or immeasurable things that underlie the material processes).[61] Here, Coffey locates a key concept introduced by Teilhard, namely, "radial energy," the guiding force of nature that propels the evolutionary process.

Teilhard's use of radial energy stems from his observation of evolutionary processes. Coffey mentions two. The first one pertains to the idea of complexity.[62] According to Coffey, Teilhard saw that, in the cosmic process, both inorganic and organic matters are evolved into more complex entities, organizing, growing, and multiplying themselves into more sustainable, sophisticated, and complex things. The second part and following from the first pertains to the notion of a critical threshold.[63] Coffey explains that Teilhard was interested in the way these evolved entities develop into something new that clearly distinguishes them from their predecessors, once a critical threshold of complexity is reached. In my opinion, what Teilhard is describing is very similar to the theory of emergence. However, rather than calling this distinction between the lower and higher layers of emergent properties, Teilhard labeled it as the "critical threshold," and this idea plays an important role in Coffey's appropriation of the entelechy of the Spirit.

Next, Coffey turns to a more pressing question raised by Teilhard. Why does the simple evolve into the complex, or the less into the more? For

---

60. Coffey, "The Spirit of Christ," 368.
61. Coffey, "The Spirit of Christ," 372.
62. Coffey, "The Spirit of Christ," 372.
63. Coffey, "The Spirit of Christ," 372.

Teilhard, the answer is simple. There is radial energy that guides the process of evolution to its telos, that is, complexification and threshold crossing. In relation to Teilhard's conception of radial energy, Coffey directs his attention to Teilhard's description of the final telos of the natural process, which is called "hominization," a subset of the ultimate telos, the Omega Point.[64] Here, we can see a preliminary thought of Coffey's understanding of transcendence. In nature, as Teilhard describes it, all things have a habit of transcending their environment, from the less complex structure to a higher level of complexity. Moving continually with upward mobility, this complexification finally reaches its telos of hominization. What we need to note is that these upward movements are both naturally active and supernaturally guided.

Since Karl Rahner reinforced the idea of the divinely guided process of evolution, Coffey finalizes the concept of the entelechy of the Spirit based on Rahner's work. He points out several key features of Rahner's work, but due to the limited space, I mention one that explicitly deals with the concept of the spiritual entelechy. Correlative to Teilhard's idea of "radial energy," Rahner describes the "entelechy" of the Spirit as the divinely inspired spiritual guidance inherent in the cosmic process that propels the evolution to its final telos, that is, hominization.[65] That is not all. Even after hominization is completed, the Spirit continues to fuel the onward march of "evolution," which is now headed toward the hypostatic union of and with Jesus Christ. Hence, the coming of Savior in the world is the climax of the spiritual entelechy.

Coffey takes Rahner's theory and uses it as the support of his own paradoxical claim that the Spirit of Christ is activated before the advent of Christ. He notes, "This means that the Spirit is always and everywhere the 'entelechy' of the history of revelation and salvation."[66] He continues, "That is to say, the communication of revelation and salvation is universally oriented to the cross of Christ, and since this entire process is guided and directed by the Holy Spirit, the Spirit, in this sense and even before the

---

64. Teilhard's Omega Point is where Christ draws all things into himself. The Omega in this respect actually points to Jesus Christ, the source of radial energy. For more details, see Teilhard de Chardin, *Activation of Energy*, 111–4.

65. According to Coffey, Rahner saw that the "cosmos comes to consciousness in human beings." Rahner is essentially affirming Teilhard's theory of hominization. Coffey, "The Spirit of Christ," 378.

66. Coffey, "The Spirit of Christ," 381.

Incarnation, is the Spirit of Christ."[67] Hence there is a dual dimension of the Spirit's incarnational work: (1) the Incarnation of Christ actualized in the historical personage of Jesus by the guidance of the entelechy of the Spirit, and (2) the Incarnation of Christ anticipated in the cosmic process leading up to Christ. The second point is what Coffey has been talking about in relation to the natural end being sublated to the supernatural end in his other works.[68]

Furthermore, the principle of duality is explained in terms of the eschatological unity between the natural end and the supernatural end. Coffey explains,

> If the anticipation of Christ and the acceptance of him once given historically constitute a true unity, and if both phases are accomplished in the power of the Holy Spirit, and indeed the Holy Spirit as the Spirit of Christ, then the action of the Spirit of Christ as the entelechy and that of the same Spirit as sent by the risen Lord constitute no less a unity.[69]

Put differently, the anticipation of the Son's Incarnation and the actual Incarnation of Christ in history mutually condition one another—e.g., the Spirit of Christ, which is actualized after the resurrection, is retroactively impacting the process of evolution as it directs toward and pursues the Incarnation of Christ. Hence, according to Coffey, we are not talking about two different process of the Spirit of Christ, but a single process with two distinct phases. The first phase is the Spirit of Christ working in the complexification process as a relative ordination of grace, and the second phase is the Spirit of Christ working in hypostatic union of Christ (and by implication, our union with Christ) as an absolute ordination of grace.

This is as far as I would go with Coffey. It is because he takes another step and crosses the line that undermines his theory. Let me explain further. Grounded on the theory of the entelechy of the Spirit, Coffey accepts wholeheartedly Rahner's theological program that claims, "Jesus Christ is always and everywhere present in justifying faith."[70] By this he means that the Spirit becomes the inner, subjective, and transcendent agent in the world who anticipates and completes the objectivization of the Incarnation. With

---

67. Coffey, "The Spirit of Christ," 381.

68. Coffey, "The Whole Rahner," 95–118.

69. Coffey, "The Spirit of Christ," 383.

70. Coffey, "The Spirit of Christ," 383. See also Rahner, *Theological Investigations*, 17:46.

this idea of spiritual interiorization, Rahner was able to say that "Christ is present and efficacious in the non-Christian believer (and therefore in the non-Christian religions) through his Spirit."[71] Coffey agrees with Rahner. He even endorses Rahner's assertion that "absolute love of neighbor, the acceptance of death, or hope in the future bespeaks an implicit faith in the absolute bringer of salvation."[72] An implicit faith, for Coffey, fulfills the criterion for salvation, and it applies to not only non-Christian religious people but also, "people of good will but with no religion at all."[73]

I cannot accept Coffey's application of the entelechy of the Spirit to grant salvation to non-Christians and the "good willed" people of no religion. Even though Coffey says that the criterion of salvation is an implicit faith, it sounds very much like a semi-Pelagian theological criterion. His implicit faith is identified with "good will" and "spiritual interiorization," and for me, this criterion defies Paul's claim: "Faith comes by hearing, and hearing by the word of God" (Rom 10:17). So, for me, the prerequisite of faith, which is the union with Christ being led by the entelechy of the Spirit, is the explicit exposure to the word of God. The word of God as I interpreted closely aligns with Barth's dictum—i.e., God's self-revelation in and through Jesus Christ as testified by Holy Scripture. Without this exposure to and acceptance of God's word, it is inappropriate to say that the person has a saving faith.

Where does this leave us with the explanation of self-transcendence? Coffey's work, despite its flaws, is exemplary in the way we can explain the key characteristics of self-transcendence, as long we as know its limit. Even with the help of the Spirit of Christ, the final critical point, that is, the union with Christ, cannot be achieved with an implicit faith. It requires an explicit confession of christological faith and the true exposure to and the acceptance of the saving word of God.[74] So, the zenith of self-transcendence is

---

71. Rahner, *Theological Investigations*, 17:43.
72. Coffey, "The Spirit of Christ," 388.
73. Coffey, "The Spirit of Christ," 388.
74. This leaves us with a question. What happens to those who have not heard the gospel, such as the unreached peoples or those who lived in the pre-Christian era in which no gospel was available? This question requires a book of its own to address the full scope of its theological implications, but I would comment briefly to note that there is no "unreached" people. The offer of grace is given to all (at least, unthematically). For more details on the unthematic dimension of God's grace, see Coffey, "The Whole Rahner," 95–118.

the level of implicit faith, an inferior stage to the final stage of the threshold crossing, that is, the level of explicit faith.

Returning to the theory of the entelechy of the Spirit, we can see that it describes for us why the entire creation is self-transcendent. Due to the supernatural guidance of the Spirit that beckons the natural process to move from the less to the more complex level of activities by crossing the necessary thresholds, all natural processes are disposed to self-transcend its environment. Simply put, we are self-transcendent because we are both doing it habitually, and at the same time, pressed forward by the entelechy of the Spirit. So, the transcendentalization is not just a natural process, but also spiritually charged. Because of its complexification and threshold crossings, it does not let us be constricted to one system but allows the natural process to move beyond its own system to the higher system in which the order of the lower system no longer explains the order of the higher system. The higher and lower systems are still interrelated though. For instance, the higher system can function as a new system of order imposed upon the lower system to assist in its complexification all the while the lower system continues to be the propitious ground for more novel emergence, as in the case of the brain and mind relationship.

The theological significance of the spiritual entelechy closes the gap left behind by Barth. We can now explain why self-transcendence is part of our nature. As Coffey has shown, we have the natural ability to seek higher grounds upon which we can at least arrive at a rudimentary knowledge of God because of the beckoning of the infinite Spirit.

At this juncture, I need to end with a word of admonition. Our openness to higher and greater things are not always trustworthy, even if it is spiritually guided. Stanley Grenz makes this point. He notes that "the human sense of infinite dependency and of directedness beyond the finite confines of the world may in the end be nonsensical and meaningless."[75] Surely, our orientation toward what is beyond this world could have a negative consequence, and as a result, we may end up seeking the things that have nothing to do with God. However, contra Barth, such a negative potentiality of self-transcendence should not be the reason for its complete dismissal; rather, because of the fallibility of self-transcendence, all the more we need to rely on the entelechy of the Spirit so that we can arrive at the truth that there is the "infinite, world-transcending Someone, who alone is

---

75. Grenz, *Theology for the Community*, 132.

the answer to our infinite dependency."[76] So according to Grenz, despite the possibility of misguided transcendence, we must at least acknowledge the other possibility, that the world has the potential to reach out to God with the help of the Spirit.

The Usefulness of Natural Theology: The Analogical Relationship between God and Nature

Acknowledging the usefulness of natural theology, I want to say in this section that there is an analogical relationship between God and nature. An analogical relationship between God and nature permits us to move from God to nature as well as nature to God without confusion and without change. Thus, we may do away with a complete equivocation between the two while heeding Barth's warning to keep God and nature as distinguishable systems. If we view the God-nature relationship analogically, the order of creation can be decided based on the principle of similarity-and-difference as it holds together the commonality emerging from the comparison of analogues that discloses certain similar cognizable patterns and relations, and the difference arising from the particular feature of analogues that conveys multiple meanings as a result of not only contrasting features in analogues but also our approach to each analogue with various motivations and from different perspectives.

For instance, if we assume that there is a logical order in the divine system, this intelligibility of God in some sense is correlatable to the intelligibility of nature. As it is affirmed by Augustine, this is precisely why we can discern God's order from nature. Augustine spoke of the vestige of God in the things of this world from which we discern the reality of God.[77] Surely, if there is no correlation between God and nature, there is no way we can make any sense of God's order. As an illustration, let us look at one particular aspect of the order of God. God is who he is in himself (and by implication, God cannot be *not* God). Although this statement seems trivial, it is one of the key orders in God that qualifies God. Because there is nothing in this world that qualifies God, we can only say that "God is who he is in himself," and this statement is the only true viable option for describing God (e.g., Ex. 3:14). However, logically, this is also true of the order of nature, which we call it the principle of identity. Like God, we

---

76. Grenz, *Theology for the Community*, 132.
77. Augustine, *The City of God*, 431.

can say the same thing about a "mountain." A mountain is what it is in itself, and by implication, it cannot be something other than a mountain (e.g., a dog or a man). So, without hesitation, we can say that God has a similar order as nature, namely, the principle of identity. Notwithstanding this similarity, we should not forget that there is a difference between God and the mountain. God exists as an uncreated singularity (e.g., Isa 45:5). By contrast, a mountain is a derived entity. It is a byproduct of plate tectonic movements. So we cannot speak of the mountain in terms of an uncreated singularity like God. Hence, the logic of God's order, while similar to the logic of nature, is utterly different from it. If we keep this analogical duality in mind, we can avoid the errors of contemporary theology confusing the order of God with the order of creation.

For instance, the order of process has been erroneously imported to God, and as a result, it has confused God's order with nature's order. The order of process is brought to our attention by Alfred North Whitehead in the early twentieth century, and more recently, by his theological followers such as Joseph A. Bracken, John B. Cobb, and David R. Griffin.[78] Whitehead's key tenet is that everything is in the process of becoming as the actual entities rise from the lower level of activities to the higher level of more complex activities. It sounds very much like Teilhard's theory of complexification. Like Teilhard, for Whitehead, nothing remains the same or static. All things are moving to a greater or higher level, propelled by the creative force that guides the entire process of cosmic becoming. All is good thus far. There is nothing wrong with viewing the world as a process of becoming. In fact, I believe Whitehead is on target. We should move beyond the static notion of ontology and come to a more realistic view of our world, which is constantly fluctuating, changing, and shifting. However, the problem occurs when he equates the order of nature with the order of God.

Whitehead claims that, like nature, God is in the process of becoming. Although God is differentiated from the rest of worldly entities as he has an infinite quality as opposed to the finitude of the world, Whitehead still sees God following the same order as the rest of the created things. This means that God's "singularity" is no longer appreciated. Like any other temporal entities, God is subjected to the same course of history and is determined by the creative outcome of history. Joseph Bracken, an avid follower of Whitehead, goes even further and states that God is eternal because God's

---

78. For more details, see Bracken's *Society and Spirit* and Cobb's *God and the World*.

process of becoming stretches to infinity. For Bracken, God will never stop growing and expanding as he gathers the finite process into his own life.

I do not know how Bracken can sustain the claim of the God of process when there is no biblical precedence. The Bible does not testify to a process God. Rather, the Bible is clear that God is who he is in himself, and he is already God-is (Exod 3:14), not a being that needs to become something more. What I can conclude here is that Bracken as well as Whitehead have pushed the natural analogy too far and broken the similarity-in-difference principle of analogy. The similarity between God and process was pressed too hard, and as a result, God's order has turned into nature's order. This is what Barth wanted to avoid, and for sure, we must do the same.

Does this mean that the concept of "process" has no relevance to God's internal order? As I have said before, the order of nature is functionally useful, and thus, it can be analogically applied to unveil the order of God. In this case, the analogical relationship between God and process can be established based on the concept of "sequence," because the idea of process reveals the fact that there is a sequential activity in the process of becoming. For instance, Whitehead talks about the stratification of actual occasions. He mentions at least four levels: (1) the elementary process which involves the influence of gravity and other natural forces, (2) the process of inanimate things which is a more sophisticated version of the elementary process, (3) the organic process that sustains the order of living things, which reveals a raw form of conscious intentions, and finally, (4) the process of "presentational immediacy," which is the subjective experience that human beings go through.[79] There are multiple implications of this order, but what I want to focus here is the sequential order of nature. Whitehead recognizes that there is a sequential event of things, one event leading up to another event, and each event having its own distinct properties and characteristics, though interrelated to the whole.

I can take this process analogy and apply it to God. In God, we can say, like nature, that there is a sequential order. From a trinitarian perspective, we can denote that the Father is God's firstness, the Son is God's secondness, and the Holy Spirit is God's thirdness. This sequential order maintains within God his own personal distinction. This is the same with nature. As Whitehead has shown, in nature, sequential logic plays a critical role in the way we understand the world. Without sequential logic, we would not

---

79. Mays, *Whitehead's Philosophy*, 81–104. Also see Whitehead, *Process and Reality*, 511–43.

be able to *distinguish* one thing from another. I do not think we can even imagine a world where there is no sequence. Similarly, the sequence in God *distinguishes* God's oneness into three persons. Without the sequential order, God could not be differentiated in himself. More clearly, without his sequential logic, God cannot be the God of the Trinity.

Again, we need to be careful here. Nature's order needs to be well qualified so that it is not confused with God's order intentionally or unintentionally. As Whitehead has shown, nature's order always carries the hierarchical implication. Nothing in nature is uniform. All things are varied in nature. There are peaks and valleys as there are highs and lows of life. This is what we observe in nature. However, this is not so with God. Unlike nature, God is perfect in his unity, and his oneness cannot be subjected to nature's order of hierarchy. There are no peaks and valleys in God. God remains who he is, regardless of where he is and what he does in himself or for us. Thus, the firstness of God should never be treated as the higher order of the secondness or thirdness of God.

To advance my point further, let me introduce another useful aspect of natural analogy in relation to the *ordo salutis*. Allow me to show that the natural analogy of self-transcendence can unveil the order of salvation, though in a limited way. To bring the matter closer to Christology, I revisit the core tenets of self-transcendence. To recap, we know that nature has an innate ability to transcend and reach various levels of thresholds. Things in nature can cross thresholds, synthesizing and becoming more complex as they move from one level of activities to another. Coffey has located the source of this transcendence to the entelechy of the Spirit, which is spread out to every corner of the universe, beckoning the natural process to come to its final telos, that is, the level of hominization. I also mentioned that a push from the natural transcendence cannot help us cross the limit of explicit faith. Salvation is no place for self-transcendence. It belongs to the realm of explicit faith, the "graceful" transcendence in and through Jesus Christ by the power of the Holy Spirit.

Although the idea of "self-transcendence" cannot be pressed any more than to the place of implicit faith, it nonetheless could serve as a natural analogy to the order of salvation. Since there are many different orders of salvation, I work with Paul's order of salvation (Rom 8:30) as a test case. Paul's order of salvation is predestination/calling–justification–glorification. I treat predestination and calling as two facets of a single order of God's election because I do not split up God's election into two distinct categories of supralapsarianism and infralapsarianism. In my judgment, God's election is always eschatologically conditioned, involving predestination, calling, and fulfillment as continuing and interrelated events. This will be more apparent when I deal with open theism in the last chapter, so I defer its details until then.

In Paul's view, the first transcendence is God's predestination and calling, moving out of the bounds of God's inner life and coming to the natural system of this world as "calling."[80] Eschatologically speaking, God calls as he presupposes and anticipates predestination, and God predestines as he presupposes and anticipates calling. In other words, what God wills in the immanent Trinity is revealed as the presupposed and anticipated actualization in the economic Trinity, because God's action in himself is God's revelation for us. I call this movement in God "formal transcendence." What I mean by this is that this transcendence does not belong to us. It belongs to God only, so from our perspective, it is a formal transcendence that prepares the way for our own transcendence.

In the context of God's formal transcendence—his free offer of grace *ad extra*—we are now ready to accept or reject God's offer of grace. God's movement from his own being to the creaturely realm becomes the template upon all other transcendence occurring in the world. For this reason, justification as the second transcendence becomes possible for us because of God's first transcendence. We are justified because God has predestined and called us, not because we call ourselves to be saved or we are transcending our existential limitations to be like God. The critical point has been reached, as God is pushing our existence from the level of ordinary existence to the level of supernatural existence, as we accept his call and come into his presence to be in union with Christ. Paul labels this transcendence as a "justified" reconciliation that leads to a new creation (2 Cor 5:17–19). We are made new as we moved from sinfulness to "justified" righteousness because of the reconciliation ministry of Jesus Christ. The new person now has both a new ontological status (the sonship of God) and a new

---

80. Often, God's election is denoted in a deterministic sense. This is true of Calvinism. However, if we view God's election not as the source of the separation of the chosen and the not-chosen before the creation of the world, but as the source of God's calling that respects our free choice, God's election becomes more inclusive and dynamic than Calvinistic determinism. What we have to recognize is that God's election operates on the principle of duality. It has both deterministic and indeterministic dimensions. It is deterministic since God's election cannot *not* happen. It is indeterministic since God's election needs to recapitulate the whole of God's salvific work, that is, predestination, calling, and justification, which is awaiting its fulfillment at the eschaton.

telos (eternal life) that is distinctively different from the old person, which consists of the old ontological status (the enemy of God) and the old telos (death). This is our transcendence, since we have come into God's presence by faith in Christ, although justification-reconciliation is really the work of God. We are justified by faith, indeed. But avoiding the legalistic connotation, we can translate this phrase in terms of divinely caused transcendence. Saving faith is the transcendental push initiated by God that permits us to cross the threshold from death to life.

Paul's order of salvation does not end with the second order of transcendence. There is more, namely, glorification as the third order of transcendence. There are many different ways of interpreting what Paul means by "glorification" here. Without being bogged down by the controversy associated with this term, I want to emphasize Paul's desire to press on and continue to transcend until we finish the race (2 Tim. 4:7). As the final telos, Paul connects this idea of continuing transcendence with justification and sanctification. He notes, "Those whom he justified he also sanctified, and those whom he sanctified he also glorified." Glorification, as the final telos, is reached when we are continually renewed "beholding the glory of the Lord, and are being changed into his likeness from one degree of glory to another, for this comes from the Lord who is the Spirit" (2 Cor. 3:18). According to Paul, from the life of justification, we move onto the life of sanctification. And this is possible because glorification as the future is already impacting justification in and through the Spirit. In other words, for Paul, justification, sanctification, and glorification are not three discrete events, but a single flow of the Spirit driven transcendence. We become new everyday as the Spirit moves us ever closer to God's glory. For this reason, our spiritual quest is on-going, moving from one degree of glory to another.[81]

Of course, once again, in accordance with the principle of analogy, we have to recognize that there is the independent and dependent relationship between God's transcendence and our own transcendence. As with the relationship between God and nature, there are things that God does for us and there are things that we do and act in this world. This is the same with nature. God does not do everything for nature. Had he done so, natural causality would be non-existent. Everything will be under the rubric of divine causality. What is true of this world is that there are many different causalities. For instance, we have inorganic causality as denoted

---

81. For a similar explanation, see Macchia, *Baptized in the Spirit*, 83.

by a mechanistic law. We have organic causality as denoted by a biological law. We have social and psychological causality as denoted by the order of personalism. We have theological and metaphysical laws as denoted by divine and philosophical systems.

Thus, to emphasize God's order of singularity, although transcendence is divinely inspired, our transcendence is not God's transcendence. God's transcendence is never derived. It comes from God's own inner being. He does not need any help like us. However, to complete the order of salvation, we are hopelessly incompetent without God's help. Despite our incompetence, because of God's continuing work of transcendentalization in the world, we can move and have our being in God. Being empowered and renewed by the Spirit, we now can transcend and transform the limitations of this world.

Concluding Remarks

What I had shown in this chapter is that God's order and nature's order are not entirely discordant. They are related and relatable, though analogically. My claim is that we can discern certain aspects of God's order through the examination of nature's order. In fact, we cannot even begin to talk about God's order without recognizing that our intelligibility depends on the order of nature.[82] Hence, the discussion of God's order ought to begin with knowledge of nature. By this claim, I do not intend to undermine God's special revelation as it is testified by Holy Scripture. Despite the fact that there is an analogical correlation between God's order and nature's order, this correlation is only a heuristic device that serves to clarify and explain what God has revealed to us through Jesus Christ and Holy Spirit. It can never replace God's special revelation. Neither can it fully reveal the order of God.[83] As Barth has pointed out, the order of nature cannot truly give us

---

82. To add, this claim is never meant to prove the existence of God based on natural knowledge. The existence of God is already assumed. It is a presupposition to all my claims. Following William P. Alston, I do not think that we can ever prove God solely on the ground of natural knowledge. In order to prove God's existence, we have to have a non-natural Archimedean point, for God is beyond nature. But this defies the requirement of naturalism, so there is no natural way to prove God.

83. Even with a special revelation, Emil Brunner notes that God is unknowable. In this regard, Brunner introduces *Deus nudus*, a part of *Deus absconditus*. He writes, "*Deus nudus*, of whom is intolerable for the sinful creature, 'God merely and apart from Christ.'" Brunner, *The Christian Doctrine of God*, 1:171–2.

the Archimedean point. Nature without the intrusion of God's revelation can never be able to see anything else but nature. This is the limitation of nature's self-transcendence. This is our limitation. Though we may transcend some internal grounds of nature moving from the empirical to the theoretical level, we would still be under the matrix of nature. Without the supernatural injection, such as the intervention of the Spirit of Christ, we would never be able to fully understand the order of the Trinity nor the order of God's salvation.

What I have demonstrated in this chapter is that the order of nature provides us with the intellectual ground upon which we can start to think about God's order. The order of nature, as it is discussed previously, at least grants us the principle of identity, the principle of duality (or eschatology), the order of sequence, and the order of transcendence that can be applied to God. These orders, though unique to God, are readily visible in nature. We glean these orders from the way we observe the world exterior to us and the world within us. For this reason, I had to counter Barth's disclaim of natural theology. Barth's anathema against natural theology regrettably missed the usefulness of natural analogy. In doing so, he failed to recognize that our understanding of God cannot avoid going through natural analogues.

The key implication of this study then is that God has a logic that is correlatable to the logic of this world, albeit analogically. This logic cannot but be discerned from natural analogy. In other words, nature reveals God. Even if we say that natural revelation may not lead to saving faith, it nonetheless serves as a guide to unveiling God's order. At this point, we may ask: Why is the natural order correlatable to God's order, if there is an infinite qualitative difference between the two? The only response I can give to this question is that God has come and left the trace of his order in the world, which is evidenced by the entelechy of the Spirit. With God's continuing involvement with the world as creator, redeemer, and renewer, nature is moving along with God to some extent. So, from a theological standpoint, we cannot say that the order of creation is purely natural. As Coffey's entelechy of the Spirit has shown, we can only say that it is also spiritually and supernaturally charged. In this respect, we can learn of God from both general and special revelation. The words of B. B. Warfield are especially insightful in this regard. He said that general revelation is designed to "meet and supply the natural need of creatures for knowledge of their God," whereas special revelation is given to "rescue broken and deformed sinners from their sin and its consequence."⁸⁴ As Warfield notes, we need both natural and special revelation to configure God's order. If we dismiss one at the expense of the other, we would lose the chance to see the wider picture of God working in the areas of creation, redemption, and renewal.

Ultimately then, God is a God of order. Order is an inherent feature of God's existence. Although we may never be able to fully grasp the complete scope of God's order, nevertheless, by correlating the order of nature and the order revealed by God via his two hands (Son and Spirit) in the world, we can confirm that there is a unique set of orders in God. Of course, we cannot impose the concept of natural order onto God without qualification, but by way of inference from natural analogy, we can at least say that there is a specific principle in God that may shed some light of who God is and how he acts with or without us.

With this idea of the order in God, we are now in position to tackle more in-depth the order of God's inner life. Our encroachment to God's inner life must be done with utmost prudence. Taking Barth's warning seriously, we have the duty to outline God's order not as the projection of our own image but the true reference to God himself. For this reason, in the next chapter, we return to Barth's work again, and this time, we extrapolate his positive contribution to this area of study.

---

84. Warfield, *Revelation and Inspiration*, 6.

CHAPTER 2

The Prius of God's Ontological Order

IN THIS CHAPTER, I will attempt to justify the *prius* of God's ontological order based on the principle of identity, the principle of duality, and the order of sequence in God. As I had stated in the previous chapter, there is a logical order of God. What is evident from the last discussion is that God's order is discernible via our examination of nature's order. What is also true is that there is a distinct logic of God that is not of nature. For this reason, we can never equate God with nature, though they are correlatable to a certain extent. The question at this point to ask is, what is so unique about God's order? What makes God's order distinct from that of nature? In order to address these questions and their cognate issues, I move beyond the discussion of natural analogy and dive into the very essence of God to search for the underlying structure of God's order.

Moving into the world of God's essence, however, is not encouraged in the climate of today's theology. The consensus is that we may not be able to define God's ontological order at all. Why is this the case? As David Coffey once lamented, "We cannot simply put ourselves in the place of God and see things as he does."[1] Likewise, Philip Clayton quips that the contemporary scholars dismiss what they often refer to as "the God's-eye view, the illusion of the view from nowhere, the confusion that arises when we forget that we always speak out of a language game."[2] He adds that modern philosophers like Hilary Putnam demanded "a treatment of 'reason, truth, and history' that is based on dispensing with the 'God's eye point of view' altogether."[3]

---

1. Coffey, *Deus Trinitas*, 25.
2. Clayton, *The Problem of God*, 351.
3. Clayton, *The Problem of God*, 90.

The problem that today's scholars are talking about is the speculative nature of theology—and surely, the discussion of God's ontological order falls under this category. Like what Kant had questioned, they are skeptical of accessing the inner nature of God (e.g., the thing-itselfness of God) by way of reason alone. As Kant had noted, the thing-in-itself or the realm of noumena was off limits to any reason-abled activities.[4] Thus, according to Kant, even if we "know" something about God, it will not be "reason" that allows us to arrive there. Rather, for Kant, we may need some sort of moral or aesthetic sensibility that puts us in touch with God from which we can deduce God's existence.

Against the post-Kantian sentiment, despite the unpopularity of tackling the world of noumena, the goal of this chapter is to search for the ways in which we can speak of God's "thing-in-itselfness." I base by pursuit on the work of Karl Barth. As we have seen in the previous chapter, Barth spent his lifelong study to make the claim that the movement between God and the world is irreversible, in that we must start from God in himself rather than the reverse; thus, it is proper that we involve Barth in this discussion. My intention here is not just to take his theology for granted but scrutinize his work to see what sort of theological principles drive his theological program that allows him to promote the priority of God's ontological order. I end the chapter with my own view of God's ontological order especially seen from a pneumatological perspective.

Barth and the Prius of God's Ontological Order

There is no better place to start the discussion of God's ontological order than Barth's famous dictum: "God is who he is in the act of his revelation."[5] Despite its simplicity, due to its complex theological backing, it needs a further explanation. Before I flesh out what it means, I need to introduce Barth's specific thought forms. As Hans Urs von Balthasar once said, Barth has certain key thought forms that guide his theological writings,[6] so we

---

4. Kant, *Critique of Pure Reason*, 165.

5. Barth, *Church Dogmatics* 4/1, 257. Primarily, Barth states this dictum to promote his christological thinking, e.g., Jesus as the "Word made flesh" is God, for God is who he is in the act of his revelation. However, I carry this theological implication further to note that there is a specific ontological principle that allows Barth to sustain this dictum, which is the principle of identity and duality.

6. Balthasar, *The Theology of Karl Barth*, 59.

should choose some specific criteria that may assist us in unpacking the meaning of this statement. For this purpose, I bring up George Hunsinger's categorization, not because he stands tall above all other Barthian scholars; rather, in my judgment, he has provided a good starting point for us to discuss the particularities of Barth's theological program without placing Barth in a one-size-fits-all paradigm.

Hunsinger lists Barth's "thought forms" in the following way: actualism, objectivism, realism, particularism, personalism, and rationalism.[7] Although I am using Hunsinger's categorization, I have nuanced them differently to suit our purpose, stretching his definitions even further to include what I think is important to Barth that Hunsinger did not mention in his book. Of course, we cannot blame Hunsinger for leaving out some of the details that I am going to mention here, for his book is not an exhaustive account of Barth's work—neither is mine. Adding my own expansion and simultaneously condensing Hunsinger's categorization, I begin with an actualism-personalism combination, or what I call personalist actualism. This particular category denotes Barth's tendency to put together God's being and act as an inseparable whole. For Barth, God is not a static, inactive being.[8] Rather, God, as a person, acts freely and his free action makes him who he is. For God always involves his personal act, Barth unequivocally reads God's being from God's action, and vice versa. So, Barth's God is always performative, relational, personal, or eventful.

The next in line is Barth's objectivism-realism combination. Contra Hunsinger, for me, these two are too closely related to separate them into distinct categories, so for now, we shall call it objectivist realism. It basically emphasizes Barth's distinct view of God—i.e., God's own reality impinging upon us, rather than our own subjectivity determining the form and shape of who God is and what he does. Drawing upon a generic realist definition, we can say that, for Barth, God's self-existence is independent of our imagination, and since God is always active, his own reality "speaks" and "shows" who he is before our speech-act. The implication of objectivist realism is

---

7. I put objectivism and realism under the same rubric here for the purpose of highlighting the ontological order of God. My point here is that Barth's ontological order of God follows the path of theological realism, for he starts with God's own reality which exists independently of our existence and knowing.

8. According to Barth, to equate God with "being itself"—e.g., a lifeless and inert entity—is to equate God with death. See Barth, *Church Dogmatics* 2/1, 494. He is essentially arguing against the Thomist view, namely, the categorization of God as "unmoved mover."

that we may perceive God standing as an actual independent entity, rather than a conceptually constructed being that depends on human imagination or natural phenomena for its conception. For this reason, we can say that Barth's God has thing-itselfness, that is, noumenon (e.g., God is who he is in himself, or for short, God in himself) that is differentiated from phenomenon (e.g., God's experience of the things in this world).

Speaking of God's thing-itselfness, Hunsinger mentions Barth's particularism, which in my opinion, is the most important category of all. Since it is so pervasive in Barth's writing, it could be integrated into the rest of Hunsinger's categories. This is what I am going to do in the following sections, but for now, it suffices to say that Barth's theological particularism deserves a singular attention. From my reading, particularism speaks about Barth's focus on God's own logical center that is distinct from any other centers we know. For Barth, God is not known because of us, nor is he determined by anything that is other than himself. He is just who he is. In a classical sense, we may say that Barth advocates God who is uncreated and self-existing. Consequently, for Barth, God is nothing like us, or anything in this world. This divine particularism is the linchpin of Barth's theology, which allows him to maintain theological particularism—i.e., the particularity of doing theology only within the context of *analogia fidei* or Christology[9] as well as the particularity of biblical language that must be treated differently from the rest of literature.

Moving on to the final category, we find Barth's rationalism. I pair this with realism to emphasize Barth's rationalistic realism, for Barth is advocating not just any rationalism but a particular rationalism, that is, *intellectus fidei*. To borrow the words from Hunsinger, "the nature of the *intellectus fidei*—faith's critical understanding of itself through rational reflection—can be presented, in the sense Barth conceived of it, under two organizing rubrics: 'no knowledge without faith' and 'no faith without knowledge.'"[10] The former describes "faith seeking the limits of understanding, faith seeking to understand the extent to which we actually can understand, and thus faith seeking to understand precisely what it is that we cannot understand," and the latter "meant to suggest that faith was never conceived (in *Church Dogmatics*) as anything other than intrinsically rational."[11] I add christological realism here to emphasize that Barth's rationalism is always based

---

9. Balthasar's made this point well. Balthasar, *The Theology of Karl Barth*, 114.
10. Hunsinger, *How to Read Karl Barth*, 49.
11. Hunsinger, *How to Read Karl Barth*, 49, 54.

on what God reveals to us in history through Jesus Christ. So, unless our theological statements refer to the actuality of God revealed in and through Christ, Barth will not consider them as "real" or "rational."[12]

Before I move to the heart of the matter, I want to mention one additional comment about Barth's theological principle. Barth treats theology dialectically. There are essentially two ways to describe Barth's dialectic. The first way is Barth's incorporation of philosophical concepts for the sake of expanding his theological thought. Although Barth does not build his theology upon "philosophy," he does "assimilate" some of classical and modern philosophical ideas such as the concept of "being" and "infinity" into the doctrine of God. It is critical here to note the qualifier "assimilation."[13] As Barth brings philosophical concepts into theology, he changes its original meaning to fit the idiom of the church. Thus, in the context of *Church Dogmatics*, Barth's philosophical terms may carry different meanings as they have been moved from the realm of the secular to the sacred.

The second aspect of Barth's dialectic is his integration of two opposing concepts into a single unified statement—this is what we are going to concentrate on. How does it work? For instance, he often notes that God holds together the thesis and antithesis together without destroying one at the expense of the other, such as being and becoming, eternity and time, selflessness and self-relatedness, or God *in se* and God *pro nobis*. This is his dialectic, which keeps the tension between the different ideas of God all the while enforcing their commensurability. Barth likes the dialectical approach because two seemingly antithetical ideas about God can be linked together to create a healthy tension so that the integrity of the two categories in question is preserved without conflation and without separation. What we need to realize is that Barth's dialectic is tied to his theological particularism. For Barth, it is God, and only God, who can hold together thesis and antithesis without marginalizing one at the expense of the other. For some, Barth's dialectic resembles that of Hegelian dialectic,[14] but I disagree. Barth's particularism does not allow him to pitch his tent in the prox-

---

12. Thomas Torrance calls it an *a priori* method. This method tries to fit God into a prefabricated box that we have created. Thus, God is placed on a Procrustean bed of artificiality, and reconfigured in such a way that he is no longer recognizable from a Christian biblical perspective. Torrance, *Theological Science*, 88, 340.

13. Hunsinger, *How to Read Karl Barth*, 61–63.

14. E.g., Ward, "Barth, Hegel and the Possibility for Christian Apologetics," 56. I would rather say that Barth may have been influenced more by Søren Kierkegaard than Hegel. To note, Kierkegaard was an avid distractor of Hegelian dialectic.

imity of the Hegelian camp, though he may have visited Hegel and drawn water from his well.[15] How can Barth's particularism concede to Hegel's abstract idea of the *Geist* that blurs the two opposing components of being and non-being by the introduction of the third category of becoming?

Going back to Barth's dictum, we are now ready to unpack the significance of his statement: "God is who he is in the act of his revelation." We can decode this statement first from the vantage point of personalist actualism. Here, Barth connects God's being ("God is who he is") with God's act ("his self-revelation"). In other words, God is who he is because he is active and revealing. Moreover, God is personally involved with us, since he comes to us as who he is, an active and revealing agent.

Going further, from an objective realist vantage point, we can also see that Barth starts with God himself. Unlike modern apologists, Barth's point of departure is an assumption that God exists. He never tries to defend the existence of God apologetically. So, free from making a case for God's existence, Barth simply states that "God is."[16] Barth confirms this approach unequivocally. "The Christian knowledge of eternity has to do directly and exclusively with God himself, with Him as the beginning before all time, the turning point in time, and the end and goal after all time."[17] For Barth, God-is does not need any further support, because "God is God's own, belonging to and dependent upon no other or upon no thing."[18] Hence, Barth's objective realism points to his particularism. Barth clearly emphasizes that God has his own unique world, ontological status, and logic, that is starkly different from that of our own ontological status and logic, and as a result, God-talk has to start from God himself. This is Barth's rationalism, his way of explaining the logic of God's being and act, his way of fulfilling the demands of *intellectua fidei*. This approach, however, begs a question. If Barth starts with the proposition of God-is and claims that this is a non-inferential belief of God, is he advocating foundationalism?

Often Barth has been labeled as a theo-foundationalist.[19] This is something we must examine before we move to the next topic, since foundationalism in the modern world is outrightly rejected as an untenable

---

15. Because of this difference, to avoid confusion, I may not use the language of "dialectic" but instead the language of "duality."

16. Barth, *Church Dogmatics* 2/1, 257.

17. Barth, *Church Dogmatics* 2/1, 639.

18. Titus, "The Perfection of God," 207.

19. Diller, *Theology's Epistemological Dilemma*, 88.

theological epistemic structure. This is clearly the thesis of Stanley Grenz and John Franke's analysis of the current condition of foundationalism.[20] Notwithstanding other theories of foundationalism, for our purpose, we need to be concerned with a foundationalism that revolves around unjustified beliefs. Unjustified beliefs are those beliefs that have no backing, and if they are substantiated, they are backed up by other unjustified beliefs. We can clearly see the error of creating a vicious circle or falling into the deep abyss of *reductio ad absurdum*. More dangerous is its implication of "anything goes." Without clear justification, one's belief can be as outrageous as "Caesar is God," and becomes a source of indoctrination that controls the minds of the public. This is one of the reasons why foundationalism is untenable in today's theological climate.

Is Barth really a foundationalist? On the surface, Barth's claim of God-is seems that he is, but he is not. Although Barth relies on a basic belief, he is not structuring his theology upon unjustified beliefs. For Barth, the claim of God-is is a direct consequence of what God has revealed himself to us. It is not a derivative of "our beliefs" or our speculations. This is why Barth's theology falls under the rubric of objectivist realism. As an illustration, the statement, "the mountain is rocky," is a true statement if the mountain is made up of rocks. In this respect, in accordance with Barth's claim, we cannot start with the belief that "the mountain is rocky" without an encounter with the mountain itself. We must rely on what the mountain is revealing itself to us to know that it is rocky. Had we refused to do so, we would be speculating. So, when Barth says that God-is, he is not stating about his guess work—God is something like what we assume to be. Rather, he is stating that God is who he is in himself as he is historically disclosed to us through the God-man Jesus Christ. Surely, an atheistic naturalist would not accept this proposition, since he or she denies the existence of God. However, in Barth's world, there is no such thing as non-existent God. God exists. His existence has been fully revealed in and through Jesus Christ, so for Barth, it is naturalists who are blind as bats living in a cave unable to see the true light that has been disclosed to us already by Jesus Christ.

There is one more issue that lingers with Barth's theology, the problem of criticizability, which is related to the first point. Wolfhart Pannenberg is one of the key theologians who brought this point against Barth. According to Pannenberg, Barth's theological statement such as God-is is so complete in and of itself, it can never be tested or criticized. He writes, "By appealing

---

20. Grenz and Franke, *Beyond Foundationalism*, 3–56.

to the commitment of faith, theological thinking ultimately escaped any rational critique. This position was justified by the assertion that all thought rests ultimately on unprovable assumptions."[21] Basically, Pannenberg is calling Barth an irrational fideist. I agree with Pannenberg to some extent, which has to do with Barth's incessant effort to build his theology within the premise of "faith knowledge" that eschews all forms of natural theology. As we have seen, Barth is nowhere near the camp of natural theologians. Indeed, Barth does not build his theological case based upon secular science such as psychology, sociology, or physical science, even though he may interact with their findings. In this regard, I depart from Barth's paradigm. However, I do not think Pannenberg is fair here.

In my judgment, Pannenberg does not see why Barth is rejecting natural theology. Barth's theological statements are *not* criticizable due to the fact that he discounts the criticism coming from modern empiricists, rationalists, or idealists. It is because, for Barth, they lie outside the faith circle, so they do not have the qualification to "criticize" theological statements. How can they? They do not consider "revealed history" as appropriate scientific data, and reducing theology into discrete pieces of natural phenomena, they have dismissed God's miracles. Without God's miracles, as far as Barth is concerned, they are not really doing full justice to theology. In this respect, Barth is right to say that theology is not criticizable.

By contrast, from a different perspective, Barth's theological statements are criticizable. If the critics work within the premise of faith knowledge, Barth allows his theology to be criticized and investigated by others. This is confirmed by Hunsinger.

> Theology so conceived [by Barth] is a form of coherentism in the sense that no theological assertions and beliefs can be justified independently of other theological assertions and beliefs—all of which are rooted directly or indirectly in faith. Theology as a set of internal logical and cognitive relations can thus be explained by noting several 'rationalist' procedures: deriving, grounding, testing, and assimilating.[22]

Hunsinger details the identification of Barth's deriving, grounding, testing, and assimilating in the rest of his chapters, but in summary, he is showing that Barth's theological claims are criticizable and substantiated by critically investigating and self-assessing his theology as well as others

---

21. Pannenberg, *The Historicity of Nature*, 12–13.
22. Hunsinger, *How to Read Karl Barth*, 55.

within the Christian faith tradition. In the final analysis, we cannot say that Pannenberg's criticism captures the full scope of Barth's theology. He is neither an irrationalist nor a fideist. Rather, his rationalism is grounded on theological particularism.

With the contours of Barth's theology clarified, we are now in position to discuss Barth's conception of God's ontological order. According to Barth, God has a logical order. His order starts from God in himself. Here, Barth recognizes that God is a "free" being. This is the thing-itselfness of God which is free from all worldly contaminations. In this light, Barth's description of God's attributes with the concept of "perfection" contrasts well with the imperfections in this world.[23] This is not the end of the story for Barth.

Going further, Barth denotes that, although God is in himself, God moves *ad extra* and reveals himself to us. At this juncture, we must pay close attention to Barth's principle of identity. What is Barth's principle of identity? For clarification, let me restate Barth's dictum this way: God remains who he is even in his self-revealedness. So, from Barth's perspective, it is proper to say that God follows the principle of identity. I agree with Barth here, for this is the logic of God. God is who he is, as he declared, "I am who I am" (Ex. 3:14), regardless of what he does for us. The implication of the principle of identity is that the beginning and the end of God are the same (e.g., Rev 22:13). God enters history as God and exits as God, despite whatever process he may go through in between. There is no change in God in himself. God can only be God, and he cannot be *not* God, or any other being other than God. If we keep this principle of identity in mind, we would not be making mistakes and confuse God with the things of this world, as many contemporary scholars have done. For this reason, I value Barth's theology highly. Christian theology owes a great debt to Barth in this regard.

Realigning Barthian Scholars' Interpretation of God's Order

From my reading, according to Barth's dictum that says, God is who he is in his act of revelation, Barth's conception of God's ontological order begins with God's freedom to be himself and then moves *ad extra* to God's freedom to be with us. However, this ordering has been contested by several Barthian scholars such as Robert Jenson and Bruce McCormack. Since

---

23. Barth, *Church Dogmatics* 2/1, 322.

McCormack's argument is based on the most updated interpretation of Barth's theology, I will use his proposal to see why this ordering principle is contested.

The essence of McCormack's theological proposal is that God freely chooses to be with us and this status explains God's essence. He argues that "the eternal act in which God gives to himself his own being as Father, Son and Holy Spirit and the eternal act in which God chooses to be God in the covenant of grace with human beings is one and the same act. These are not two acts but one."[24] This statement aligns well with Barth's theology of election. For Barth, the "election of grace is the eternal beginning of all the ways and works of God in Jesus Christ."[25] If this is true, which McCormack believes so, then as God's being is God's act, God must be a self-determinate being as God-for-us. However, in my opinion, McCormack has overstretched Barth's theology of election, claiming that God-for-us determines God's inner trinitarian life, neglecting the fact that there is God's freedom to be without us. Going back to McCormack, he says that "it is God's act of determining himself to be God for us in Jesus Christ which constitutes God as triune."[26] Hence, God's aseity (e.g., God's triunity) is determined by God-for-us. Kevin Hector sums up McCormack's view succinctly: "McCormack claims that God's economic triunity reveals that God is eternally self-determined to be God-with-us, such that God's being is eternally being-toward the economy of grace."[27] Hector affirms that McCormack's God cannot be anything other than what God reveals himself to us, following Barth's principle of identity.

I have no quarrel with McCormack's utilization of Barth's principle of identity, that God must be God in himself as well as in his revealedness. Also, epistemologically, McCormack is right to start with the economic Trinity, which grants us access to the immanent Trinity, so that we can turn back to the economic Trinity from the immanent Trinity. This is McCormack's hermeneutical circle. Without it, our knowledge of God will be too abstract and speculative. We need to depend on God's revelation (the economic Trinity) to know who God is in himself (the immanent Trinity). However, there are two areas of his argument that in my opinion needs reworking in order to take advantage of Barth's theology fully.

24. McCormack, "Seek God," 66.
25. Barth, *Church Dogmatics* 2/2, 94.
26. McCormack, "Seek God," 67.
27. Hector, "God's Triunity," 246.

The first one has to do with merging Barth's principle of identity with his dialectical theology. It is true that Barth enjoys the principle of identity, but he does so only in light of the principle of dialectic—this duality essentially preserves the distinction even when the principle of identity is applied.[28] I believe that Thomas Torrance, one of his renowned disciples, has caught this idea and made use of it in the development of his theology of *homoousion*. Torrance writes, "Just as the *homoousion* expresses at once the distinction and the oneness between the incarnate Son and the Father, so it enables us to speak both of the distinction and of the oneness between the economic and the ontological Trinity and without detracting from the crucial significance of either."[29] Torrance is basically saying that the logic of Trinity (e.g., *homoousion*) reveals that God's oneness and God's distinction go hand in hand without separation and without confusion. Thus, the only way to express the logic of the Trinity is to merge the principle of identity and the principle of duality in God.

McCormack, in my judgment, did not merge these two principles carefully. When he says that God with us is the determinant factor for God in himself, he applies the principle of identity with no regard for the principle of duality, for God with us and God in himself cannot simply be conflated into "one and the same act." The "one" part is correct, but the non-distinguishable aspect is wrong. God is distinguishable—e.g., God has taken on something new in his act of revelation.[30] I will come back to the

---

28. Note that the principle of duality is biblically attested. For instance, Kavin Rowe detects the principle of duality at work in the Lukan usage of the term κύριος. He asserts that "one can distinguish between θεός and Ἰησοῦς—they are not, as we will see, vermischt [blended]—and yet they can and do share an identity as κύριος." Rowe, *Early Narrative Christology*, 21–22.

29. Torrance, *The Christian Doctrine of God*, 30. In the Bible, God is revealed as the Trinity (e.g., the baptismal formula), not as triunity. In order for us to go from the Trinity to triunity, we must combine two biblical attestations: (1) God is one, and (2) the Father, the Son, and the Holy Spirit are three persons of the Trinity. According to Torrance, the doctrine of *homoousion* accomplishes this task. However, the Nicene Creed simply declares *homoousion*, which states that the Father, the Son, and the Holy Spirit are of the same substance. We need to move further than *homoousion* and state that the same substance is spirit (which Torrance does not say).

30. Here, I am following Torrance's christological thinking, for he pointed out that Jesus did not just reveal something of God already there but became something new without which our salvation may have not been possible. See for instance, Torrance, *Theology in Reconstruction*, 130. For this reason, in my judgment, the doctrine of God always needs two pillars to sustain its weight: God's presupposition of redemption (his election in and through the *logos asarkos*), and God's actual act of redemption (our salvation in

order of the Trinity later but it suffices to say that there is an order of distinction in God as it is revealed by the logic of the Trinity.

Translated to God's ontological order, we should say that God is who he is even when God is with us and for us. However, we should not say that God in himself and God with us are not distinguishable. They are distinguishable because the latter includes an incurred event. We do not belong to God in himself necessarily. We are surely created beings. As God the creator must be distinguished from his creation—Barth can't say enough about it—God's inner self must be distinguished from God with us; otherwise, we will violate God's principle of identity by reading "us" into God and make "us" a necessary component in God's life. What I am afraid of is that "man" becomes God's necessary ingredient in which anthropology determines God's ontological order. This is precisely what Barth was fighting against, and so, we must not make this error if we are to be faithful to Barth. Barth confirms: "God is also the One who is event, act and life in His own way, as distinct from everything that He is not Himself, even though at the same time He is its source, reconciliation and goal."[31]

For this reason, I also disagree with McCormack's formula: the *logos asarkos* is the *logos incarnandus*. I will flesh out this relationship in more detail in the following section from a pneumatological perspective, so I make a brief interjection here. Certainly, the *logos asarkos* is the *logos incarnandus*, again due to the principle of identity. However, the *logos incarnandus* cannot precede the *logos asarkos* due to the fact that "flesh" does not belong to God in the first place. McCormack may say that deleting "flesh" from God in himself would violate the principle of identity. That is not true. Even though something new was added to God, God is who he is in himself. He remains who he is and he cannot be something else even as he becomes God-man. In other words, God did not change from God in himself to God-man in Christ. Nor can adding something to God make him any lesser or greater deity. More clearly, even as God-man, God is who he is in himself, though "man" is added to him. According to the divine principle of identity, God is who he is, and he comes to us as who he is. Thus, the Word made flesh, or the *logos incarnandus* does not make the Son any lesser God because the divine Logos assumed a human body. It is just that the Logos without flesh precedes the Logos with flesh, to emphasize

---

and through the *logos incarnandus*).

31. Barth, *Church Dogmatics* 2/1, 264.

the order of God's love. God did not have to assume the flesh for us, but he did. This is the logic of God's grace.[32]

McCormack may worry about the *logos asarkos* disappearing into the thin air of speculation, since, if we distinguish the *logos asarkos* and the *logos incarnandus*, we may find some indeterminate God hiding behind the *logos asarkos*. My answer to this issue again is that the priority of God-is (e.g., the *logos asarkos*) does not invite speculation per Barth's understanding of revelation. According to Barth, the priority of God-is is a revealed truth because God comes to us as he in himself in the act of his revelation. The talk of God's aseity may be treated as theological abstraction had we considered the fact that God's aseity is only accessible to us via theological imagination. However, when we affirm that our understanding of God's aseity depends on God's self-revelation, we are already out of the waters of abstraction, at least, according to Barth. So, we do not need to worry about an "indeterminate" God hiding behind the concept of the *logos asarkos*. God has revealed himself fully in and through Jesus Christ, that is, God-without-us-but-for-us. What we need to remember is that the immanent Trinity is the controlling center due to its priority over the economic Trinity, so even after we read the immanent Trinity from the economic Trinity, we must take into consideration the proper "order" of God as the economic Trinity contains the "contingent" factors such as the addition of "flesh" that was not there before in God's life.

To reiterate, Christ's assumption of human flesh is a new event for God. To say it is "new" to God, I am talking about God's new event in the sense that "man" who is distinct from God became part of God as he has been drawn into God by Christ, and that God and man were not united before as it had been done through Jesus Christ by the power of the Holy Spirit. As Barth says, the God-man union in Jesus Christ is a singularity. It has not happened before and will never occur again, except the way it did in the God-man Jesus. This does not mean that the newness that God has experienced changed God's being to something other than he is not. The Chalcedonian definition of the hypostatic union between God and man in Jesus Christ attests to the fact that God and man in Jesus Christ are united without confusion and without change. This means that, although there is a thorough "integration" between God and man in Jesus Christ, they are

32. The logic of grace is this: God did not have to assume flesh. He did not have to redeem us through the death of God-man Jesus. Consequently, the Christ-even is a new event for God. The logic of grace accords with God's essence, but nonetheless, it is a novum in the sense that God has taken up that which he is not (e.g., the death of humanity).

nevertheless distinct. Again, the principles of identity and duality play a key role here. Jesus has one nature of God-man, but God and man are distinct. God has this new feature, that is, the new nature of God-man, which is already introduced to God *in se*, not as an intrinsic event but an event of grace, revealing God's freedom to join us to himself.

The second point that I want to mention is that McCormack confuses Barth's ontological order of God with God's economic order. McCormack reads God-for-us as the ontological starting point for God, for this is what God reveals himself "to be." I agree with McCormack that once the immanent Trinity is decided, it controls the whole of God's economy, or at least, our understanding of it. However, we have to note an additional requirement from Barth.[33] Barth insists that we have to start with God-is rather than God-for-us. He states it in this way. "God is who he is in his works. He is the same even in Himself, even before and after and over His works, and without them. They are bound to Him, but He is not bound to them."[34] This is another clear statement about Barth's principle of identity, but with a caveat, that we should not start with God's work so that he may be bound by it. In other words, God is who he is in his work for us, but his work for us does not precede God in himself, since God is not bound by it. Barth clarifies with an added comment. "He is not, therefore, who He is only in His works. Yet in Himself He is not another than He is in His works."[35] This is Barth's duality. God is both without and with us. With this statement, Barth prevents us from reading God's work into God in himself indiscriminately.[36] What Barth recognizes is that there is precedence in

---

33. McCormack correctly notes that Barth's earlier writings have a different understanding of God than his later writings. See McCormack, "The Actuality of God," 218. However, although there may be a theological gap between early and later Barth, there is still continuity, at least, with respect to Barth's conception of the principle of identity and the principle of duality. For a similar argument, see Terry L. Cross' *Dialectic in Karl Barth's Doctrine of God*.

34. Barth, *Church Dogmatics* 2/1, 260.

35. Barth, *Church Dogmatics* 2/1, 260.

36. A brief logical illustration may help. Assume that there is "before" and "after" God, as the Lord God said, "I am the Alpha and Omega" (Rev 1:8). For brevity, let us focus only on what is "before" God. According to the principle of identity, ontologically, what is before God must be God, because before God, there was nothing but God. God was all that there was to be. However, if we follow McCormack's logic and say that God is essentially toward-us, then creation (e.g., God's toward-us) must be "before" God. However, nothing exists "before" God, except God himself. So, logically, McCormack's argument is faulty. For this reason, God's toward-us cannot be *de facto* but only *de jure*, according to God's logic of grace.

God's ontological order. This order is biblical attested. The Bible speaks of the Father begetting the Son, not vice versa. The Son neither begets the Father, nor sends the Father to us. The order is clear. The Father is first and the Son the consequence, albeit they are one.

The precedence of the Father, however, does not mean that the Father is greater than the Son or the Holy Spirit.[37] This is the reason why I insist that the trinitarian ordering principle of God must be accompanied by God's identity principle. In the economy of God, the Father sending the Son does not mean that the Father is above and beyond the Son. Though taking upon himself the mantle of human flesh, the Son is God, the same God as the Father. The oneness of God the Father and God the Son is not violated because, in the immanent Trinity, God who is one in essence is distinguished as the firstness of the Father, the secondness of the Son, and thirdness of the Holy Spirit. The order in God simply emphasizes the logical distinction in God, not his ontological status. As I have said before, the order of nature and the order of God is different because of it. Unlike the natural system, there is no hierarchical ontology in the life of God. God is who he is in himself even as three persons, and only this principle of identity-and-distinction determines God's ontology.

To make myself clear, I repeat that, even though God makes his own distinction by disclosing himself to us in history, we cannot simply read God from his economy to formulate God's order of aseity. Because of the novum that God experiences in this world, we must be cautious in the way we read God's ordering principle from God's economy for us, though our knowledge of God depends on God's act in history. It is understandable that McCormack wants to read God's aseity from God's economy perhaps to prevent theological abstractions concerning God as we may impose our own ordering principle onto God, which can set off a great chain of messy controversies and errors such as subordinationism and adoptionism. However, I introduce the principle of the ontological *prius* precisely to prevent these errors. As long as we stay on task and keep in mind that God has the

---

37. Jesus' exaltation of the Father is evidenced by his sayings such as "the Father is greater than I" (John 14:28). Based on Jesus' sayings, often biblical scholars, like Dale Martin, assume that Jesus was not a divine figure, or at least, he was not equal to the Father. In my judgment, theologically, this is wrong. In the economic Trinity, there is a sense of "subordination" as the Son and the Spirit are doing what the Father wills. However, once again, we cannot read the immanent Trinity strictly from the economic Trinity, because of the addendum factor. For this reason, we must read John 14 vis-à-vis the principle of identity. As the principle of identity affirms, Jesus is who he is (our Lord and God) even in his service to us and the Father.

principle of identity-in-distinction, our reading of "order" in God will not fail us, avoiding theological abstractions as well as hierarchism like that of Neoplatonic gods. God has order, but this order is an at-once event. We can compare it to God's eternity. God's order is eternally identical and at the same time eternally distinguishable as a logical sequence. From a trinitarian perspective, God is at once one and three; likewise, he is who he is in his works, and at the same time, his essence *without us* precedes his work *for us*, for he is free to exist *without us*.

Speaking of God's freedom, Hector mentions the dispute between Paul Molnar and Bruce McCormack about the interpretation of Barth's conception of divine freedom. Hector writes,

> McCormack and Molnar thus move in nearly opposite directions; though both agree that God's economic triunity must be the starting-point for claims about God's immanent triunity, each sees something different in this economy. For McCormack, God's economic triunity discloses the fact that God's being is eternally oriented toward being-with-humanity, whereas for Molnar the economic Trinity reveals that the God who is with us is *freely* with us, such that God could have been otherwise.[38]

He goes further and restates this difference in terms McCormack's emphasis on God's freedom-for-us, and Molnar's God's freedom-from-us.[39]

If Hector's assessment is true, McCormack and Molnar, as well as Hector who raises McCormack's hand in the end, all have a winning card, though incomplete. The trophy can be handed to the one who has upheld Barth's "both-and" attitude regarding God's freedom. Barth denotes that God is free for us as well as free from us. As an example, he writes, "God is free to present with the creature by giving himself and revealing himself to it or by concealing himself and withdrawing from it."[40] As this statement confirms, Barth understands that God is both free to be with us and free to be without us.[41] For this reason, in Barth's theology, there is continuity between God who is free for us and God who is free to be himself, all the

---

38. Hector, "God's Triunity," 254.

39. Hector, "God's Triunity," 256–7. For clarity, I will change Hector's language from God's freedom-from-us to God's freedom-without-us.

40. Barth, *Church Dogmatics* 2/1, 314–5.

41. Note that we cannot say that God without us is one of many possibilities in God. We cannot let the "possibility" be the limiting factor for God, which will undermine God's sovereignty. The only "limiting" factor for God is who he is not—e.g., God cannot be *not* God, or God cannot be *not* good.

while recognizing that there is distinction between God is free for us and God is free without us. Once again, Barth's principle of identity and duality come together here.

So, McCormack is right to say that God is free for us, but the card he holds is not complete. He needs an additional card that says, "God is free without us." Likewise, Molnar is right to say that God is free without us, but his theology is not complete also. He does not have the card that shows God's freedom for us and God's freedom without us as a single event. More clearly, Molnar's depiction of God in himself and God for us as two independent acts of God is wrong.[42] As Barth has pointed out, God in himself and God for us cannot be two acts of God, but a single act. The principle of identity cannot be violated. It is a distinguishable act, but nonetheless a single act.[43] That is the reason why we need to be cautious in our depiction of God. God has a unique logic, the principle of identity and the principle of duality working co-operatively as a commensurable logic. God in himself is God for us though not without qualification. This is what Barth is claiming. If we want to follow Barth, we cannot say that God's distinction pans out as two independent acts.

In summary, my introduction to Barth's conception of God's ontological order reveals the fact that Barth has pushed his theological paradigm far and wide to include the principle of identity and the principle of duality within the scope of his particularism, realism, and rationalism. Barth's theological paradigm provides a good stepping stone for me to rethink about the ontological order of God. For this reason, I build my own conception of the *prius* of God's ontological order based on Barth's theological paradigm. However, as with all other constructive work, while I appreciate Barth's contribution, I want to move beyond Barth and rethink God's order from a pneumatological perspective.

---

42. Molnar, "The Electing God," 216. He states, "God's self-determination to be God for us is a distinct and new action on God's part as the beginning of his ways and works *ad extra*. Therefore, we have two acts of God here and not just one." I agree that God for us is a "new" action on God's part, but we still need to emphasize that God is who he is even when he tags onto himself something "new."

43. Perhaps, the language of Thomistic virtual distinction may be helpful. This is what David Coffey has done to explain the at-once-one-and-distinct principle of God. God's immanent relations and God's economy are a one single event, and the two are only virtually distinct, the former having a logical precedence over the latter. See Coffey, *Deus Trinitas*, 75.

A Pneumatological Vison of God's Ontological Order

As the one who advocates doing theology from the vantage point of Third Article Theology, I feel that pneumatology will not only support Barth's cause, but at the same time, expand our understanding of the *prius* of God's ontological order by pushing it to the unreached realm of God's spiritual order. Surely, Barth has captured not only God in himself, but also God for us, connecting many theological dots in between, skillfully applying the principle of identity and duality, which is further supported by his particularism (e.g., realism, actualism, and rationalism), but there is one thing lacking, that is, doing theology from the perspective of Third Article Theology. However, as Myk Habets notes, if Barth had time, he would have done so. He quotes Barth in this regard.

> What I have already intimated here and there to good friends, would be the possibility of a theology predominantly and decisively of the Holy Spirit. Everything which needs to be said, considered, and believed about God the Father and God the Son in an understanding of the first and second articles might be shown and illuminated in its foundations through God the Holy Spirit, the *vinculum pacis inter Patrem et Filium*.[44]

So, as a bold step forward, in this section, I will attempt to do what Barth had planned to do, to recode the doctrine of God by structuring God's ontological order pneumatologically, all the while meeting Barth's demand for particularism. Also, I demonstrate that the pneumological approach is much more fluid and expansive than Barth's Second Article theological approach, which potentially prevents the one-sided reading like that of McCormack's or Molnar's theology, as the Spirit follows the principle of identity and duality, without marginalizing one at the expense of the other. I start with my own description of the pneumatologically driven *prius* of God's ontological order, which will be followed by a critical engagement with pneumatologists from other traditions, namely, Sergius Bulgakov, an Eastern Orthodox scholar, and David Coffey, a Jesuit scholar.

Spirit and God's Ontological Order

In order to unpack God's ontological order pneumatologically, I start with the biblical statement that says, "God is spirit" (John 4:24). As Henry

---

44. Habets, "Prolegomenon," 4.

Thiessen comments, God-is-spirit defines God's nature, that is, God's essence.[45] If God is spirit in nature, we can restate it with respect to Barth's dictum: God is spirit in himself and God is spirit in his act of revelation. What I have stated here is the affirmation of the principle of identity. God is spirit in himself as well as in his act of revelation. Even if we reverse the order, the statement still retains the continuity between God *in se* and God for us, as God is spirit in his act of revelation and God is spirit in himself. This logic affirms the biblical attestation that God is "I am who I am" (Exod 3:14). God is affirmed by who he is in himself spiritually and who he is in his act of revelation spiritually. God's being and act are one and the same because God is spirit in his being and in his act.

God-is-spirit also attests to God who is the wholly other. Simply put, divine spirit is not of this world (finite things). Being not of this world, divine spirit is wholly differentiated from the things of this world. For this reason, in the words of David Coffey, God is "absolute spirit."[46] Because of God's absoluteness, divine spirit cannot be produced, created, or formed. God-as-spirit just is. This aligns well with Barth's theological particularism. Spirit is the thing-itselfness of God. There is nothing else like it. There is nothing else that can describe it. Spirit is God and God is spirit. In other words, spirit's thing itselfness explains that God is who he is in himself and

---

45. Thiessen, *Lectures in Systematic Theology*, 75. Exegetically, the meaning of the phrase πνεῦμα ὁ θεός is highly controversial. There are essentially two opposing views. The first view is that πνεῦμα ὁ θεός designates the nature of God. Thiessen's view fits into this category. Andreas Köstenberger explains it more in detail: "God is a spiritual rather than material being" as John 4:24 contrasts the place of worship between a geographical location and a spiritual qualification. The second view states that πνεῦμα ὁ θεός is a specific statement denoting the third person of the Trinity, the Holy Spirit. Benny Thettayil presents this interpretation. He demonstrates exegetically that πνεῦμα ὁ θεός signifies "God is the Holy Spirit," since the article in front of the word θεός implicitly affirms his reading. Wayne Johnson follows Thettayil's interpretation, but with an added note that, since John 4:24 focuses on the new locus of worship, πνεῦμα ὁ θεός should be interpreted as the new locus, that is "the Father in union with Jesus and the Holy Spirit." Although Johnson makes his case for the latter position, he admits that πνεῦμα ὁ θεός is highly ambiguous phrase, and it may not be clearly discernible from an exegetical analysis alone. My stance is that, like Johnson, πνεῦμα ὁ θεός should be read in a trinitarian term, but it needs to be nuanced differently than what Johnson provides—e.g., πνεῦμα ὁ θεός denotes the union in the spiritness of the Father, the Son, and the Holy Spirit. For this reason, I follow Bulgakov's interpretation of πνεῦμα ὁ θεός (God's essence is spirit), which will be analyzed in detail in the following section. For more details, see Wayne Johnson's paper, "John 4:19–24: Exegetical Implications for Worship and Place," presented at the Annual Meeting of the Evangelical Theological Society.

46. Coffey, *Deus Trinitas*, 75.

remains so in his act of revelation. God is spirit before and after; therefore, it justifies God's principle of identity.

Although God's spirit is absolute, the order of divine spirit is distinguished, as God is spirit in himself first and God is spirit in his act of revelation second. As we have shown above, we cannot begin with God is spirit in his act of revelation, because there is a distinction between God *in se* and God for us. Pneumatologically, we can describe this relationship as God-is-spirit-in-himself and God-is-spirit-for-us. God-is-spirit-for-us is further related to Holy Spirit, which is distinguishable to the one spirit substance of triunity. We require a trinitarian logic to flesh out what this means.

The doctrine of the Trinity states that not only the Father and the Son are God, but also the Holy Spirit is God. But the Bible also attests to the fact that the Father is spirit (e.g., Matt 10:20)[47] and the Son is spirit (e.g., Rom 8:9)—it goes without saying that the Holy Spirit is also spirit. Hence, the oneness of God is affirmed spiritually as God is one in spirit, and the threeness of God is affirmed spiritually as Father-spirit, Son-spirit, and Holy Spirit, respectively in that order.[48] In other words, divine spirit's oneness defines the principle of identity, and the spiritual personal existence defines God's principle of distinction.

If we understand that God is sprit, unlike McCormack's proposal, we can see that God's self-determination (God's act) is not prior to God's triunity (God's being). Nor can God's triunity be the result of God's act—i.e., God is triune only because he reveals himself to us as triune. Rather, God is triune because God is spirit. In other words, God is intrinsically and necessarily spiritual as well as God is inherently and necessarily triune. Moreover, contra Molnar, because God-is-spirit is at once event, we cannot have two discrete acts in God and emphasize the independence of the immanent Trinity from the economic Trinity. Because God is spirit, they are one act of God, albeit distinct. They are one but distinct, since God is spirit

---

47. I read the Father's spirit not merely as the Holy Spirit but the Father *as* spirit. According to the principle of identity, Father's spirit is equivalent to the Father as spirit in God's life, since for God, to be is to act, and to act is to be. So, to be of spirit is to be spirit.

48. Appropriately, pneumatology enhances the trinitarian order that is faithful to both ontological and personalistic ideas of God. The term "spirit" in the Bible presupposes and identifies the personhood of man and God, that is, the living, thinking, and feeling subject. Also, in support of the trinitarian dynamics, the Bible attests to the common as well as distinct spirituality of the Father, the Son, and the Holy Spirit. Moreover, *pneuma* in the Bible normally denotes the essence of God or man. Thus, the concept of spirit underwrites the principle of *homoousion*. For more details, see Kim, *The Holy Spirit in the World*, 1–66.

and God's spiritness is ordered in terms of three distinct persons, namely, Father-spirit, Son-spirit, and Holy Spirit, respectively.

The pneumatological ordering also solves the issue of relating the *logos asarkos* to the *logos incarnandus*. If we retrieve the pneumatological language of Son-spirit, we can clearly see that there is continuity and discontinuity between the two. The starting point of the *logos asarkos* makes sense, since the Son-spirit does not have the flesh in his essence. So the *logos incarnandus* is an event that is "new" to the *logos asarkos*. Hence, the *logos asarkos* precedes the *logos incarnandus*. This does not mean that we have two logos' events that are mutually exclusive. Rather, we have one logos event, as the Son-spirit (without human flesh) is the *logos asarkos*, and the Son-spirit (with human flesh) is the *logos incarnandus*, in accordance with the principle of identity. The distinction is that the Son-spirit has assumed man into his life (thus, into God's life) as the *logos incarnandus*. In this respect, the spiritness of the Son could be considered as a merger of the *logos asarkos* and the *logos incarnandus*, being able to unite the two as one (e.g., one nature of God-man spirit), and at the same time, without confusion and without change, keeping the distinction of God and man (e.g., infinite Spirit versus finite spirit) in Jesus Christ. Hence, the doctrine of the hypostatic union needs to be fleshed out pneumatologically as well.[49]

To make an additional comment about the "at once" trinitarian logic, I believe that both Barth and Torrance do not explain the "at once" component pneumatologically, which is vital to our understanding of God's trinitarian ontological make-up, since it sustains the logic of the Trinity. Barth simply explains it mostly in terms of his actualism, in his non-apologetic fashion, declaring that God is at once Trinity in Unity and Unity in Trinity, whereas Torrance explains it with the doctrine of *homoousion*, drawing upon the Nicene Creed that affirms the *homoousion* of the Father and the Son (and by implication the Holy Spirit). Torrance has done well to relate the doctrine of *homoousion* to the doctrine of the Trinity, but he does not go further and explore the possibility of this "same substance" may be God's spirit-substance as it is implied in the statement, "God is spirit." Thus, from a pneumatological perspective, we can move beyond Barth's actualism and

---

49. This project has taken up by David Coffey, and he states that the hypostatic union of God-man is spiritual, for the Holy Spirit bonds God and man as one God-man nature, which he calls "theandric." For more details, see Coffey, "The Theandric Nature of Christ," 405–31.

Torrance's *homoousion* and state that divine oneness or "substance" (*homoousion*) is spirit.[50]

If the *homoousion* is spirit, then the Father, the Son, and the Holy Spirit are at once one spirit and three distinct spirits, because each person in the Godhead is spiritually distinct from one another without dividing up the oneness of spirit-*homoousion*. To put it differently, we can say that each spirit-person of the Godhead does not add up and make the triunity-spirit whole. Each spirit person is fully God and each person in the Godhead is fully spiritual. This is the pneumatological principle of identity and distinction, which confirms the "at once one and three" principle of the Trinity. The trinitarian continuity once again is possible because God is consubstantial in spirit, the common denominator for the three persons in the Godhead. Furthermore, distinctiveness is possible also because of the three logical orders of spirit—e.g., the firstness of Father-spirit, the secondness of Son-spirit, and the thirdness of Holy Spirit. In sum, the spirit-*homoousion* is the "at once one and three" component of the triunity.

To reiterate, we can see that the distinctiveness of spirituality in each person in the Godhead does not divide God into three parts. Spirit by definition is a non-discrete entity. Even metaphysically, it is a quality of relations.[51] Thus, it cannot be divided or treated like billiard balls. It can be participated but not divided. Therefore, spirit ontology does not allow us to think discretely, but fluidly and dynamically, defying the logic that three-ness means three different parts to a whole. The problem of separation in the Trinity that leads to tritheism, adoptionism, or hierarchism, is resolved if we understand that God is wholly spirit, even if God is distinguished into three spirit persons—e.g., the Father-spirit, the Son-spirit, and the Holy Spirit. To put it in Barthian idiom, God is spirit in triunity and God is spirit in each person of the Godhead, without separation and without confusion.

---

50. Following John S. Feinberg, I believe that the theological terminology of God's essence, nature, and substance all connote God's aseity. Feinberg, *No One Like Him*, 37–80. Sergius Bulgakov also portrays this continuity by surveying the work of patristic fathers. See Bulgakov, *Comforter*, 1–94. Although we must be cautious in the way we use the term "substance" so that it does not conflate with the Neoplatonic sense of the static immaterial matter, if we hold to the idea that God's "substance" is his uncreated essence, then like Feinberg, we can use the term to denote God's being. Hence, contra LeRon Shults, "substance" should not necessarily viewed as the antithesis to relational ontology. We may even say that God's "substance" is relations, or more specifically, trinitarian relations. For more details on the development of God as an immaterial substance, see Shults, *Reforming the Doctrine of God*, 15–40.

51. Loder and Neidhardt, *The Knight's Move*, 10.

Realigning Pneumatologists' Interpretation of God's Order

At this juncture, let me critically review some of the ways in which God-spirit is viewed by pneumatologists from different Christian traditions and show that the model I presented here can adjust the pneumatological problems that we have inherited from our predecessors. In this section, I am going to examine those issues that pertain to the ontological order of God particularly seen through the lens of pneumatology—I defer the problems associated with the epistemological order until the next set of chapters though we may be mentioning it in passing here. Relevant to our discussion, I inspect two views. The first one belongs to Sergius Bulgakov and the second David Coffey, to whom I give credit for rethinking pneumatology from a holistic perspective.

To begin, I review Sergius Bulgakov's pneumatological approach. As an Eastern Orthodox scholar, he tackles many controversial issues that are related to pneumatology, especially arguing against the Catholic tradition. There are just too many arguments denoted in his book, *The Comforter*, which may require another book to lay out all his contributions to pneumatology, so I bracket it within his portrayal of God's ontological order and his understanding of God as spirit.

Sergius Bulgakov and the Pneumatological Trinitarian Order

Bulgakov certainly recognizes the priority of God's ontological order. He does not deny that God's essence takes priority over God's revelation. He even rightfully connects God's essence to God as spirit. He writes, "God is spirit and spirituality is the essence of God."[52] He goes on and says, "Spirituality is proper to the First and Second hypostases not less than to the Third."[53] His rationale is similar to what I have been describing about the nature of God's spirit-*homoousion*. Spirit neither decreases nor increases even if spirit is shared by the three persons in the Godhead. God remains as one spirit despite being shared by the three persons. For this reason, Bulgakov is able to say that "God is spirit in his entire trihypostatic being, not

---

52. Bulgakov, *Comforter*, 153. Bulgakov's dictum makes more sense if we say that the Spirit-substance is the essence of God, and from the context of his writing, God's Spirit-substance and spirituality are synonymous.

53. Bulgakov, *Comforter*, 153.

only as the Third hypostasis, but also as the First and Second."[54] All is good thus far. The problem occurs when he notes that "the Holy Spirit actualizes the spirituality of God, without retaining it, exhausting it, or ever defining it, for his own spirituality is that of the Father and the Son."[55] In order to flesh out what he is saying here, we must go back to his understanding of the trinitarian order.

Bulgakov has an unconventional way of understanding the order of the Trinity. By unconventional I mean that he deviates from the classical understanding of God, because in his study of patristic fathers, he found that there are two errors that plague the early theological thinkers. The first error he mentions is the introduction of "degrees" to God. From his own historical survey, he has found that the patristic thinkers were heavily influenced by Neoplatonic philosophy, and as a result, the hierarchical system has been incorporated into God's trinitarian life, in which God the Father is made the supreme "originator" and the remaining two persons of the Godhead as the "generated ones." The supremacy of the Father is then highlighted by his productive personhood, and to a lesser degree, the inferiority of personhood is accentuated by the "barren" hypostases of the Son and the Spirit.

The second error he mentions is the dependence on the concept of causality (*aitia*). Again, Bulgakov blames the Neoplatonic doctrine that brought this idea to early Christian thinkers. The concept of causes, to which the Catholic traditions have adopted, insists Bulgakov, all the more emphasizes the idea of "origination" in God. He notes, "The Father is the cause of the Son and the initial cause of the Holy Spirit (*principium imprincipiatum*); the Son is the derivative cause (*principium principiatum*) of the Holy Spirit; whereas the Holy Spirit is not a *principium* at all."[56] Bulgakov rejects this order. In fact, he wants to do away with the idea of "origination" altogether. Bulgakov is on the right track to erase the concept of "origination" and pull its roots out of the divine ontological system, because it does not do full justice to who God is and how God is related within the life of the Trinity. We simply cannot have subordinationism or hierarchism in God, which are the two main implications of "origination." The language of "origin," even if we say that it is implicated by the biblical idiom of the Father begetting the Son, does not belong to God's ontological order, since

54. Bulgakov, *Comforter*, 153.
55. Bulgakov, *Comforter*, 153.
56. Bulgakov, *Comforter*, 69.

the language of "begetting"[57] is the language of the *logos incarnandus*, not the logos *asarkos*. What distinguishes God's essence from revelation is the newness that has incurred in God's life. God taking on human flesh, as I have explained it already, is a new event for God, which distinguishes the *logos asarkos* from the *logos incarnandus*, albeit the continuity between the two. So, we cannot make the mistake and carry the human image back to God's triunity as if it is a necessary component of God's life.

What does Bulgakov do to correct these two errors? He ingeniously redefines the meaning of "procession" and "generation" not as "origination" but as "mutual revelation." He says that he can do away with the language of origination and still talk about the order of God if we accept the self-revelation of the Holy Trinity as the guiding principle. He explains,

> This self-revelation is accomplished in the three interrelated hypostases. This interrelation is defined as trine: the Father revealed in the generation of the Son and the procession of the Holy Spirit; the Son revealed in the generation from the Father and in the reception of the Holy Spirit; the Holy Spirit is revealed in the procession from the Father and the reposing upon the Son. Generation and procession, both in the active and the passive sense, have the significance not of *origination* but of modes of *mutual revelation*.[58]

However, despite the removal of the language of origin, he keeps the idea of "generation" and "procession" as a means to identify the distinctive mutuality of the triune relationship.

In my judgment, Bulgakov's theory of mutuality is not effective due to his reliance on the idea of "generation" or "procession." In order to account for God's mutuality, the idea of generation or procession needs to be either entirely removed or supplemented with a return metaphor, as we shall see later in our discussion of Coffey's model. If we follow Bulgakov, we would not be able to remove or eschew the implication of "emanation," because the Father is still seen as the generator and the Son and the Spirit as the generated hypostases. To be truly mutual, in the inner trinitarian life, we need to see the dual movement of *ad intra* and *ad extra* for each person of

---

57. The eternality of "begetting" has been promoted by Kevin Giles. See Giles, *The Eternal Generation*, 15–37. Giles is on target to talk about the order in God's eternal realm but misses the mark as he ties "begetting" language to eternity without removing the "origin" implication. Not all biblical language can be carried into God without qualification. It is acceptable to talk about the begetting of the Son in God's economy, as long as we remove its "origin" implication in God's inner trinitarian life.

58. Bulgakov, *Comforter*, 69–70.

the Trinity. In the economic Trinity, this duality can be viewed as the Father sending the Son and the Spirit to the world, and later, the Son returning to the Father in the Spirit. In the immanent Trinity, this duality can be viewed as the Father presupposing and anticipating the Son and the Spirit, the Son presupposing and anticipating the Father and the Holy Spirit, and the Holy Spirit presupposing and anticipating the Father and the Son.[59] For this reason, mutuality cannot be established just based on the order of God *ad extra*.

Going back to Bulgakov's statement, we now know why he says that "the Holy Spirit actualizes the spirituality of God, without retaining it, exhausting it, or ever defining it, for his own spirituality is that of the Father and the Son." Based on his mutual revelation theory, he wants to say that the Holy Spirit is only a guiding principle, who is identifiable by deferring himself to the Father and the Son. In other words, Bulgakov's understanding of God's spiritness depends on the spirituality of the Father and the Son that is consummated only after the procession of the Trinity revealed in history. Granted that the hierarchical relation implied in the procession metaphor that Bulgakov mentions here retains the principle of identity (or equi-divinity) in God and avoids the mistake of subordinating the Son or the Spirit to the Father, nonetheless he misinterprets trinitarian spirituality, for the Holy Spirit does not "actualize" the spirituality of God, though we may say that the spirituality of the Holy Spirit is that of the Father and the Son (e.g., the commonness of God's spirit). We need to recognize that the spirituality of God is always and eternally triune, and because of it, we can say that the Father is the spirituality of God always, the Son is the spirituality of God always, and the Holy Spirit is the spirituality of God always. They are already and always spiritual. For this reason, trinitarian spirituality is never constituted by the spirituality of either the Father, the Son, or the Holy Spirit.

The problem of Bulgakov's trinitarian theology lies in his retention of the language of God's economy for us to explicate God's inner life, unable to renounce the Father as the "generator" and the remaining two persons of the Godhead as the "generated." In the end, I could not say that Bulgakov

---

59. Note that I have removed the language of "sending" and "generation" in the immanent Trinity and substituted with the metaphor of the principle of identity and duality (presupposition and anticipation). I have chosen the metaphor of presupposition and anticipation because they belong to the language of eschatology. As I have said elsewhere, eschatology operates on the principle of identity and duality, that is, the principle of God's trinitarian eternity.

has successfully moved away from the concept of "emanation" in the Godhead, partly due to his Eastern Orthodox tradition, being faithful to the doctrine of divine procession. The idea of origin cannot be removed if we explain God's ontological order based on the language of God's economy for us. Even the biblical language of God's economy, such as "begetting," as I have pointed out, cannot be transported into God's inner life. The language of "begetting" belongs to the *logos incarnandus* only. We cannot import this idiom into the *logos asarkos*. Pneumatologically, there is no "begetting" in God's life. God is spirit intrinsically and necessarily. In the pre-temporal context, the Father-spirit does not "beget" the Son-spirit; rather, he simply presupposes the Son-spirit due to the fact that the Father and the Son coexists as spirit from eternity to eternity, and at the same time, anticipates the Son-spirit due to the fact that the Son-spirit is the logical "consequence" to the Father. This is why, as we have seen, the *logos asarkos* and the *logos incarnandus* are one but distinct. Consequently, we cannot simply move from the *logos incarnandus* to the *logos asarkos* because the *logos incarnandus* carries a new event that does not belong to the *logos asarkos*.

Therefore, the only way to remove the concept of "origin" in God's inner life is to see that God is spirit in essence. God is already and always the Father-spirit, the Son-spirit, and the Holy Spirit. God does not need the concept of "begetting" in the immanent Trinity to have this distinction. The language of "begetting" or "generation," which belongs only to the economic Trinity, does not determine God's distinction, or interrelation. God is interrelated as he in himself and as he is for us. To put it pneumatologically, we can say that God is necessarily related to each other spiritually and mutually since they all have the same spirit, and that God is necessarily related orderly and distinctively since they have a particular trinitarian sequential order of firstness, secondness, and thirdness.

On a positive note, Bulgakov's ontological order, though troubled at a critical point, provides us with the theological support that God's ontology begins with pneumatology. To restate Bulgakov's point, we can say that God is spirit and God's spirit-*homoousion* is God's essence.[60] Hence, according to Bulgakov, God's ontological order starts from God-is-spirit. The pneumatological starting point means that the thing-itselfness of God is spirit. The implication of this message is that spirit is objective and real in the sense that God's being is grounded pneumatologically in himself and in his revelation, not based on an abstract principle of this world. The objectivity

---

60. Bulgakov, *Comforter*, 153.

of God defies the modern caricature that spirit is only a subjective category. Rather, God as spirit is the divine thing-itselfness, the uncreated substance, the source of all created things, as well as the subjects of the Trinity. For this reason, divine spiritness defines objectivity and subjectivity in the life of the Trinity. The Trinity is at once one spirit-substance, and three spirit-persons. This understanding is what Bulgakov confirms and positively contributes to the pneumatological Trinity.

David Coffey's Mutual Love Theory

Speaking of the pneumatological Trinity, we move to David Coffey's work on the doctrine of the Trinity. As a Jesuit scholar, Coffey has written more extensively than Bulgakov, but fortunately, he has summed up his doctrine of the Trinity as well as pneumatology in his book, *Deus Trinitas*, so I concentrate my investigation on the materials provided by this monograph. Even though Coffey presents his case in a concise manner using less than 200 pages, *Deus Trinitas* nonetheless contains a treasure trove of data on the doctrine of God, so we need to narrow it down even further. For this reason, we focus primarily on his "return model" of God, which is based on Augustine's mutual love theory.

Drawing upon Augustine, Coffey claims that the Holy Spirit is the mutual bond of love. From an Augustinian perspective, this is understandable, since Augustine pictured the trinitarian relationship in terms of love, which is shared by the Father and the Son, the lover and the beloved, respectively. Staying close to Augustine, Coffey develops his own trinitarian principle: The Holy Spirit is the Father's love for Jesus and the Jesus' answering love for the Father.[61] He comes up with this model to complete the trinitarian puzzle that has been left behind by the patristic scholars due to their preoccupation with the "procession" model of the Trinity. In the procession model, according to Coffey, the attention is given to the originator of the Son and the Holy Spirit, that is, the Father, and as a result, the theological *prius* is riveted to the act of procession without any regard for the act of return. To compensate this gap, Coffey introduces his own paradigm of Jesus' return to the Father in the Spirit. This return is expressed in terms of the love of the Son for the Father. So, he supplements descending theology with ascending theology vis-à-vis the mutual love theory.

---

61. Coffey, "The Holy Spirit," 193–229. Also see, Coffey, *Deus Trinitas*, 48–49.

The implication of Coffey's paradigm is significant. For one, it has the potential to close the gap between descending theology and ascending theology. If he is right, the procession and the return of the Son in the Spirit could merge and create a constructive hermeneutical circle that does not marginalize one at the expense of the other. It means that theory and experience, the immanent Trinity and the economic Trinity, revelation and natural knowledge, can live together not as foes but as mutually supporting partners, and surely, we need this mutuality to complete our understanding of God.

However, due to several setbacks in his theological program, I do not see that Coffey has succeeded in accomplishing what he set out to do. I see three problems. First, there is a problem of "order" in his theology. Coffey's theological order goes like this: the Bible, the immanent Trinity, the economic Trinity.[62] Why is he following this order? Of course, like Barth, he wants to start with revelation, so opening his theological chapter with the Bible is understandable. But how is it that he could jump from the Bible to the immanent Trinity? Logically, should we not move from the economic Trinity to the immanent Trinity, since the economic Trinity is a part of God's revelation?[63] The rationale for taking this approach is that he wants to follow the method provided by Bernard Lonergan.[64] According to Coffey, Lonergan's order of knowing follows the taxis of experiencing, understanding, and judgment. Experiencing involves the "matter to be known," understanding defines the "matter to be known," and judging affirms this understanding. Based on the Lonergan's order of knowing, Coffey produces his own theological taxis, the order of biblical theology–the immanent Trinity–the economic Trinity. The Bible plays the role of providing the "matter to be known," the immanent Trinity its understanding, and the economic Trinity the final judging.

In the light of our conversation with Barth and Barthian scholars, Coffey's rationale for choosing this method does not make sense, for the proper order should be the Bible, the economic Trinity, and the immanent Trinity. But we have to be careful here. Coffey's interpretation of the Bible, the immanent Trinity, and the economic Trinity differs from that of Barth and his

---

62. Coffey, *Deus Trinitas*, 33–45.

63. Torrance is a good example. Torrance, *The Ground and Grammar of Theology*, 166. To note, for Coffey, the biblical materials do not provide a well-polished form of the immanent or the economic Trinity.

64. Coffey, *Deus Trinitas*, 16–17.

followers like McCormack and Molnar. For Barth, God's revelation consists of God's self-disclosure for us. Thus, biblical data and the economic Trinity fall under the common matrix of God's revelation for us. The immanent Trinity is different, however. For Barth, if we follow Molnar's interpretation, the immanent Trinity is a pure form of God, or God's absoluteness. God's absoluteness is free from the contamination of the world, albeit it is known via God's economy for us. Despite the fact that God has embraced "us" into his inner life, God is still absolute and perfect, free from the contamination of the world. Hence, as I have stated before, although Barth moves from the economic Trinity to the immanent Trinity, once the immanent Trinity is identified, without including the contingency factor included in the economic Trinity, the immanent Trinity becomes the controlling center for the economic Trinity, as God remains who he is *even* in his act of revelation. Hence, the order of God coming to us from himself is first and irreversible in Barth's theology.

By contrast, Coffey does not consider the Bible on par with the immanent or economic Trinity. For Coffey, the Bible is just a raw material, ready to be shaped and formed by us the theologians. In Coffey's reading, the Bible contains no doctrinal formulation like that of the patristic writers. The key here is Coffey's view that the immanent Trinity was chiseled out into its current form by the patristic theologians, many years after the completion of the Bible.[65] The economic and the immanent Trinity, insists Coffey, are not heavenly sent revelations that we simply receive by faith and recognize them immediately by reading the Bible. Rather, they are a by-product of many years of thinking, arguing, and formulating. So for Coffey, the doctrine of the Trinity as we know it today is a more of a collaborative, constructive artifact of past theologians than a pre-configured idea of the Bible.

Therefore, unlike Barth, Coffey is more in line with cognitive constructivism rather than objectivist realism. I do not mean that Coffey is a non-realist. I believe Coffey is a realist since he does not dismiss the fact that God's essence exists regardless of what we think of it. However, regarding Coffey's ontological order that relies heavily on human constructive efforts to outline the contours of the idea of the immanent Trinity, he follows more closely to the Kantian distinction of noumenon and phenomenon. For him, God's aseity belongs to the world of noumenon, the inaccessible thing-in-itself. As any realist would confirm, he accepts the fact that God's

---

65. Coffey, *Deus Trinitas*, 19.

absolute reality impinges upon the way we think about him. However, he leaves God's thing-in-itself behind because it has little relevance to our life. He states it this way. "Because we human beings realize our personhood through relations, the relative personhood of God is more interesting and relevant to us than is his absolute personhood."[66] I will review Coffey's distinction between God's absolute and relative personhood in the next point of this discussion, but for now, it suffices to note that Coffey is making a distinction between God's noumenon, the absolute God of whom we know little, and God's phenomenon, the relative God of whom we know enough to control our theological programs. Like Kant, Coffey categorizes the immanent Trinity as an implicit dimension of theology that needs to be refined and turned into an explicit expression by the economic Trinity.[67] For me, this is a clear sign that the priority of God's ontological order has been undermined. Its outcome is unwarranted dualism.

As a continuation of the first point, secondly, Coffey's doctrine of God carries unresolvable theological dualism. We can see his theological dualism come into play in his distinction of God's absolute and relative personhood. Taking cues from the Bible, Coffey believes that "in God there are one absolute person and three relative persons."[68] He is reconciling the Old Testament witness to one person of God and the New Testament witness to three persons of God. The immediate issue I have is the soundness of his exegesis to interpret the Old Testament witness to *one* God as *one personhood* of God. The biblical testimony truly implies the fact that God is one (e.g., Deut 6:4). The biblical emphasis on God's singularity is uncontested. However, to say that God's oneness implies God existing as a single absolute person is making a huge theological jump.

The problem gets worse as Coffey grounds his argument on Rahner's dictum: "In God there is one subjectivity (or absolute subjectivity) but

---

66. Coffey, *Deus Trinitas*, 76.

67. I would recast Coffey's order in this way: the Bible–the economic Trinity–the immanent Trinity. I agree with Coffey that the Bible is the raw material for theology, but the economic Trinity is not our telos, but a means to the end (e.g., God in himself). Besides, even if I were to follow Coffey's rationale and assume that theology progresses over time, the immanent Trinity should be the most focused and well-developed theology, albeit provisionally since it is where we find the true shape and form of God, which in turn, controls and refines the interpretation of the Bible and the way we understand God's economy. I read patristic theology like that of Athanasius, Irenaeus, and Augustine to follow this order rather than what Coffey has asserted.

68. Coffey, *Deus Trinitas*, 72.

three (relative) subjects."[69] Rahner's original saying is without the parenthetical remarks, which were added by Coffey. So, from this statement, we can see that Rahner's one absolute subjectivity was translated into Coffey's one absolute person, and Rahner's three subjects into Coffey's three relative persons. Based on Coffey's argument, I can only conclude that he has read the economic Trinity (developed by Rahner) into the immanent Trinity (Coffey's re-appropriation of patristic theology), and as a result, he opened up an unbridgeable gap between the absoluteness and relativeness of God.[70] What we have is God's noumenon separated from God's phenomenon as Coffey concentrates on God's phenomenon rather than God's noumenon.

Coffey's dualism is in violation of God's principle of identity and duality. On the one hand, the principle of identity is violated. It is true that Coffey equates God's one absolute person with God's three relative persons, since he says that God's one absolute person "contains" three relative persons.[71] The identity of God seems to be established as God's one absolute person is equal to God's three relative persons. But the principle of identity will never work with this idea because what is absolute is completely differentiated from what is relative. According to Coffey's rule, we can never say that God is three absolute persons, because he is just one absolute person. This is due to the fact that only when all three relative persons are added up to one can God be absolute. So there is the break between God's absoluteness and relativeness. For me, this is a clear telltale sign that Coffey suffers from theological dualism.

On the other hand, the principle of duality is also violated in that God cannot be one and three at the same time. God is either one absolute person or three relative persons. If he is one absolute person and three relative persons at the same time, we have four persons in God, which is specious to Christian theology. Coffey avoids this problem by saying that God's one absolute personhood equals to God's three relative persons. So Coffey is asking to choose one, either God as one absolute person or God as three relative persons. If we choose God's absoluteness, we see one person, but if we choose God's relativeness, we see three persons. Simply put, Coffey's paradigm is based on the either-or principle, which violates the principle

---

69. Coffey, *Deus Trinitas*, 76.

70. He writes in this regard, "There is no known philosophical principle that can be used to integrate absolute personhood and relative personhood in God." Coffey, *Deus Trinitas*, 76.

71. Coffey, *Deus Trinitas*, 73.

of duality. The principle of duality—we can also call it the "both-and" principle or the "at once" principle—recognizes that there is distinction in God as such, but without marginalizing the continuity between the distinction. The principle of the Trinity attests to the fact that God is at once one and three, not that he is either one or three.

Thus, to avoid Coffey's theological dualism, we need to say that the Trinity is at once absolute and relative. In other words, whatever is predicated on one person must be predicated on all three persons both absolutely and relatively.[72] Because God is absolute, three persons of the Trinity are also absolute—e.g., all three persons are God from eternity to eternity. In a Barthian term, God is free to be himself eternally, as the absolute Father, the absolute Son, and the absolute Holy Spirit. They are all univocally absolute. And at the same time, they are relative. They are relative in the sense that the three persons of the Godhead are active and dynamic as three distinct persons in history. As with Barth's theory of appropriation, though every person of the Trinity is involved in the work of each person in the Godhead, there is an appropriately distinct mode of each person. McGrath explains the doctrine of appropriation succinctly. "Despite the fact that all three persons of the Trinity are implicated in creation, it is properly seen as the distinctive action of the Father. Similarly, the entire Trinity is involved in the work of redemption. However, it is appropriate to speak of redemption as being the distinctive work of the Son."[73] In this way, God is both absolute and relative.[74]

Therefore, like Barth's dictum, we can say that God's is both absolute and relative in himself and in his act of revelation. Even though God comes to us and mingles with the things of this world, God's absoluteness remains intact. He does not change into something that is "relative." God's relativeness without absoluteness of this world could imply that God can be a shape-shifter, changing into something he is not in his relativeness. God's

---

72. I follow Barth here. He notes that the three divine persons "mutually condition and permeate one another so completely that one is always in the other two and the other two in the one." Barth, *Church Dogmatics 1/1*, 370.

73. McGrath, *Christian Theology*, 252.

74. To note, Coffey seems to distinguish God's absolute person as incommunicable subsistent person from God's relative persons as communicable. But in other places, he notes that a person subsists as both communicable and incommunicable entity. Had he kept the duality of the latter, he would be free from the error of theological dualism. A trinitarian personal relationship, in my judgment, is both communicable and incommunicable. The communicability of the person allows the three persons to retain the principle of identity and the incommunicability the principle of distinction.

duality of absoluteness-relativeness prevents the error of God as a changing entity. God can come and assume human flesh to be in union with man to reveal his "free" relativeness, but at the same time, God is also freely absolute, because even in his relativeness he still remains our absolute God. So, the divine logic is clear: God is absolute even in his relativeness and relative in his absoluteness.

Third and the final issue I have with Coffey is his mutual love theory. The earlier two arguments come together here to show a weak spot in his mutual love theory. I agree that God is essentially mutual and relational. The doctrine of the Trinity affirms it, and at the same time, it affirms the doctrine of the Trinity. The problem I have with Coffey is that his mutual love theory reveals that the mutuality of God is completed in the Holy Spirit. In fact, the Holy Spirit is the mutuality of God for him. I concede to the fact that the Holy Spirit is by nature mutual, since "spirit" is necessarily mutual due to its "at once" perichoretic property. However, the mutuality of God lies also in the Father and the Son as well. Are they not spirits also? Besides, to be in line with the principle of identity, we must say that if one person is the mutuality of other persons, then the remaining two persons are also the mutuality of other persons. Although Coffey has done well to define divine mutuality within the sphere of Holy Spirit's mutuality, he has come up short to show that this mutuality belongs to all three persons in the immanent Trinity.

In this respect, I find Coffey's mutual love theory limiting. I give credit to Coffey for his unbiased depiction of divine spirituality in terms of God's mutuality as he sees that the Holy Spirit is the give-and-take transaction between the Father and the Son—a better option than Bulgakov's one-way transaction—but as I have said before, divine mutuality is not sustainable if it does not fully speak about the dynamics of *ad intra* and *ad extra* of all three persons.

This begs a question. How can we talk about the mutuality of all three persons without being bogged down by the concept of origin? We can answer this question with the language of God's sequential order of firstness, secondness, and thirdness. To recap, in God's triune life, there are Father's firstness, Son's secondness, and Holy Spirit's thirdness, and this ontological order is only logical, which means that God's firstness, secondness, and thirdness do not define an ontological degree or a temporal differential in God. Despite the orderliness in God, the three persons of the Godhead are equally divine, because they are one in spirit. This trinitarian order implies that in God the logic of monism applies. Because God is who he is in himself through and through, there is no qualifier other than God himself.

What is also revealing about God's sequential logic is that the trinitarian distinction satisfies the ontological irreversibility of God, for the Son cannot precede the Father. Despite the ontological irreversibility, paradoxically, there is the mutuality of God. The significance of this duality is that the three persons of the Godhead is both communicable and incommunicable. They are communicable because of the oneness of divine spirituality—e.g., they are one in spirit. However, they are incommunicable in the sense that the firstness of the fatherhood belongs only to the Father. Likewise, the sonship and spiritship of the Son and the Holy Spirit, respectively, are not communicable to others. So, to be faithful to God's order, we must satisfy these two aspects of God. In order to fulfill this requirement, we need to state the trinitarian relationship in the following way: Father's firstness is the mutuality of the Trinity as the first order of the trinitarian dynamics from which secondness and thirdness are presupposed and anticipated. Likewise, Son's secondness is the mutuality of the Trinity as the second order of the trinitarian dynamics from which firstness and thirdness are presupposed and anticipated. Finally, Holy Spirit's thirdness is the mutuality of the Trinity as the third order of the trinitarian dynamics from which firstness and secondness are presupposed and anticipated. The sequential order and mutuality are univocally present in all three persons because God is spirit.[75] This is only pneumatologically possible. Each person in the Trinity is mutually related to one another, and at the same time, remains distinct, only because God is spirit.

Consequently, we see that divine mutuality is presupposed and anticipated spiritually. In other words, God is mutually conditioned *in himself* absolutely (e.g., his presupposition) and relatively (e.g., his anticipation) due to the fact that God's presupposition of one and three as well as God's anticipation of one and three are always an at-once spiritual event. More clearly, God's mutual transaction from one to three and three to one is necessarily simultaneous and distinguishable. The give-and-take is always fluid

---

75. This statement accords well with Coffey's understanding of *esse*. For Coffey, "to be" (*esse*) is to be spirit. He explains, "The word 'spirit' denotes, in this case, that qualified transcendence and independence of matter that allows its possessor to be and to become a 'subject.'" In this respect, God is absolute spirit whereas human beings "relative spirit" who participate in a "transcendental relation to God as absolute spirit." Moreover, *esse* is to be in relations to one another. Thus, from Coffey's interpretation, spirituality can be defined as "being in mutual relations." Coffey, *Deus Trinitas*, 74–75.

and completely unitive as all three persons are always spiritually one and distinct. Therefore, when we understand that the Son's procession from the Father in the economic Trinity is controlled by the immanent Trinity, we can see that behind the language of procession in the economic Trinity lies the order of God's spirit in the immanent Trinity from which the Father-spirit presupposes and anticipates the Son-spirit in the context of the Spirit of God, that is, the Holy Spirit, but not exhaustively so. Thus, the mutuality of the economic Trinity is justified by the immanent trinitarian mutuality, and vice versa, since each person's order of presupposition and anticipation in the inner life of God can be translated as the Father's sending and receiving the Son and the Spirit, the Son's receiving and sending the Spirit from the Father, and the Holy Spirit as the mutual bond between the two. This unitive correlation is important, for it preserves the ontological order without the concept of origin like that of the Neoplatonic theory of emanation.

Concluding Remarks

I put so much effort into pruning the order of the economic Trinity that does not belong to the order of the immanent Trinity for the purpose of re-appropriating pneumatologically driven God's ontological order that prioritizes God *in se* rather than God *pro nobis*. I introduced Barth's program to show that there is an ontological *prius* of God. Because of the ontological priority, we must allow God's aseity to control God's economy, or more precisely, our understanding of who God is in himself rather that what God does in the creaturely realm. Although our understanding of God's aseity starts from God's economy, we must preserve the principle of duality and mutuality, that is, the disposition of God's spirituality, clarifying the logical "order" in God that does not violate the trinitarian sequence and the pneumatological logic. As I have pointed out, the pneumatological logic moves from the order of *asarkos* and ends up embracing the incarnation as God's own. Even in this act of embracing, God is both absolute and relative since he is who he is in the act of revelation.

Surely, the starting with spirit and the inner life of God is a methodological move that defies the current theological trend, which prefers Christology or the economic Trinity as the controlling center of our theology. Even pneumatologically, ascending theology is in vogue due to the fact that pneumatology is tied closely to the experiential dimension of the Holy Spirit. However, at least for the development of theology proper, that is, the doctrine of God, we cannot neglect the importance of keeping God's aseity distinct from and prior to God for us. Without it, we will falter, as we have already seen, and confuse God with the things of this world.

Those of who are tired of working in the area of speculative theology may detest the idea of splitting the Trinity into two sectors, the immanent Trinity and economic Trinity, and giving the priority to God's ontology. What I have in mind here are two scholars, Catherine LaCugna and Michael Welker, who respectively refused to talk about the inner life of God.[76] The former emphasizes God-for-us with little regard for God's aseity and the latter God the Spirit as the public person working primarily in the real-life settings. However, whether we like it or not, our clear and precise understanding of God's aseity is critical in the way we understand not only God as our Subject of worship but also God as our Object of study. The stake is too high. If we misalign God's aseity to something that he is not, our entire theology would be skewed. This is precisely the issue I have with both LaCugna and Welker. Speaking nothing but God as the one who is working in the sphere of our cultural context could mislead us to think that God is moldable any way we wish vis-à-vis our cultural conditions. God cannot be for us unless he is for us in himself, but as we have seen, God is more than *for us* in himself, for he is also *without us*. Likewise, God as Spirit cannot be a public person unless he is a God who is public in himself first. But God is more than a public person in himself because he is God who he is, having the freedom to turn away from us (Matt 27:46)[77] as well as turn toward us. In my opinion, contemporary theology is continually suffering from the ills of reading God with us without any regard for the possibility of God without us, even if God without us is not veiled in total mystery. Christian theology today, as well as in the past, is being misaligned without knowing who God really is, mostly due to the error of indiscriminately reading God from the perspective of our own existence.

What I see is the need to emphasize the distinction between God *in se* and God *pro nobis*. This proposal sounds specious to Christian theology, but it is not. We have been so in tune with theology that opts for continuity

---

76. For more details, see LaCugna, *God for Us*, 1–20, and Welker, *God the Spirit*, 1–49.

77. This is the thesis of Jürgen Moltmann's theology of the cross. Moltmann, *The Crucified God*, 200–73. Like Moltmann, I believe that there is "forsakenness" of God, but contra Moltmann, I do not believe that such forsakenness is an inherent quality of the Trinity. For more details, see my upcoming book, *God in Our Likeness: The Duality of Christ*.

between God in himself and God for us, which is not entirely wrong, that we have forgotten about what I call the addendum factor in God. The addendum factor means that God has taken upon himself in this world something other than who he is. God's addendum denotes God taking up to himself something other than who he is. For instance, in the economic Trinity, "the Word came in human flesh."[78] The addendum component is "flesh" that does not belong to the divine Logos. Had it been the essential component of God, God does not have to assume or "come in" to it. So, as the Word coming in flesh shows, we have two different aspects of God, one before the assumption and the other after the assumption of flesh. Therefore, we have two aspects of God that are distinct yet commensurable.

My emphasis on two trinities is never meant to advocate a theistic dualism like Whitehead and defend the two distinct realities of God, one primordial and the other temporal. We cannot say that God has two distinct realities. God is one, and because of it, we must keep in mind that God is who he is in the act of his revelation. The same rule applies to the *logos incarnandus*. God is who he is even if the addendum factor is attached to God. However, when we move from God-for-us back to God-in-himself, we must recognize that the addendum is just an addition to God, not a necessary component of God; thus, we should not determine God's essence based on God with an addendum factor. In this respect, the *prius* of God's ontological order is an important matter for the discussion of God.

This does not mean that we are going to dismiss theology from below. As I have shown in the previous chapter, our study of nature as well as the raw data of the Bible underwrites the analogical relationship for us to access God. We need theology from below as the primary source for doing systematic theology. However, my point of bringing the *prius* of God's ontological order to the forefront of our theology is to recognize that our trinitarian God is one and at the same time three spiritually and dialectically,

---

78. The flesh-addendum of the incarnation is well attested by ὁ Λόγος σὰρξ ἐγένετο (John 1:14). J. Ramsey Michaels translates ὁ Λόγος σὰρξ ἐγένετο as "the Word came in flesh." He writes, "The point is not that the Word was *transformed* into flesh, for (as Schnackenburg points out) 'the Logos remains the subject in the following affirmation ("and dwelt among us") and made his divine glory visible—in the flesh—to believers.' Rather, the meaning is that the Word came into the world *as* flesh, or *in* flesh. The affirmation is much the same as the confession of faith by which the utterances of prophets are to be tested according to 1 and 2 John: 'Jesus Christ come in flesh' (1 John 4:2), or 'coming in flesh' (2 John 7)." Michaels, *The Gospel of John*, 77. So, theologically, Torrance is right when he says that the divine Logos assuming the human flesh is a new event for God.

and that this reality drives the doctrine of God as a whole. Only when we establish this fact on the solid ground, as what Barth has done, we can move forward and make sense of God's work of salvation in this world. We must understand that God's economy is not the end, but a means to the end, that is, our return to God in himself. It is our return to God's inner life that is the goal, not to be satisfied with knowing God's act in this world. Unless we know the precise nature of who is waiting for us at the end, our talk about the things we do for God and knowledge of God in this world would be meaningless. So, as we move to the order of God's communication for us, we will continue to keep our eyes on the telos, the controlling center of our theology, that is God in himself who is free to be with us and without us.

CHAPTER 3

God's Order of Communication and Its Relationship to the Unthematic Dimension of Human Existence

BEGINNING WITH THIS CHAPTER, we are going to explore God's order "with us." Unlike our previous discussion of God's ontological order, the following chapters deal primarily with the order of God's economy and God's self-communication for us. The mood and attitude of theological activities in this field are starkly different from the treatment of God's ontological order. On the one hand, *theologia archetypa*—e.g., our discussion of God's aseity and the immanent Trinity—was very restrictive. It was restrictive because we were dealing with the very essence of God. I purposely did not allow the intrusion of created things barging into the realm of God indiscriminately, due to the fact that God's ontology needs a clear and precise language to narrow down and arrive at the most "objective" picture of God's reality from his revealed data. On the other hand, *theologia ectypa*—e.g., our free depiction of God in the world—allows much greater freedom to imagine what God does for us in this world. It needs expansive creativity and innovative ideas that were not allowed in the previous proceedings.

Thus, we gear up and ready ourselves to explore the vast territory of God's field of activity with us in this world. However, what we need to remember is that this free exploration does not give us the license to violate God's ontological order. Even if we let our imagination roam free, we are still coming back to God's ontological status and anchor *theologia ectypa* to *theologia achetypa* which preserves *theologia perennes*. God's revelation that has broken into the realm of human history, which we have the freedom to articulate in accordance to our cultural and linguistic norm, is controlled still by his reality. We are not going to dismiss Barth's dictum but rivet our theological thinking upon God who remains who he is in his act of revelation. Because God's reality does not change even if it is intermingled with and subsumed under the process of this world, God's own unique attributes and logic can function as the guiding principle in the way we "imagine" God's interaction with the world and our depiction of it.

Keeping Barth's dictum in mind, we zoom in and pay closer attention to God's order of communication. The study here revisits the order of transcendence that I brought up in chapter 1 but sidestepped in chapter 2.[1] As we shall see, the order of transcendence and God's order of communication are correlatable. I detail this aspect by showing that the order of our transcendence is the result of God's order of communication. For this reason, I do not think we can understand God's order of communication without the order of transcendence, and vice versa. Again, I emphasize that God's order of communication is not determined by the order of human transcendence. Rather, my theological conclusion reverses this logic. God's transcendental order, that is, his order of communication with us, determines the order of natural and human transcendence.

I support my claim with the examination of the unthematic dimension of human existence. As with the ontological dimension of God, I try to unveil the core of our being, from which our God-conscious activity flows. Following the modern thought form, I examine the seedbed of our existence upon which our relationship with God is born. Furthermore, my investigation of the unthematic dimension of human existence discloses the core aspect of God's order of grace. I contend here that God's grace comes to us and stirs our being prior to any conscious activities such as our movement of free will and rational thinking.

My primary dialogue partners for this chapter are Karl Rahner, David Coffey, and Stanley Grenz. They represent the conflicting understanding of the unthematic dimension of human existence in the Catholic and Evangelical traditions. Regrettably, Catholic theology and Evangelical theology have been played off against each other ever since the time of the

---

1. As we recall, "transcendence" here denotes our ability to move out of the limitations and seek out what lies beyond this world (e.g., God). Also, note that God's "transcendence" is a different kind than ours. Since there is no limitation in God, God does not transcend like us; rather, God's transcendence has to do with God moving out of his own sphere and reaching out to the sphere of created things.

Reformation. The argument is well exemplified by the disagreement about the way we view the *imago Dei*. On the one hand, the Catholic tradition holds to the belief that, despite the fallen nature of humanity, the image of God has not been completely destroyed. It is still functioning as the *finitum capax infiniti*. On the other hand, in the Reformed tradition, a different story is told. The claim here is that the image of God is utterly dysfunctional. Hence, from a Reformed theological viewpoint, we are neither naturally oriented to God nor have the *finitum capax infiniti*. In fact, the motto of the Reformed tradition is the *finitum non capax infiniti*. All dimension of human existence is fallen and error-bound. Nothing escapes the fallout from Adam's original sin. Accordingly, we are totally depraved. As we can see, we have two different views. What we need at this point is a theological reconciliation.

To begin the process of reconciliation, I choose Karl Rahner's conception of the supernatural existential as a point of departure. To be more specific, I critically review David Coffey's interpretation of Rahner's work. So, the first section revolves around the Catholic theology of Rahner-Coffey. There is a good reason for choosing Coffey as my main dialogue partner in this section. His interpretation and reformulation of Rahner's supernatural existential fills the gap left behind by Karl Barth. Barth was extremely helpful in clearing away the unwarranted reading of human existential situations and analogies into God's aseity, because he understood that the logic of God is wholly different from the logic of creaturely things. However, Barth went too far with this attitude. His particularism restricted him to neglect the contribution of human imagination and the natural ability to pursue God. In this regard, Barth's dismissal of natural theology is well contrasted with Coffey's work, which provides for this project a clear and concise justification for taking into consideration our "natural" competency to seek God.

Moving further, in the second section, I present a critical review of Coffey's position and identify his shortcomings. Coffey's main problem, as I see it, is that he remains too close to his Catholic tradition, and as a result, in his discussion of the supernatural existential, he rarely mentions the problem of sin that extends to the very being of our existence. For Coffey, the problem of sin is thematic, that is, it is a problem that comes with the activation of human freedom. Rahner feels the same way. Even the original sin is seen as a matter of volition, not an existential issue.[2] For this reason,

---

2. Coffey, "The Whole Rahner," 108–10.

I bring Stanley Grenz to the discussion and revamp Catholic theology of human existence with Evangelical theology of total depravity. In this way, I formulate a holistic picture of our existence based on the dual core theory, which will be the main theme of my third section.

In the third section, I try to finalize the relationship between human nature and God's grace by putting together Coffey's work on the supernatural existential and Grenz's work on human existential conditions. Moreover, the presentation of the dual core theory includes my own analysis of the sin-grace relationship. This last approach is again pneumatological. I nuance the nature and grace relationship in terms of the human spirit and divine spirit relationship. I start with laying out the contours of Rahner-Coffey's theory of the supernatural existential.

Rahner-Coffey's Supernatural Existential

Rahner's writing is very difficult to decipher. I am not alone in this regard. Rahnerian scholars echo the same concern as they find philosophical abstractions, ambiguities, and unconventionalism underlying his theological project.[3] Even more challenging is to single out one idea from countless theories he has contrived during his long academic years. However, Coffey, as a Rahnerian scholar, made him accessible vis-à-vis several short articles he has written on his work, such as "Quaetiones Disputatae," "The Theandric Nature of Christ," and "The Whole Rahner on the Supernatural Existential." Especially important to our discussion is the latter, for it explicitly outlines the contours of Rahner's theory of the supernatural existential. Besides, Coffey's work is always enlightening due to the fact that he often includes his own application to Rahner's theory, which adds to the clarification as well as the value of Rahner's work. So, I base my analysis of Rahner's supernatural existential on Coffey's interpretation of it.

Coffey situates Rahner's theory in the nature and grace debate that went on between Rahner and Henri de Lubac (and his followers) in the 1960s. So allow me to briefly present the synopsis of this debate. Rahner and de Lubac were two giants belonging to the Catholic theological camp but with two distinct theological approaches. Being faithful to the Catholic tradition, de Lubac accentuated the fact that humans are naturally oriented

---

3. Nicholas Adams lists difficulties that the protestant scholars have with Rahner. See, Adams, "Rahner's Reception," 217–26. For an in-depth study of Rahner's philosophy, see Kilby, *Karl Rahner*, 1–99.

to God.[4] In fact, for him, the universal saving will was inherently present in human nature. This claim was a radical departure from the traditional view that opted for the *duplex ordo*. The *duplex ordo* is a theological idea of humans having two inclinations, one natural and another supernatural. The problem with this view is that they were considered "separate layers," to borrow the term from Coffey. For de Lubac and all those Catholic scholars associated with the renewal movement of the Vatican II, the *duplex ordo* had to be dismissed, because it unnecessarily placed a gap between the natural processes and the supernatural end. More clearly, it unnecessarily made what we do as humans irrelevant to what God does in himself. Coffey puts it this way. "That theology, designed to protect the transcendence of God, had produced the unintended effect of rendering the Christian religion and all that belonged to it, namely, divine revelation, grace, the Church, God, as irrelevant to human beings as they went about their lives in the world."[5] So, it was de Lubac's intention to move away from the *duplex ordo* and introduce his *nouvelle theologie* to make God relevant to all aspects of human life, and there was no better place for him to start than the very essence of humanity.

Rahner agreed with de Lubac insofar as the need to do away with the *duplex ordo*; however, he deviated from de Lubac insofar as the claim that the natural end is God in himself. Rahner accepted the fact that every human being, from birth to death, has to be God-oriented and God-seeking. I emphasized "every human being" to denote the Catholic teaching that God's offer of salvation extends to every corner and every individual on this earth regardless of sex, race, or religion. However, unlike de Lubac's claim, his theology of grace could not afford him to accept that God ordered human beings to the beatific vision naturally, that is, our natural end is the union with God in himself in and through Jesus Christ by the power of the Holy Spirit.[6] According to Rahner, had this been the case, we would have to throw away the theology of grace. If we are already and necessarily seeking God in himself, what is the need for "grace"?

---

4. De Lubac, "A Way," 381–94.

5. Coffey, "The Whole Rahner," 98.

6. Here, the term "grace" carries a specific connotation. It denotes God's saving grace. More specifically, Rahner uses the term "grace" in light of God's self-giving to us. Rahner's quote is helpful here. "Grace is God himself, the communication in which he gives himself to humans as the divinizing factor which he is himself." This quote is from Coffey, "The Whole Rahner," 105.

To save the theology of grace, Rahner built his case for the supernatural existential. What is the supernatural existential? Three key components hold this theory together. The first one is that all human beings are oriented toward God. This orientation is natural. It is part of human *esse*. Hence, human spirituality is transcendental. It naturally seeks and pursues God. From a theological standpoint, this claim makes sense. Why would God create a being that is closed upon itself without any possibility of communicating with him? God creates an open being, a being that can transcend the bounds of his existence, and for this reason, a human subject is spiritual, with whom God can interface and commune. As we have seen, de Lubac has no quarrel with this view. However, the difference comes next.

The second point pivots on this simple statement: God makes an offer of his grace supernaturally. Here, although we need to look deeper into the meaning of the offer of grace, I am going to defer it just for a short instance so that I can make a statement about the difference between de Lubac and Rahner. De Lubac and his followers found that it was natural for humans to seek God's beatific vision or the grace that justifies our salvation, but for Rahner, it was not true, for our pursuit of God's beatific vision is not "natural" but "supernatural." This is simple enough, so we move to the third point.

The third point, which is closely connected to the second point, is that the offer of grace starts at the level of man's existential condition. Citing Rahner, Coffey explains what this means. "As an existential of human beings 'it is present prior to their freedom, their self-understanding and their experience.'" Basically, Coffey is describing the existential as a pre-volitional, pre-rational, and pre-experiential dimension of human existence. Thus, like de Lubac, Rahner wants to reach down deep into the core of human beings so that the effect of our orientation to God is universal—e.g., it is given to everybody unthematically. From this respect, the only difference between de Lubac and Rahner is that one opts for our union with God in himself as the natural end and the other the supernatural end.

Rahner's theory demands more explanations than de Lubac since Rahner's theory has more parts than that of de Lubac's theory. For this reason, Coffey unpacks the key components of the supernatural existential. So I revert back to the second and third point I have mentioned earlier. I am not going to revisit the first point in this section, since I have already detailed Coffey's conception of the entelechy of the Spirit as the source of our self-transcendence in chapter 1.

Revisiting the second point, we see that Rahner emphasizes the "supernatural" aspect of our existence. Coffey finds the root of Rahner's supernatural addendum to our existence in God himself. Coffey writes that Rahner "must be envisioning the existential as the beginning of the self-communication of God."[7] This is supported by Rahner's own words. "Man can never even begin to have anything to do with God or to approach God without being already borne by God's grace."[8] Indeed, as Rahner pointed out, "Grace is God himself, the communication in which he gives himself to humans as the divinizing factor which he is himself."[9] So, Coffey points out that Rahner's order of the supernatural begins with God. What is lacking though in my judgment is an added qualifier, for not all supernatural things are traced back to God such as angels and the principalities of this world. But from an ontological standpoint, we can see that Coffey is highlighting Rahner's theological starting point. Rahner starts with God in himself even in his discussion of the human existential.

The supernatural addendum has another implication. Coffey talks about it in light of the "supernatural elevation." He writes, "Rahner held that, as 'God in himself,' the end required in the human person a supernatural elevation, which was not, however, that of sanctifying grace, though it implied its permanent and continuous offer. This elevation he termed 'the supernatural existential.'"[10] In this respect, we can be certain that Rahner is not talking about a mystical experience in which a person is lifted up into a heavenly realm in which he or she gains supernatural knowledge or power from beyond. Rather, he is talking about a transformation taking place in the human existence.[11] As what Rahner has been saying, the person is transformed from pure nature to graced nature. Simply put, the supernatural existential points to the fact that the natural person has been graced to the core. Thus, because of the supernatural elevation, a person with a natural end also has a supernatural end as a consequence of the grace addendum.[12] Here is where Coffey interjects. Coffey complains that

---

7. Coffey, "The Whole Rahner," 106.
8. Rahner, *Foundations of Christian Faith*, 146.
9. Coffey, "The Whole Rahner," 105.
10. Coffey, "The Whole Rahner," 110.
11. Coffey, "The Whole Rahner," 114.
12. I believe that Rahner is adding a catalysis here to prevent a direct move from nature to divinity. If we do not have a middle component, which is the grace addendum, our union with God could be seen as an immediate process. What Rahner wants to avoid, although he does not say explicitly, is process theism. Process theism denotes

Rahner does not identify what exactly is the natural end that is qualitatively different from that of the supernatural end.[13] According to Coffey, this is a critical missing piece, because without it we may be misled to think that there is no difference since both ends are oriented to God. To clarify, Coffey reinforces Rahner's theory by adding that the natural end is the God of creation and the supernatural end is God in himself. The two are different though with a common denominator, that is, God as our final telos.

Coffey's introduction of two ends seems to lead him to the direction of the *duplex ordo*, but rest assured, it does not. Coffey uses the principle of duality and states that the natural end (the God of creation) sublates to the supernatural end (God in himself), because they are one and the same, but with two different aspects, the former the lower end, and the latter the ultimate goal, thereby the higher end. He writes in this regard. "The key here is the recognition that we are not dealing with two totally different ends, but with one end—i.e., God—conceived under two aspects, one higher and the other lower."[14] Inferred in his other writing,[15] Coffey is essentially making the claim that the God of creation and God in himself should not be distinguished as "two separate layers" but one single end with two overlapping inroads, one implicitly defined and the other explicitly given, respectively. The significance of this work is that, with this duality, Coffey is able to integrate de Lubac's *nouvelle theologie* with Rahner's theology of grace.

With respect to de Lubac's emphasis on the natural inclination toward "its unconditional desire for God in himself," Coffey's presentation of the natural end as the God of creation meets this demand, since the God of creation is one of the inroads to God in himself. From the perspective of Barth's dictum, it is easy to see why the God of creation is God in himself, though distinct from it—e.g., God remains who he is even in his creation. God remains the same, so Coffey is not suggesting that there are two gods or two ends. The natural end corresponds to the supernatural end. But what makes it distinct? What does it mean to say that the natural end is lower and the supernatural end higher? Coffey needs to address these questions so that he is not dissolving the natural end to the supernatural end and

---

the immediate participation in God as each entity is prehended directly into the whole (which is God). Although Rahner's order may be charged with the error of following process hierarchism due to his emphasis on the upward mobility of things, because of this safety net, he is free from the error of panentheism.

13. Coffey, "The Whole Rahner," 111.
14. Coffey, "The Whole Rahner," 112.
15. Coffey, "The Spirit of Christ," 363–98.

wrongly depict that the natural end is just a subset of the supernatural end. If this is the case, Coffey may be encroaching the land of universalism like Rahner's theological program.

Fortuitously, Coffey is aware of this issue and interjects that the natural end is not completely dissolved into the supernatural end. He does this by introducing the material cause, which is absent in Rahner's work. Coffey spells this out in relation to the four Aristotelian causes.[16] The saving grace falls under the quasi-formal and efficient cause, which is guided by the final cause. To translate this statement into theological language, Coffey writes, "God, intending himself as the ultimate end of human beings [the final cause], creates them [the efficient cause] and communicates himself to them accordingly [in Jesus Christ as the quasi-formal cause]."[17] However, grace that is offered at the existential level is not related to any of these causes. For this reason, Coffey calls it a "deficient mode" of grace. It is deficient since it is just an offer that has yet to be transpired as the mode of either acceptance or refusal, which occurs after the activation of free will. In other places, drawing upon Rahner, Coffey calls it a "remote ordination" since the offer of grace exists in the supernatural existential as the mode of an offer not yet accepted or rejected.[18]

As a deficient mode of grace, the supernatural existential is related to the material cause. This is understandable because the deficient mode of grace works only with the material form of human existence at the unconscious level. So, the material form of human existence provides the raw material for God to elevate the human nature to the level of the supernatural existential, and with this idea, Coffey is able to explain how human nature retains its natural end "though with a relationship peculiar to itself to the God of creation."[19] In short, nature has a unique identity. Because of the material cause, it remains natural, regardless of the supernatural intervention. Nature's material properties do not change into something "supernatural" even if it is indwelt by God. It just provides grace the raw material to begin disposing the human nature to be oriented toward God. The inclusion of the material cause helps Coffey preserve the natural potency that is not confused or conflated with the supernatural existential.

---

16. Coffey, "The Whole Rahner," 115.
17. Coffey, "The Whole Rahner," 115.
18. Coffey, "The Whole Rahner," 108.
19. Coffey, "The Whole Rahner," 103.

Coffey is on target, preserving the natural end for the sake of our own existence working in tandem with the supernatural end, but my concern here is that the natural end is not always optimistic. Because of the biblical testimonies and the theological theory of total depravity, we must account for the dark side of our natural end that refuses to follow the final cause (e.g., God in himself). I will return to this matter at the end of this section, but for now, we must commend Coffey for successfully preserving the natural end with his inclusion of the material cause, so he is potentially free from the accusation of universalism or occasionalism.

Going back to the third point, we see that Rahner focuses on the unthematic existence of human life, which he calls the human existential. As we have seen, it is here that the supernatural elevation takes place, and accordingly, it is called the supernatural *existential*. An integral aspect of this theory, as Coffey unveils, is its unthematic nature, which is pre-volitional, pre-rational, and pre-affectional. He explains it this way. "[F]or Rahner the bestowal of the existential takes place at the initial moment of the human person's existence, in other words, at the moment of his or her creation."[20] So the human existential, according to Rahner and Coffey, takes place at the unconscious level, and as a result, the unconscious conditions the conscious. Consequently, God's communication moves from the existential to our conscious state.

Because the existential conditioning takes place prior to all human free decisions, Coffey rightfully calls it a "remote" ordination of grace as opposed to the "proximate" ordination of saving grace. The difference is that the offer of grace at the level of the existential is just preliminary within the breadth of God's entire salvific act, since the "form" of the offer of grace is not yet accepted or rejected. It cannot be since it takes place before the activation of human freedom and rationality. However, even if it is "remote," it nonetheless is a critical piece in the entire scope of God's work of grace, since without it, we would not have the capacity of faith—that is, our openness to receive the offer of grace. Without this divine offer that penetrates deep into our existence, it is meaningless to speak of God's grace. Had it been just an offer made after the activation of human freedom, it would insinuate that grace is always contingent upon our decision, which is anathema to both Barth and Rahner. Grace starts from God and therefore presupposes an unthematic starting point (without us) and Rahner has found it in the place called the human existential. Following Rahner, Coffey

---

20. Coffey, "The Whole Rahner," 101.

ensures that the offer of grace is the precondition of our faith. This means that even our faithful decision is not a solo flight. It demands a divine partner who needs to elevate our existence to initiate our redemptive process and follow through to the final telos, that is, God in himself.

What we glean from this analysis is that Coffey has formulated a unique understanding of God's order of communication. Building upon Rahner's principle of the supernatural existential, Coffey perceives God's communicative order having three components: raw material–unthematic dimension–explicit dimension. It is easier to see if I state it the following way. God starts his communication from himself and reaches out to the human nature (raw material). He elevates the human nature by his offer of grace implicitly at the level of the human existential (unthematic dimension). He continues to offer his grace until we accept or reject his offer (explicit dimension). This order aligns well with Coffey's trinitarian model in which the taxis is biblical theology (raw material)–the immanent Trinity (unthematic dimension)–the economic Trinity (explicit dimension).

The implication of the order of the supernatural existential is far reaching. At this point, I examine Coffey's other work that applies the concept of the supernatural existential to a wider theological topic, namely, "the Theandric Nature of Christ." This examination will unveil not only the ways in which Coffey applies Rahner's conception of the supernatural existential but also his pneumatological reworking of this theory, which is going to be propitious to my project.

The Theandric Nature of Christ

As we have seen, Coffey's re-appropriation of Rahner's supernatural existential hinges on the conceptual taxis of raw materials–implicit theology–explicit theology. A similar principle applies here when we examine Jesus' hypostatic union as the "highest" point reached by the entelechy of the Spirit. However, like Barth, because Coffey understands that Jesus' God-man trait is absolutely singular, Coffey also distinguishes the order of our union with God from the order of the union of God and man in Jesus Christ, although there is a correlation between the two. Because of the particular aspect of Jesus' hypostatic union, Coffey ingenuously reorders the supernatural existential to follow the order of creation, sanctification, and union.

At the onset of Coffey's article "The Theandric Nature of Christ," he clarifies the reason for promoting his own order of Jesus' hypostatic union. Coffey states that he wants to use his own order of hypostatic union to overturn and revise the traditional Catholic teaching. According to Coffey, the traditional taxis of Jesus' hypostatic union is as follows: creation–union–sanctification. Based on his historical survey, Coffey believes that this is incorrectly formulated. The historical background of this order has been well developed by Coffey in his article, but due to the limited space, I briefly summarize Aquinas's order of Jesus Christ's hypostatic union as the representative case for the traditional taxis and its shortcomings.

Aquinas understood that the human nature of Christ subsists in the hypostasis of the divine Word and the divine Word subsists in the human nature.[21] For this reason, he had no issue with the belief that the divinity of Christ was working through his humanity. However, for Aquinas, "Christ is very God according to his person and his divine nature. But since with the unity of person the distinction of natures remains, Christ's soul is not divine by its essence. Hence it is necessary that it becomes divine by participation, which is by grace."[22] What Aquinas was unwilling to accept is the conflation of the divine and human natures in Christ. They have to be treated differently. Aquinas's objection is acceptable since divine and human natures are incommunicable in the sense that there is an infinite qualitative difference between them. If they are treated differently, then Christ's soul must be elevated from its creaturely level to the supernatural level to be in union with the divine Logos, and as we have already seen, the only way to elevate the human nature to the supernatural end is via grace. So, as noted by Coffey, the taxis of hypostatic union for Aquinas is the "creation of the human nature, hypostatic union, infusion of habitual grace."[23] More clearly, "creation belongs to the natural order, union to the supernatural order of substance, and grace to the supernatural order of accident."[24] What we have is three distinct phases of Jesus' hypostatic union that moves from the natural, to the substantial, and finally to the supernatural elevation of grace.

However, Coffey finds Aquinas's order problematic. There are mainly three issues that Coffey mentions. The first issue is Aquinas's denial of the

---

21. Aquinas, *Summa Theologica*, 3, q.19, a.1.

22. Coffey, "The Theandric Nature of Christ," 414. Also see, Aquinas, *Summa Theologica*, 3, q.7, a.1.

23. Coffey, "The Theandric Nature of Christ," 427.

24. Coffey, "The Theandric Nature of Christ," 427.

finitum capax infiniti,[25] even though he accepts the Aristetolian principle of *operatio sequitur esse*.[26] As Coffey contends, if Aquinas esteemed the human nature and its rational capability to reach God via "faith and charity made possible by grace,"[27] there is no reason to deny ontological expandability of the finite that can be open to receive the infinite, though not naturally but supernaturally. So, Coffey laments that Aquinas's view of human nature as "capable of God by its action but incapable by its being" fails to connect "the finite nature with the patristic concept of the image of God, [that is,] openness to the absolute."[28] The second issue is Aquinas's dependence on descending Christology, or more specifically, Christology of the Gospel of John, with no regard for ascending Christology or Christology of the Synoptic Gospels. According to Coffey, descending Christology acknowledges Jesus' hypostatic union to be the work of the Son (or the Logos) only, and for this reason, he assigns Aquinas's descending theology as Logos Christology. However, as the Synoptic Gospels show, Jesus' hypostatic union is also the work of the Holy Spirit[29] and Coffey locates this gap in Aquinas's Christology. The third issue which is related to the first two issues is Aquinas's inclusion of habitual grace. For Coffey, Jesus' hypostatic union does not require habitual grace. We need to examine this point more thoroughly since his justification for changing Aquinas's order of Jesus' hypostatic union pivots on it.

Coffey claims that Jesus' hypostatic union does not need habitual grace because Jesus' human nature is theandric. Coffey's introduction of the theandric nature of Christ is based on the re-reading of Pseudo-Dionysius and Thomas Aquinas, but more importantly, Karl Rahner's Christology. Relying on Rahner's order, Coffey states that Christ is theandric because he is divine in a human way and human in a divine way. In other words,

---

25. The *finitum capax infiniti* is normally translated as the following: the finite comprehends the infinite. However, in this context, theologically, it means that the finite is capable of embracing the infinite. It is related to ontology more so than epistemology.

26. The phrase *operatio sequitur esse* is a Latin term that literally says, "operation is the perfection of being." In Coffey's sense, it simply denotes that there is a link between ontology and praxis. We can restate it in this way. We do what we are made to do. So if we are able to know God (operationally), then we must be open to the infinite (ontologically).

27. Coffey, "The Theandric Nature of Christ," 416.

28. Coffey, "The Theandric Nature of Christ," 417.

29. Coffey is referring to Luke 1:35, which reads, "The Holy Spirit will come upon you, and the power of the Most High will overshadow you. Therefore the child to be born [creation] will be holy [grace], the Son of God [union]."

Christ's human nature remains genuinely human, even though Christ's human nature is united to the divine Logos in a unique way, "to the point of the coincidence of its being with the being of God."[30] If this is true, Coffey can avoid the error of Monophysitism, on the one hand, and Nestorianism, on the other. The former conflates two natures and the latter separates them without any possibility of communicability between the two. If there is one nature in Jesus, Coffey is free from the Nestorian heresy, and if there are two distinct essential aspects in Jesus, one divine and another human, existing without confusion or without change, then Coffey is free from the error of Monophysitism. But the question remains. How is it that Christ's human nature remains integrally human when it is made coincident with the being of God?

Coffey uses three different ways to address this question. He refers to the theory of the communication of idioms, the biblical testimony, and the supernatural existential. For our purpose, Coffey's reliance on the supernatural existential will be given more attention, but nonetheless, I mention other two ways briefly here. Regarding Coffey's use of the communication of idioms, it represents the principle of duality. Coffey's own words are self-explanatory.

> In Christ there is a single esse corresponding to his single divine personhood. In as much as he is the incarnate Word of God, this esse viewed from the perspective of the communicating Word is the divine esse. But in so far as it founds Christ's human nature in existence, it is received as a human esse.[31]

To state it differently, we can say that the theandric nature of Christ is preserved because God reveals God's own esse, but at the same time, God is revealed only through the human nature of Jesus Christ. Thus, even though Jesus is divine, as Coffey points out, he is "incapable of states of being or operations that are strictly divine (hence the divine 'condescension' involved in the Incarnation)."[32] Although I do not agree with him here for he limits the scope of Jesus' divine work to his human functionality, he has

---

30. Coffey, "The Theandric Nature of Christ," 412.

31. Coffey, "The Theandric Nature of Christ," 422.

32. Coffey, "The Theandric Nature of Christ," 413. This is one of Coffey's slippery areas that I do not endorse. I would not use the phrase "incapable of states of being or operations," but it is acceptable here in the sense that Jesus chooses to work within the confines of his human capacity even though he is fully divine. We should never portray Jesus as the one who is incapable for any reason. Even in his vulnerability, he is omnipotent. This is the duality of Jesus Christ.

arguably succeeded in preserving the principle of identity (e.g., the single nature of Christ) and the principle of duality (e.g., the two aspects of the single nature, namely, divine and human communications within Christ). In regard to the biblical testimony, Coffey simply refers to the fact that the Gospels show the human limitations of Christ. For this reason, I do not think he is too enthusiastic about attributing Jesus' miracles as the display of his divine power.[33]

Finally, we come to Coffey's use of the supernatural existential. To unpack this dimension, we need to return to Rahner's conception of the supernatural existential. There are three components to which we must refer: the raw material, the supernatural elevation in the unthematic dimension of our existence, and the move from the unthematic dimension of grace to the explicit dimension of our existence. As we have seen, all these three categories function as the key pillars to the theological edifice of the supernatural existential. I show here that Coffey is using the same principle but nuanced differently to fit his theory of Jesus' hypostatic union.

I start with the raw material. In Jesus' hypostatic union, the raw material is the human nature. The aim of the supernatural existential is to elevate this raw material to the level of the supernatural so that Jesus can cross the critical threshold from what is natural to what is supernatural and be united with God in himself.

This naturally leads to the second component, the supernatural elevation. In the case of Jesus' hypostatic union, unlike us, the supernatural elevation does not depend on grace. But nonetheless, Coffey does not hesitate to say that Jesus needs this supernatural elevation. He has nuanced it differently though, as the divinization of Jesus' human nature. He writes in this regard.

> There are therefore two ways of being divine: the simply given divinity of the transcendent God, and the divinity achieved by divine grace in humanity. Achieved divinity is itself found in two ways, expressed by the Scholastics as "substantial" in the case of Christ, and "accidental," that is, by habitual grace, in the case of other human beings, or expressed by the Church Fathers as hypostatic or personal for Christ, and by participation (in him) for others, that is, they become sons or daughters in the Son.[34]

---

33. Coffey, "The Theandric Nature of Christ," 421.
34. Coffey, "The Theandric Nature of Christ," 413.

I need to add my own comments to explain what he means by "achieved divinization." This language may sound specious to the Protestant circles, but it is not at all different from the Barthian idiom. Correlative to the supernatural existential, achieved divinization is Coffey's way of saying that the human nature needs God's supernatural intervention before we can communicate with God. Of course, in the case of Christian believers, we are ultimately "divinized" by saving grace as we become sons and daughters of God. Thus, we do not actually become gods but incorporated into God's life. This is the achieved divinity that Coffey is talking about. However, in the case of Christ, this is different. His humanity is elevated in such a way that it is assumed by the divine Logos. Hence, it is literally "divinized." His human nature is coincided with the divine being without confusion and without change. For this reason, Coffey says that the hypostatic union of God and man in Jesus Christ is substantial rather than accidental. He puts it in another way. "[H]ypostatic union is realized absolutely in the case of Christ, and relatively in the case of others."[35] Translated to Barthian language, Coffey is trying to say that Jesus' hypostatic union is different because of its absolute singularity as opposed to our creaturely relativeness. Also, we must note that "divinization" here does not mean that Coffey is blurring the distinction between God and man. Although Christ's human nature is divinized, Christ is still remains human, but with qualification. He is human in a divine way and divine in a human way.

This view complements nicely with the third point, the move from the unthematic dimension of grace to the explicit dimension of grace. Coffey has shown that, in the unthematic dimension of human existence, grace makes our nature open to receive God prior to the activation of human freedom and cognition. This means that the supernatural elevation takes place at the unconscious level, which prepares the way for the conscious, explicit actions. Likewise, Jesus' hypostatic union also has an unthematic dimension, but without the language of consciousness since Coffey has moved beyond the work of saving grace to the level of absolute divinization. Coffey borrows from Rahner the language of "*actus primus*" to accentuate that Jesus' hypostatic union begins at the implicit spiritual level, which prepares for the explicit level of the divine Logos' assumption of the human nature.

Theologically, Coffey describes the unthematic dimension of hypostatic union this way. "And for this concrete human nature to be assumable

---

35. Coffey, "The Theandric Nature of Christ," 413.

by the Son, it must be theandric. In other words, its substantial sanctification by the Holy Spirit is logically prior to its assumption by the Son, its last 'disposition' to assumption."[36] What follows from this logic is Coffey's order of Jesus' hypostatic union: the creation of human nature, the sanctification of the Holy Spirit, which elevates Jesus' human nature to be assumable by the Son, and the Son's assumption of Jesus' human nature. In short, Coffey's order of Jesus' hypostatic union is creation-sanctification-union.

Compared to Aquinas's order, which is creation-union-grace, Coffey's order does not have the "grace" component. The habitual grace, which is only applicable to us, has been correctly removed, but Coffey still retains the unthematic dimension of Jesus' human nature by adding the work of the Holy Spirit as the "remote ordination" of Jesus' hypostatic union. So Jesus' hypostatic union begins not with the Son but with the Holy Spirit. In other words, the single act of union has two distinct parts, beginning with the Holy Spirit's prepatory work on the human nature-to-be-assumed and ending with the Son's actual assumption. Again, this is Coffey's recognition of the principle of the supernatural existential framing the whole structure of Jesus' hypostatic union.

In sum, I have shown that Coffey has been faithful to his theological taxis underwritten by the principle of the supernatural existential, that is, raw materials–implicit grace–explicit grace. What we need to recognize is that the order of the supernatural existential is the order of our transcendence. It is the crossing of the threshold, from the human and natural level to the level of the supernatural. According to Coffey, we owe this supernatural elevation to the work of the Spirit. The Spirit thus is depicted not only as a compass that aligns us to God but also the supernatural empowerment that elevates us to be in union with God. Even in the event of Incarnation, the same principle applies, as Coffey overturns the traditional Catholic order and promotes the taxis of creation-sanctification-union. The Spirit again is the implicit catalyst that makes Jesus' human nature divinizable for the Son's assumption.

This is Coffey's way of fleshing out the unthematic dimension of human existence. It is not only pneumatologically driven but also holistically constructed. It ties together the work of the Spirit in creation, human nature, and God in himself, without marginalizing one at the expense of the other. Coffey's work in this area of study is extensive and thorough. I have not seen any work that is comparable to Coffey's theological program, and

36. Coffey, "The Theandric Nature of Christ," 428.

for this reason, his contribution to pneumatological studies is valuable. His pneumatological principle is almost ready-made to apply to any theological situations. However, as I have mentioned before, there is one lack. He has not mentioned the unthematic dimension of human depravity. The key to Coffey's neglect in this area is his misunderstanding that the problem of human depravity lies not in the unthematic dimension of human existence but in the explicit dimension, that is, in the conscious dimension of human freedom and rationality. This is where I depart from Coffey. In order to demonstrate why the discussion of human depravity belongs to the unthematic dimension of human existence, I critically review the work of Stanley Grenz, with which I defend my claim.

The Unthematic Nature of Human Depravity

Although Grenz speaks of neither "the unthematic dimension of human existence" nor "the supernatural existential," there is a clear-cut theological stance in Grenz's hamartiology that points to the unthematic dimension of human depravity. This is what we are going to unpack in this section. Moving forward, I focus on the two key aspects of Grenz's hamartiology: the meaning of "sin" and the reformulation of the Reformed understanding of total depravity. These two aspects of Grenz's theology of sin will unveil his desire to not only reformulate the standing theory of total depravity, but more importantly, rethink about the very essence of human being. My analysis of Grenz's work will fill the gap left behind by Coffey's work and finalize the dual core theory as the holistic version of the unthematic dimension of human existence to which God makes his first contact with us. I open up with the analysis of Grenz's definition of sin.

According to Grenz, the topic of sin is difficult to handle theologically and exegetically. Theologically, it is complex due to the fact that different theological traditions carry mutually exclusive interpretations of sin. Also, "sin" comes as a huge theological package, filled with a philosophical, sociological, or cultural assortments. Exegetically, it is extremely diverse due to the fact that "sin" has been defined not with a single term but multiple terms and phrases in the Bible. Grenz's first task then is to clear away the ambiguity and lay out clearly what he can say about the concept of sin. As a proficient systematician, Grenz starts with the biblical depiction of sin.

Grenz examines the key biblical terms that are associated with "sin," and in his exegetical analysis, he finds two important dimensions of sin that weave the Old Testament and the New Testament terms into a single tapestry. The first one that he mentions is the definition of sin as "the missing the goal."[37] It should come as no surprise to Christians in both Protestant and Catholic circles. Sin is commonly seen as a deviation from God's purpose (the chief implication for the Hebrew word, "chatha") or missing the target set before us by God (the chief implication for the Greek word, "ἀμαρτία"). Consequently, Grenz concludes that we are goal-driven, fulfilling a certain given task, albeit that we are "missing" it.

To a certain extent, Grenz's exegetical study parallels Coffey's theology. For Coffey, what is true of human nature is that it is always oriented toward God. It is open to God. It is our natural end. Grenz also believes that human beings are open to God but with one added condition. Our openness to God is tied to our inherent ability to transcend the limitation of this world. He writes in this regard. "Humans are characterized by the restless quest to move beyond every specific form of the world. The quest points toward both our ultimate dependence on God and our special God-given destiny."[38] What this implies is that human beings are intrinsically transcendent beings. They are not satisfied with maintaining the status quo as mere "animals" with high-powered rational capabilities. They try to overcome this critical threshold and move beyond the boundary of nature within which they are kept. So, like Coffey's threshold crossing, Grenz sees that humans are preprogrammed with a final telos, moving from the worldly realm to the divine kingdom. What is important for me is that, according to Grenz, the desire to self-transcend is imputed in human beings at the unconscious level, which drives human beings to seek after higher things in the world at the conscious level, and such an unconscious desire will be realized at the end as they reach its apex, that is our union with God.[39] It sounds very much like Coffey's principle of the supernatural existential. Its resemblance is patent if we put Grenz's concept of the dual telos this way. God-consciousness is implicit, and the open world-consciousness is explicit; the latter leads to the former, if all goes well.

The similarity between Grenz and Coffey ends here, however, as Grenz moves beyond the harmony of the dual telos. Surely, for Grenz there are two goals, one worldly and another divine, the former leading up to the

---

37. Grenz, *Theology for the Community*, 184.
38. Grenz, *Theology for the Community*, 206.
39. Grenz, *Theology for the Community*, 206.

latter as the latter is the ultimate goal.⁴⁰ However, Grenz adds one additional category, that is, the category of sin, which is a natural tendency that makes us miss the goal. Grenz is a realist and knows that the world is not perfect. That is certainly true of who we are. Surely, "there is no one righteous, not even one" (Rom 3:10). For this reason, Grenz's general tenor for the human condition is not just about having a goal, but the "missing the goal." As interpreted by Grenz, the worldly goal, which is the community life living in a righteous and loving fellowship with one another, and the divine goal, which is related to the worldly goal but more in tune with the fellowship with God, are not met. These goals are broken from bottom up, because something has gone awfully wrong with us. Grenz examines the very core of our being in which he locates the problem.

This leads to Grenz's second point, that is, sin affects "the core of our being."⁴¹ He writes in this regard. "Repeatedly the Scripture writers link sin with the core of our being. Sinful acts arise from within us, from the center of our existence."⁴² What we need to pay attention is Grenz's focus on the "core" of our being. What is this core? What defines the core? There are two hints that suggest what he is talking about here. The first hint is his association of sin with the corruption of the heart and the second point is his description of human nature. I examine them respectively.

Grenz insists that the center of our being is dysfunctional. Grenz correlates the center of being with the biblical term of "heart." For Grenz, this term points to our "personal control center."⁴³ He is not referring to the physical dimension of human reality, but an unthematic dimension of human essence, out of which comes our ability to reason and think. For this reason, Grenz assigns the dysfunctional heart as the cause for the erroneous movement of the mind and affection. Our mind and affection are not flawed just because we did something to it. Rather, Grenz is emphasizing the fact that the error begins at the core of our being, in the unthematic dimension of human existence.

Grenz's attention to the unthematic "center" of our being highlights the precondition of human existence that determines our active engagement of

---

40. Grenz was a pupil of Wolfhart Pannenberg, and he has been influenced by Pannenberg's work. It shows in this adoption of Pannenberg's anthropology. Pannenberg has fleshed out the nature of human being in terms of its openness to the world. Pannenberg, *What Is Man?*, 1–13.

41. Grenz, *Theology for the Community*, 188.

42. Grenz, *Theology for the Community*, 184.

43. Grenz, *Theology for the Community*, 185.

sinful activities. For him, it is a seat of disposition rather than a seat of our volition or rationality. It is the pre-cognitive and pre-volitional "center" upon which our decisions and thoughts are determined. We will see later in our discussion of Reformed theology of total depravity that he takes this unthematic understanding of our center as the key motif for changing the standing theory of total depravity. It plays a critical role in Grenz's hamartiology, but what I want to focus here is Grenz's desire to unveil the deep-seated flaw that controls our misbehaviors. Bolstered by biblical data, Grenz understands that the theory of total depravity has to start with the ontological status of our being.

This brings us back to the discussion of the nature of human essence. What is the ontological status of our nature? Although Grenz does not invest much on this aspect, he attempts to unpack the very essence of our being by examining one controversial biblical statement: "we were by nature objects of wrath" (Eph 2:3b). Despite the exegetical uncertainties and ambiguities associated with this verse, Grenz concludes that the word "nature" (φύσις) suggests "a state that has become a natural part of our existence or that is now 'naturally' our situation."[44] Hence, for Grenz, our corruption is internally disposed first and externally determined as we consciously sin, being influenced by the depravity inherent in our nature. Does this mean that human essence has always been this way?

Grenz answers this question negatively. He argues against Reinhold Niebuhr who translated the philosophical concept of "finitude" as "physical death." In other words, rather than counting death as the result of the "disposed" depravity that trickled down from the Fall of Adam to us, Niebuhr simply equated "death" with human essence, in this case, its finitude. Grenz says that this is wrong. The concept of "finitude" does not necessarily bind our being to death. This is true since the Genesis narrative makes clear that "death" was not part of human existence at the beginning (Gen 2:17). It was the result of sin (Rom 6:23). Hence, our depravity, though it is seated at the center of our being, according to Grenz, has been internalized by an external event, which for Grenz is the Fall of Adam. I would need to modify this aspect of Grenz's claim slightly from a pneumatological perspective because the Fall of Adam is not the ultimate source of death in this world, but regarding "depravity" or "corruption" not being considered as the original component of human existence, I agree with him wholeheartedly. They are divinely and anthropologically external, not a necessary component of

---

44. Grenz, *Theology for the Community*, 203.

Godness or humanness. Besides, the concept of "finitude" in and of itself is too vague to determine the content of human essence. It may be right for Grenz to say that "finitude" simply means our contingency as opposed to God's self-sufficiency.[45] As finite beings, we are surely dependent upon the infinite nature of God.

With a biblical basis, Grenz is now poised to reformulate the Reformed doctrine of total depravity. Here, he is even more effective in the way he portrays the unthematic dimension of human depravity. Grenz's key contention is that Reformed theology of total depravity does not have a good biblical and theological ground. I have already looked at Grenz's biblical analysis, so I attend to Grenz's theological argument at this point.

Grenz interprets Reformed theology of total depravity this way. "The dominant position in the Reformed tradition postulates that all Adam's offspring inherit both a depraved nature (the pollution of sin) and actual guilt."[46] At the onset of his argument, he differentiates the depraved nature and actual guilt by denoting the former as the unthematic dimension of human sinful condition and the latter as our conscious rejection of God that leads to condemnation.[47] In Thomist language, we can categorize the former as the potential to be guilty and the latter the actuality of guilt. The potential does not make us guilty, however. It needs to be activated by our conscious choice to be "actually" guilty.

Thus, for Grenz, we do not inherit both depravity and guilt from Adam. Rather, what comes from the progenitor of humanity is depravity. By contrast, guilt is consequential of each individual's free act of "missing the mark." This is Grenz's theological position, and with it, he wants to do away with the idea that we inherit both depravity and guilt from Adam. The concept of original sin for Grenz is limited to our discussion of depravity, not our guilt. Grenz has good theological reasons for staking out his position as such.

Grenz surveys the history of Christian theology and concludes that the patristic scholars did not adhere to the Reformed view. In other words, Grenz does not see a good theological precedence of the Reformed view from the early years of the theological development. According to Grenz, even Augustine who carved out a sophisticated theology of sin and pushed the theory of depravity to its limit by hinting that we all participate in the

---

45. Grenz, *Theology for the Community*, 193.
46. Grenz, *Theology for the Community*, 202.
47. Grenz, *Theology for the Community*, 199.

Fall of Adam, he did not go so far as to say that God has imputed Adam's guilt to us. Grenz reads Augustine correctly, for Augustine at one point confirmed that God does not charge Adam's guilt to our account.[48] For Augustine, guilt belongs to each individual's action. Sin is the result of what we do with the dysfunctional free will. For Augustine, although we have a dysfunctional free will, unless we actually do something wrong with it, we are not guilty of our sin.

If there is no theological precedence in the patristic writings, where did the Reformed tradition receive the idea of total guilt? Grenz traces the historical root to John Calvin, the pioneering figure of the Reformation. In Grenz's judgment, the dominant Reformed view of total depravity comes from Calvin's reformulation of Augustine's theory of original sin. According to Grenz, Calvin declared that "both guilt and corruption have spread to all Adam's offspring, being transmitted from parent to child."[49] Although there have been new readings of Calvin's theology that tone down the harshness and determinism associated with the doctrine of total depravity,[50] Grenz's assessment of Calvin's conception of total depravity is fair to what Calvin said in *Institutes of Christian Religion*.[51] Calvin was unequivocal about the relationship between sin, depravity, and guilt. For him, they are inherent qualities that belong to all of us since the Fall of Adam.

Moving away from Calvinistic theology, Grenz implicitly sides with Arminianism. We can detect this attitude from his writing: "Arminius reasserted the semi-Pelagian position that Adam's offspring do not share in the guilt of the sin of our first father."[52] It is safe to note that Grenz is following the Arminian position since he does not believe that we have inherited both depravity and guilt from Adam. However, he is not thrilled about Arminius's semi-Pelagian move. We can infer this from his identification of semi-Pelagianism: "The semi-Pelagians asserted that all human beings are indeed tainted by Adam's sin and therefore inclined toward evil. Yet we are not neither totally unable to do good nor involved in the guilt of Adam."[53] As we have seen, Grenz opts for total depravity, meaning that we are totally

---

48. Augustine, *Concerning the City of God*, 10.
49. Grenz, *Theology for the Community*, 200.
50. Basil Hall's *John Calvin: Humanist and Theologian* is a good example.
51. E.g., Calvin, *Institutes*, 1:246–50.
52. Grenz, *Theology for the Community*, 200.
53. Grenz, *Theology for the Community*, 200.

unable to do good. This is Grenz's thesis as he states that sin has infiltrated the core of our being.

Taking an added step, Grenz correlates semi-Pelagianism to Arminianism by saying that "[Arminius] theorized that present to the individual is a special prevenient grace from God," which "makes it possible for us to overcome our inherited depravity."[54] The concept of Arminius's prevenient grace is similar to Coffey's idea of the supernatural elevation, but with an added component, that is, the supernatural elevation that overcomes our depraved traits. I will factor in this idea when I develop my own theory about the relationship between sin and grace, but Grenz seems to dislike this claim since he relates it to semi-Pelagianism. However, Grenz's misapprehension is unfounded. As Coffey has shown, as long as we are talking about the "elevation" as a supernatural means of grace, we are free from the error of semi-Pelagianism.

In the end, Grenz re-defines the sin-depravity relationship. He writes, "We must include under the category of original sin the corruption in human nature as derived from Adam, that is, from our common inherited humanity. Our failure to measure up to God's design is not merely an external force [thematic] but also inherited part of each person [unthematic]."[55] He understands that we are both depraved and guilty before God. However, Grenz wants to be clear that there is a sharp distinction between depravity and guilt, though the former disposes the latter. For him, if we do not distinguish the two, we would make God an unjust judge, punishing for the things we have not yet done wrong. For Grenz, this is not a good theological proposition to accept, for the "great judge renders his verdict not on the basis of our fallen nature, but because of our deeds, which we do as our depraved nature expresses itself in thought or overt action."[56] This proves that Grenz's theology of total depravity pivots on the unthematic dimension of sin.

Putting Together Rahner, Coffey, and Grenz: The Dual Core Theory

We are now in position to lay out the contours of the dual core theory. What I have done so far is to show that there are two standing theories of the

54. Grenz, *Theology for the Community*, 200.
55. Grenz, *Theology for the Community*, 206.
56. Grenz, *Theology for the Community*, 206.

unthematic dimension of human existence. The first theory belongs to Coffey and Rahner. The key tenet of Rahner-Coffey's supernatural existential is that grace is offered at the unconscious level first, and then, it affects the conscious level of human decision-making activities. Likewise, the second theory, which belongs to Grenz, is presented in such a way that depravity is seated at the core of our existence. For Grenz, depravity is a fallen state of human beings that impacts our essence as well as our physical existence. What is important to Grenz is that depravity and guilt are not the same, the former as the unthematic condition of human beings and the latter as the conscious actions that may lead to our condemnation. These two theories seem to be at odds with each other without any hope of reconciliation. However, my contention is that they are reconcilable. In fact, if we are to be faithful to the biblical witness, at least to Pauline letters, we must reconcile these two theories and come up with a single theory that can embrace both concepts as non-contentious theology. Thus, my next task is to consolidate these two findings, and rethink about the relationship between sin and grace from a pneumatological perspective. My approach is to modify Coffey's theory of the supernatural existential by incorporating Grenz's theory of total depravity. Through this synthesis, I demonstrate that we have two cores that occupy the center of our being, namely, grace and depravity.

I begin with Coffey's theory of the supernatural existential. The core of this theory is that there is a specific order of God's communication—e.g., material causality, the implicit dimension of grace, and the explicit dimension of grace. Because of material causality and the implicit dimension of grace, Coffey insists that human beings are naturally and supernaturally oriented toward God. The question at this point is that if we are naturally and supernaturally oriented toward God, why do we "miss the mark"? Coffey's answer lies not in the condition of our existence. The issue of sin for Coffey depends on our volition. This means that "sin" does not belong to the realm of the unthematic dimension of human existence. For him, we sin consciously and purposely. It is an overt action that derives from our rational, affective, and volitional determination.

As Grenz has shown, this type of hamartiology is very difficult to accept if we examine closely both Old and New Testament data on this topic. The problem of sin is existential through and through. It invades the core of our being. Even if we deny that the Fall of Adam is not responsible for the demise of humanity, there is no doubt that something is awfully wrong with our existence. Had our existence been sound, Jesus would not have come.

The truth is that he did come and he had to undo the things that are already irreversibly crooked. This is our current status and we cannot neglect this fact. As Calvin once said, we are so "envenomed by sin that it can breathe out nothing but corruption and rottenness; that if some men occasionally make a show of goodness, their mind is ever interwoven with hypocrisy and deceit, their soul inwardly bound with the fetters of wickedness."[57] Grenz agrees with Calvin here, and following Grenz and Calvin, I locate the roots of our wickedness in the center of our being. So, Coffey may have missed the mark and did not account for depravity that lies in the core of our being. What I am saying is that there may be two cores at the center of our being. How can this be? Can we divide the human nature into two distinct poles? I am not dividing the human nature into two distinct poles. Let me unpack further the concept of the dual core pneumatologically.

We can speak of the core of being as "spirit." Like God, our ontological status is constituted by "spirit." If we recall, God's essence has been depicted as spirit, for out of it flows the threeness of God, that is, the Father-spirit, the Son-spirit, and the Holy Spirit. The priority of spirit is emphasized due to the fact that it is the matrix of "essence" that presupposes and anticipates the distinctive personal existence. Likewise, taking into consideration the priority of "spirit," we can denote the unthematic dimension of human existence pneumatologically. To borrow Coffey's language, spirit can be viewed as "that qualified transcendence and independence of matter that allows its possessors to be and to become a 'subject.'"[58] As God is ontologically spiritual (the Subject), we are also ontologically spiritual (a subject). Simply put, spirit makes us who we are. We are thoroughly a spiritual entity.

Because we are spiritual in nature, spirit is the core of our being (e.g., Prov 20:27; Jas 2:26). To nuance it differently, I add that spirit is the seedbed of all our dispositions and attributes. Out of it flows freedom, reason, and affection. Spirit is that objective-subjective qualification of our existence, and for this reason, it is where our consciousness is shaped and birthed. Furthermore, as an unthematic dimension of transcendence, which is affirmed by the movement of the entelechy of the Spirit, it is oriented toward God. We move spiritually from one level to another, finally reaching out to God. Consequently, Coffey rightly notes that our spiritual realization is always dependent upon a transcendental relation to God as absolute spirit. We will not be able to know our spiritual form and shape unless we are

---

57. Calvin, *Institutes*, 1:291.
58. Coffey, *Deus Trinitas*, 75.

reflected upon God's absolute spirit. This is one of my main reasons for bringing up the prius of God's ontological order in the previous chapter. Without clearly outlining God's ontological make-up, our spiritual conditions cannot be measured properly, because our spirituality is a reflection of God's spirituality.

Having said this, what is our spiritual condition? It is bleak. If nothing is wrong with us existentially, we should all be oriented toward God and be in a harmonious and righteous fellowship with God and each other. However, the fellowship has been broken and we are perpetually missing the final telos. As Grenz has said, depravity has infiltrated the core of our being, and as a result, we are spiritually dysfunctional. Let me illustrate this with a medical analogy. Depravity has come in like a cancer cell. It has attached itself to the core of our being and introduced death to our spirituality. Consequently, our spirituality is dying, if not dead already. The telos of our spirituality is no longer life eternal (God), but decay, decomposition, and death (depravity). But what is the source of this depravity?

Grenz points us to the Fall of Adam. But from a pneumatological point of view, I would go ever further. Adam sinned because of the temptation of the devil, the fallen angel. In this respect, I trace its source to the devil. The devil here represents the power of de-spiritualization.[59] I stress the point that *de*-spiritualization is antithetical to the way of God-spirit, because it entices us to "miss the mark."[60] Hence, de-spiritualization is simply the power that disposes us to miss the mark. In Paul's terms, it inclines us to satisfy the desires of the flesh, which is the against the way of the Spirit (Gal 5:17). For this reason, in Paul's view, spirit and flesh are at odds with one another, the former seeking the ways of God, and the latter seeking the ways of the world. For the lack of a better term, I call the unthematic dimension of de-spiritualization the supernatural non-existential. The supernatural aspect of de-spiritualization signifies that the ultimate source of depravity is not of this world (Eph 6:12b), and the non-existential dimen-

---

59. Welker, *God the Spirit*, 85. Welker notes that, although it may not be "always possible to distinguish immediately and clearly between the good Spirit of God and the evil spirit," "it seems plausible to conclude that the good Spirit of God is a Spirit who leads to the unity and community of a people or to the powerful, positive influence of an individual person. By contrast, the evil spirit leads to disintegration and destruction of a community. The evil spirit torments individual persons and induces them to act aggressively."

60. Sin originated with Satan (Isa 14:12–14) and entered the world through Adam (Rom 5:12), and thus, it is universal (Rom 3:23).

sion signifies that depravity leads to death, whether eternal or temporal. The non-existential dimension also denotes that the source of depravity is parasitical. The devil has no existence on its own. As Anselm has pointed out, evil is quasi-ontological.[61] It does not have its own reality, but it obtains reality from our depravity.

The supernatural existential thus plays an even more critical role than what Coffey has asserted. Rather than just elevating the natural tendencies to the level of the supernatural, it defies the effects of depravity. As a matter of fact, the offer of grace is the only means to defeat the influx of de-spiritualization that drives the existential to its demise. The healing of our depravity thus begins at the level of our unthematic existence, not at the level of guilt. In this sense, Rahner was on target to promote prevenient grace, that is, grace offered and affecting our existence even prior to our free decision. Also, it is safe to assume that Calvinism's conception of irresistible grace is not far from the truth. Since the order of our existential healing starts from the unthematic level of our existence, God's salvific healing grace is surely irresistible. It is irresistible because grace affects us even before we come to its realization. The key implication of the order of this existential healing—a form of regeneration—is that it resolves the issue of the *ordo salutis*.

The *ordo salutis* has been divided into largely two ways: monergism and synergism. On the one hand, the monergistic order of salvation starts with God's self-giving, which in turn, activates the process of regeneration at the existential level. Thus, salvation is initiated at the pre-cognitive and pre-volitional level. On the other hand, the synergistic order of salvation begins at our conscious level, upon which we respond to the offer of grace. So, the order of salvation in this respect bypasses the unthematic dimension and focuses on our cooperative act with God's salvific work. Which one should we choose? Can we choose both? If we adopt the order of existential healing, we can see that the order of salvation incorporates both dimensions. The unthematic dimension of grace satisfies both the monergistic order, as the process of regeneration begins at the unconscious level, and the synergetic order, as the process of regeneration is fully effectuated when we actively respond to the offer of grace. What we need to remember is that the unthematic dimension does not finalize the offer of grace. It only disposes us to either accept or reject the offer. Only at our conscious level can we actually accept or reject the offer. Thus, in light of the principle

---

61. Anselm, "On the Fall," 205–7.

of the supernatural existential, monergism and synergism become critical ingredients for the *ordo salutis*.

There is another dilemma associated with the *ordo salutis*—whether our salvation is instantaneous or progressive. I do not think we can explain the *ordo salutis* with either choice. If we are regenerated instantaneously, then we have to discard all aspects of God's prepatory work for our salvation. Likewise, if we are regenerated progressively, then we have to discard the once-and-for-all (Rom 6:10) proclamation of Paul. What we need here is a consolidation of the two views again, and the order of existential healing can unite these two theological themes as a single theory. According to the order of existential healing, we are made new as soon as we accept the offer of grace, and at the same time, the order of regeneration is progressive in that it starts at the unthematic dimension of human existence and finds its completion at the conscious level. Pneumatologically speaking, as we are disposed by the Holy Spirit and elevated to the level of the supernatural, we are made ready to align ourselves to Christ and finally united with him when we respond positively to the Holy Spirit's offer of grace. However, we need to remember that the progressive nature and immediate effects of the Holy Spirit are not two mutually exclusive events, but one and the same event, albeit distinct. The material causality of the unthematic dimension stands in the path of the final causality of the Holy Spirit, so if there is no hindrance, the two causalities will ultimately reach the common telos in God.

Since I mentioned the "hindering" factor, let me review this aspect further. Why is it that God does not remove the hindrance of de-spiritualization at the unthematic level so that our choice will be much more "free" from sin than the current condition of man? Although God's healing reaches deep down to our existential level, since this is only a remote work of God's grace, it still needs its completion at the conscious level. More clearly, the hindrance of de-spiritualization affects not only the unthematic dimension of our being but also our conscious dimension, and the de-spiritualization always further aggravated by our faulty conscious choices. Thus, God has to deal with two fault lines in our being, one in our unthematic dimension of existence and the other in our conscious dimension, before he can completely do away with our "hindering factor."

However, to our consolation, as Paul notes, "where sin increased, grace increased all the more" (Rom 5:20). Furthermore, this depravity is not a permanent fixture. Once again, to borrow Paul's declaration, "if anyone is in Christ, he is a new creation: The old has gone, the new is here" (2 Cor 5:17). This newness is nothing less than to "become the righteousness of God" (2 Cor 5:21). Translated theologically, it means that, once we accept the offer of grace, we are no longer depraved, for grace ultimately removes depravity, which is attached to the unthematic dimension of our being. When we consciously accept the offer of grace, depravity is at last removed from the human nature. However, as Paul laments, we still grapple with the issue of depravity even though we have put off the old self and become new in Christ by the power of the Spirit. Paul writes that "what I hate, that I do" (Rom 7:15). Why is this the case? If depravity has been removed at the unthematic level by the offer of grace, why are we Christians still disposed to "miss the mark"? Why are we still subjected to de-spiritualization? We Christians struggle with this issue, and it has become an unconquerable critical threshold for many believers.

In my judgment, the answer to this question lies in Paul's next set of comments. He says in Romans 7:20, "it is no longer I who do it, but sin that dwells in me." He adds that the "law of sin" is "with the flesh" (Rom 7:25b). Although these verses are highly controversial, if I take what Paul is saying at face value, I may conclude that Paul is simply denoting that depravity is transferred from "I" (inner being) to the flesh. This is evident when Paul says that it is not him who is doing things wrong, but sin that dwells in his body. But who is this "I"? Here I would need to insert a theological interpretation.

Since Paul is making a differentiation between himself and sin, he has already separated depravity from himself—e.g., "sin" has become an external thing to "I." In other words, "sin" no longer flows from within. The identity of "I" is then, in my judgment, the unthematic spiritual dimension of his being, which is distinguishable from the "flesh." More clearly, Paul is saying that our spirit is no longer depraved. So, where did depravity transfer to? It has transferred from the unthematic dimension of our being to the physical dimension of our existence. Simply put, it has moved from spirit to flesh. It is because our previous state of spiritual depravity in the unthematic dimension of our being already had a disposed physical reality to be depraved, and consequently, as Grenz articulates, "We may say that it [depravity] lies in our gene pool."[62] For this reason, although we have become new in the unthematic dimension of our being in Jesus Christ by the power of the Holy Spirit, our flesh is still in the process of catching up

---

62. Grenz, *Theology for the Community*, 205.

to it, until we put on the glorified body like that of Christ's resurrected body (Phil 3:21). In this respect, we can say that for believers' depravity is gone at the core of their existence, but it is still active in the realm of their physical and mental activities.

Furthermore, in spite of it, the power of depravity is not greater than grace. Rather, it is an object to be transformed. It seems as though grace is too weak to oust depravity completely out of our lives, but this is not true. An illustration of wheat and tares (Matt 13:24–30) may help. The owner of the field refuses to uproot the tares that were planted by the enemy. Instead, he lets them grow together with the good grain until the time of harvest. If the workers uproot the tares prematurely, then the good grain may be uprooted as well, since the roots of wheat and tares are entangled. Likewise, grace will remove depravity completely at the right time, that is, when our flesh is transformed into something new. Meanwhile, as Paul says, although sin may flourish through "flesh," grace abounds even more. Hence, our transformation and transcendence are still active in spite of depravity. We are still elevated to the level of the supernatural in spite of depravity. This is the renewal of the image of God in humanity. It is not a mere restoration since we are not simply going back to the prelapsarian state.[63] It is more like a healing via re-creation in which our broken image has been recreated in the likeness of Christ, thanks to grace that overcomes depravity. This does not mean that we should sin all the more so that grace may be abound even more. Romans 5:20 is not a license to sin, but a declaration of God's character. God is infinite in love, and from it flows grace that envelops the finitude of this world, including the things that are crooked. Sin is still anathema to God, but he is overcoming it by the power of his grace.

---

63. Not too long ago, there was a heated debate concerning the doctrine of justification. It is known as the Piper-Wright debate. With the risk of oversimplification, this debate can be characterized by the interpretation of what Paul meant when he said about "righteousness" in Romans 4. John Piper stands firm to declare that Paul's righteousness refers to what he calls "imputed righteousness." By contrast, N.T. Wright rejects this interpretation and claims that Piper is not exegeting the Scripture on its own terms but rather reading the doctrine of justification by faith that we inherit from the Reformed tradition. For Wright, Paul's understanding of righteousness pivots on the idea of the people of God working out the covenant relationship that God had established with the Israelites. Thus, we will be judged righteous in accordance with works (Rom. 2:6). As a theologian, I view justification having both aspects, that is, it involves God's "imputation" in the form of an existential offer of grace, and in accordance with works, which involve our conscious actions. The two theories have to correspond to form a complete view of justification. For more details on the Piper-Wright debate, see Wax, "The Justification Debate," lines 1–20.

Because of God's grace, despite our depraved nature, our ability to seek God still remains active. Although the image of God has been utterly damaged and deemed useless, our existence has been renewed by the self-giving of the Son and the Spirit sent by the Father, and because our renewal starts at the level of unthematic existence, our conscious acts that include cognition, affection, and volition, are still oriented to God, though with a hindrance called depravity that always blocks the way. Moreover, due to the renewal at the unthematic level, our orientation to God is universal. All humans are the same in this respect across the board. Christians or Muslims, we all are intrinsically oriented to God due to the supernatural elevation. This is a critical piece for an interfaith dialogue, since it implies that our experiences of God, though varied, could have a common ground. Perhaps, Kim Kirsteen is right to identify the character of the Spirit such as reconciliation, liberation, and inter-relationality that may be channeled through the non-Christian faith.[64] Thus, our ordinary experience of God cannot be dismissed since God's outreach extends to the very core of our being as he is to every corner of the world.

Despite the fact that we all are oriented to God, our rational, affective, and volitional directions are nonetheless warped. We have to remember that depravity remains in our physical and mental level. Hence, unless we are united with Christ, there is no way for us to reach the final telos, that is, God in himself. We need to cross this final critical threshold and move from the implicit ordination of grace to the explicit ordination of grace. The implicit ordination of grace in and of itself is not enough. It is only a means to an end. Consequently, the final piece of the order of salvation is spiritual "empowerment" that is, our union with Christ by the power of the Holy Spirit. It entails the order of the unthematic supernatural elevation, conversion, and continued sanctification. Without the final piece of continued sanctification, we will fall once again to the error of Deism. God does not stop working when we come to Christ. His work extends from yesterday to today and continues to tomorrow. Until the eschaton, the Spirit is poured out upon all flesh for the sake of preserving and expanding his kingdom. Consequently, the Spirit-spirit relationship is always dialectical and eschatological. It presupposes and anticipates our union with Christ. The presupposition emphasizes the already aspect of salvation and the anticipation of the not-yet component, which will be fulfilled at the eschaton.

---

64. Kim, *The Holy Spirit in the World*, 162–76.

We are there already in his kingdom because of our spiritual renewal, but we are not there yet due to the depravity in the flesh.

To finalize the order of God's existential healing based on the dual core theory, I denote the taxis of God's communication this way: creation—unthematic regeneration—continuing regeneration. The process of existential healing begins with God's self-communication. Without God's initiation, there is no creation or renewal. Thus, God's self-communication is a critical ingredient for our existence. More importantly, God's communication reaches down deep into our core of being, as his Spirit extends to our spirit. It is a Spirit to spirit communication. In other words, it is an ontological communication. God is communicating his very essence to our essence. So here begins the process of regeneration, at the level of the unthematic dimension of our existence. The process then moves to our conscious level. At the conscious level, even after grace is accepted, the process of regeneration continues. The renewal is now focused more on our mental and physical dimensions more so than the unthematic dimension of our existence. In other words, as Michael Welker notes, the work of the Spirit moves into the real-life settings, transforming us as well as the others, including all walks of life.[65]

Concluding Remarks

In this chapter, we have examined the unthematic dimension of our existence and found that there are two cores affecting the very nature of our being, namely grace and sin. This dual core theory is presented to reconcile the difference between Rahner-Coffey's principle of the supernatural existential and Grenz's theory of total depravity. It is an honest attempt to understand how God interacts with us at the very core of our being with a pneumatological twist and without marginalizing the theological value of both the supernatural existential and total depravity. My conviction is that only when the spiritual condition of our being is fully disclosed can we proceed to talk about our epistemological order. As I have said before, ontology precedes knowledge, though the conception of ontology depends on our knowledge. Therefore, as I have highlighted the ontological *prius* of God as spirit in the last chapter, the focus in this chapter was on the ontological *prius* of human existence as spirit, and how they are related to God.

---

65. Welker, *God the Spirit*, x.

The added benefit is that it addresses the question of the order of salvation and the order of regeneration.

This approach begs a question. Can we really know our unconscious state? Are we not dwelling in the land of abstraction if we rely on the unthematic dimension of human existence to unpack God's order of communication? A French philosopher, Jean-Paul Sartre, had a similar concern. He lamented that we can never catch the "unconscious I" since it will always elude us.[66] If we try to catch it, the "conscious I" will always get in the way and block the view of the unconscious. So, for Sartre, if we think we are seeing the unconscious, we are actually seeing our own conscious state of mind. I disagree. Sartre, like any good philosopher of the Enlightenment, had fallen into the dualism of the either-or principle. His either-or philosophy rejects the order of duality. The order of duality revolves around the principle that it is not necessary to disjoint the two events but see it as a single yet distinct event. So, if we follow the principle of duality, which is the way of the spirit, we can see that there is a correlation between the conscious and the unconscious. In Coffey's language, the correlation of the conscious and the unconscious can be viewed as the remote and proximate consciousness. The former accentuates the disposition of the latter, and the latter the revelation of what has been disposed in the former. More clearly, the former denotes the material causality, and the latter the efficient and final causality. This means that we can know certain aspects of our pre-disposed state from our own conscious acts. Surely, we do things according to what we are predisposed to do. In this regard, we must accept that, although the conscious state may never unveil the full scope of our unthematic dimension, it nonetheless provides some knowledge of the unconscious.

To end, I repeat that God's order of communication follows the principle of the supernatural existential. That is, God begins his communication from his own being and reaches down from the realm of the infinite to the realm of the finite as his grace is offered to us at the level of our existential. Grace as God's means of the supernatural elevation of the depraved nature continues to impact our existence as God's persistent effort to communicate his being and act to us. We transcend our depravity and its concomitant limitations by God's empowerment, which results in eschatological regeneration. We are already healed as God's future fulfillment is

---

66. E.g., Sartre, "Bad Faith," 206–20. Also, see Stephen Priest's introductory remarks in this book.

realized here and now, but still in the process of being renewed, for the total destruction of de-spiritualization awaits until the eschaton.

CHAPTER 4

God's Order of Pathos

TO FURTHER OUR DISCUSSION of God's order "with us," in this final chapter, I examine the order of God's pathos. At the onset, we can immediately see the problem with the term "pathos." It is attached to many different ideas about one's inner state—e.g., suffering, pain, and agony (its negative aspects) as well as joy, love, mercy, and compassion (its positive aspects). Moreover, it is normally understood to be capricious, irrational, inconsistent, spontaneous, erratic, and unpredictable. To explain the relationship between God who is sovereign and immutable and the world of unstable pathos seems daunting, if not, impossible.

For this reason, in the past, God was understood to be impassible.[1] God could not be conceived in the same way as humans who are constantly going through emotional changes that are unstable and unreliable.[2] If God has emotions like humans, how can anyone trust and follow him? Can

---

1. David Bentley Hart even goes further to say that "it is nonetheless striking that, in the course, say, of the great disputes of the fourth and fifth centuries concerning trinitarian dogma and Christology, divine impassibility was a principle that all parties concerned accepted without serious reservations, even though it was a principle that, on the face of it, better served the causes of what came to be viewed as the heterodox schools of thought." Hart, "No Shadow of Turning," 184–206. However, there are scholars like Daniel Castelo who read the early Christian literature recognizing that both God's impassibility and passibility played a role in the development of the doctrine of God. For more details, see Castelo, *Apathetic God*, 40–68. I agree with Castelo's assessment that the early Christian thinkers assumed a dialectical stance concerning the issue of divine impassibility—e.g., they talked about divine passibility without violating God's principle of immutability, at least, from those who sided with the "orthodox" point of view.

2. For instance, Spinoza loathed the idea of emotion interfering with the rationalistic way of doing theology. Spinoza, *Theological-Political Treatise*, 81–96.

God be reliable with the emotional baggage attached to him? Because of these difficulties, some Christian scholars had to do away with any attempt to associate God with human emotions. Besides, some aspects of Hellenic philosophy already had the idea that God could not be passible.[3] So, for the early Christian thinkers, the concept of divine impassibility seemed fitting as it allowed them to put God on a different level than us. Theologically, God's impassibility, as noted by Richard E. Creel, carries at least eight implications: (1) God is emotionless; (2) God's state of mind is imperturbable; (3) God is not susceptible to distraction from resolve; (4) God has a self-determined will; (5) God cannot be affected by an outside force; (6) God's plans cannot be thwarted; (7) God cannot be susceptible to negative emotions; (8) God cannot change even with his own will.[4] Because of the conceptual restriction granted by the doctrine of divine impassibility, theologians in the past did not see the need to relate God to the deficient form of human emotions.

However, in the contemporary scene, the old view of God has been set aside.[5] The question concerning God has become much more personal and emotional than its earlier versions. Rather than spending time preserving the impeccable nature of God who is free of emotional variations, modern scholars have turned to God who is more like us, feeling the pain and agony of life, and going through the peaks and valleys of history. The theological table has turned. We no longer perceive God as an insensitive, emotionless, dispassionate, indifferent being who sits on a throne beyond this world, reigning over us without feeling anything about what we go through and how we live in this world. Even from a biblical perspective,

---

3. There is a new development concerning early Christian studies. Traditionally, divine impassibility was accepted as the norm of past Christian theology due to its Hellenic philosophical influence. This thesis has been put forth by scholars like J. M. Hallman. See Hallman, "The Seed of Fire," 369–91. Hallman's thesis has been countered most extensively by Paul Gavrilyuk. For more details, see Gavrilyuk, *The Suffering of the Impassible God*, 1–20. As Gavrilyuk clearly lays out, only a minor sectarian belief like Gnosticism gave way to the idea of divine impassibility. Nowadays, we cannot say that Hellenism brought the idea of divine apathy and Jews the idea of divine pathos. This is surely a false dichotomy, for both Hellenism and Jewish religion carried the idea of divine impassibility as well as divine passibility.

4. Creel, *The Divine Impassibility*, 9–10.

5. Karkkainen, *The Doctrine of God*, 120. There is a group of scholars who are trying to revive the lost spectrum of classical theism. Eric Johnson and Douglas Huffman provide us with a list of these scholars as well as their contributions. For more details, see Johnson and Huffman, "Should the God of Historic Christianity Be Replaced?," 11–41.

modern scholars have begun to rediscover God who is more like us.[6] The God of the Bible is being extrapolated exegetically as the one who is loving and kind, and at the same time, angry, jealous, and wrathful. Although these qualities of God appear to be overly anthropomorphic, nonetheless scholars in today's world is retrieving the personal image of God and attending to God's pathos to move away from the classical theistic picture of an impassible God.

With the retrieval of God's order of pathos came the burden to explain the true nature of God's emotional features. Is God feeling the same way like us? If not, what is the difference? Can God suffer? If so, in what ways? Can we reconcile God's passion with his unchanging character? These questions and more like them will be addressed in this chapter. As representative figures in this field of study, I introduce two scholars in this chapter: Jürgen Moltmann and Clark Pinnock. Each of these contemporary scholars has his own approach that revises classical theism, and at the same time, defends God's passibility—e.g., Moltmann's staurocentric trinitarianism and Pinnock's open theism. I critically review their theology and locate areas of their strengths and weaknesses, and based on this analysis, I draft my own proposal to state that God's order of pathos must retain the principle of identity and duality in order to prevent creaturely order to determine the affective dimension of God. I begin my analysis with Moltmann.

Moltmann's Staurocentric Trinitarianism

Moltmann's approach to the problem of God's passibility is unconventional. He comes to the theological table with a new proposal. He wants to do theology reversing the order of history. According to Moltmann, history runs from the future to the present, while the past is realized in the present. From the perspective of the linear history, the future is the last thing in the line, waiting "to be." However, Moltmann revises this order and places the future in front of the rest of the temporal spectrum. For him, the future has the priority over the past and the present. Consequently, Grenz and Olson note the particularity of Moltmann's theology as eschatological. In fact, they argue that Moltmann adheres to a sort of eschatological ontology. Eschatological ontology simply denotes the fact that the nature of being is shaped and formed by the future. This is what Moltmann calls the

---

6. For example, see Abraham J. Heschel's *The Prophets* and Walter Brueggemann's *Theology of the Old Testament*.

"not-yet-being."[7] The not-yet-being is always in the process of becoming something new as the not-yet-realized-future imposes itself upon it. So, eschatological ontology is an open, dynamic, and relational ontology that determines the very being of our existence.

What is more important for Moltmann is that the future imposing upon the present is only possible if God is working in the world.[8] So, Moltmann is not advocating a Marxist sort of utopianism that pivots on the power of human progress and prosperity which will eventually turn the ties of human conditions and transform social unbalance and disequilibrium into a harmonious utopia. As a Christian scholar, he attributes the positive influence of the future to God rather than social optimism. For Moltmann, God who is transcendent comes to us from the future to transform the world. He is well aware that the ultimate telos of godless human life is dystopia, not utopia. Therefore, Moltmann finds that the only thing that guarantees the positive flow of history toward utopia is God. Moltmann's God of the future makes what is impossible possible for humanity. Although Moltmann operates with the same optimism as Marxist utopianism, he defers social utopianism to God's transcendence, that is, God's futurity, which proleptically impacts the world of today.

Because of God's transformative involvement in this world, Moltmann seeks to tie God to the history of the world. God is transcendent for sure in Moltmann's view, but God's immanence is all the more important for him. God's futurity is transcendent because it is beyond what is taking place today, but at the same time, God's future is already here, which means that God is absolutely immanent.[9] This dialectical order for Moltmann ensures that God is relevant to all aspects of life. According to Moltmann, God's transcendence is not his way of keeping himself away from the things of this world; rather, it is the very cause that makes God come into history, getting involved with the ebb and flow of creaturely life. So Moltmann's God is not removed from the world; rather, his God is in "all being and all that annihilates has already taken up in God and God begins to become 'all in all.'"[10] To avoid a complete panentheistic overlay, he insists that "God

---

7. Moltmann, *The Experiment Hope*, 25.

8. Moltmann, *In the End*, 83.

9. Moltmann, *The Trinity and the Kingdom*, 209.

10. Moltmann, *The Crucified God*, 277. He adds, "But a trinitarian theology of the cross perceives God in the negative element and therefore the negative element in God, and in this dialectical way is panentheistic."

is not the ground of this world and not the ground of existence, but the God of the coming kingdom which transforms this world and our existence radically."[11] Consequently, we can interpret much of Moltmann's theology as an attempt to depict God's transcendence, which is paradoxically immanent, impinging upon all things for the sake of the transformation of the world.

What is God transforming? For Moltmann, God is transforming the evil and suffering in this world. This is why God's reality and the reality of history, though related, are contradicted in his thinking. Grenz and Olson are supportive of this thesis when they explain Moltmann's theology: "Transcendence is God's being the power that transforms the present world from the perspective of its future by negating what is negative in it and by drawing it into the Kingdom of Glory."[12] The negation of what is negative is precisely the suffering and evil in this world that God is transforming into "the fullest degree of life."[13] As Daniel Castelo notes, due to Moltmann's usage of such language, he is known to follow Hegel's dialectical theology.[14] For Hegel, "God is related to reality by his contradiction of the nihil, the power of death, to which all reality is subjected."[15] The difference between Hegel and Moltmann may be that, for Hegel, God could be seen as a process of history, whereas for Moltmann, God comes from the future and recapitulates the whole natural process into Godself. Still, there is that common thread, namely, God's complete saturation of history. Moltmann juxtaposes God's history and natural history in a trinitarian fashion by saying that "he is, if one is prepared to put it in inadequate imagery, transcendent as Father, immanent as Son, and opens up the future of history as the Spirit."[16] Furthermore, he says that "if we understand God in this way, we can understand our own history, the history of suffering and the history of hope, in the history of God."[17] The implication is clear. Dialectically, Moltmann is placing our history under the rubric of God's history. God has a history that encompasses our history. In this way, there is no doubt that God is affected by our history.

11. Moltmann, "Theology as Eschatology," 10.
12. Grenz and Olson, *20th-Century Theology*, 179.
13. Moltmann, *The Crucified God*, 255.
14. Castelo, *Apathetic God*, 77.
15. Meeks, Origins, 36.
16. Moltmann, *The Crucified God*, 256.
17. Moltmann, *The Crucified God*, 256.

Moltmann's dialectical theology is also portrayed pneumatologically. He states that the Spirit is both immanent and transcendent. The Spirit's immanence is depicted as the source of life that functions as the creative and revitalizing energy of all things, and at the same time, the Spirit's transcendence is described as the power that comes from the future to redeem the lost and transform the broken into something new. For this reason, Moltmann boldly declares that pneumatology "brings christology and eschatology together."[18] Translated to the event of crucifixion, Moltmann notes that that the Spirit is immanent in the suffering of Christ as a fellow sufferer, and simultaneously, the Spirit is transcendent as the power of resurrection that raised Jesus from the dead. Thus, for Moltmann, the Spirit is the source of the bond of not only the Father and the Son but also God's suffering and our suffering. In this way, Moltmann is able to address the Spirit's universal compassion that encompasses the whole of history, which extends from before, during, and after the birth, life, and death of Christ.

What we have gleaned thus far is that Moltmann's theology is underwritten by eschatology and dialectical theology. But what does Moltmann's eschatological–dialectical theology has to do with God's order of pathos? It provides the impetus to organize God's order of pathos around the notion that God suffers with us. For Moltmann, God is a fellow-sufferer who goes through the same misery we do and experiences the same pain and sorrow we endure. Because God embraces all events in history, including our history, as the future includes the past and the present, there is no way for God to escape this fate, but rather to go through the mundane details of life that include all emotional variations. Moreover, because God's transcendence means his immanence, the negation of what is negative is a proper event of God. Hence, the negative components of life such as suffering, pain, and even death, belong to God. This is a bold claim and Moltmann drives it home with his idea of godforsakenness.

Moltmann's examination of godforsakenness revolves around the event of the cross. He asks: What happened on the cross? Who died on the cross? Was it God or man? What did the cross of Jesus mean for God himself? Did God suffer on the cross? Moltmann tackles head-on these difficult and controversial questions, and as he does this, he unveils the order of God's pathos. Due to its massive conceptual framework, I will narrow it down to his dialectical–eschatological–trinitarian reading of the cross-event. In Moltmann's theological paradigm, these three categories

18. Moltmann, *The Spirit of Life*, 69.

are mutually supporting and mutually determinative so they cannot be separated.

Going back to the theology of the cross, Moltmann explains that on the cross, there was the cry of dereliction. Jesus shouted, "Eli, Eli, lema sabachthani (My God, my God, why have you forsaken me)" (Matt 27:46)? For him, this is a clear sign that God has incorporated the pain and suffering of godforsakenness into God's order of being. He writes,

> God's being is in suffering and the suffering is in God's being itself, because God is love. It takes the "metaphysical rebellion" up into itself because it recognizes in the cross of Christ a rebellion in metaphysics, or better, a rebellion in God himself: God himself loves and suffers the death of Christ in his love.[19]

A rebellion in metaphysics is nothing more than the disclaim of God's impassibility. So, Moltmann has pulled down God from the abstract sphere of divine impassibility and set him on par with the things of this world. As a result, he has succumbed to the overpowering historical act of the cross and allowed it to determine God's ontology. As he repeatedly comments, "the Christ event on the cross is a God event. And conversely, the God event takes place on the cross of risen Christ."[20] He adds, "Here, God has not just acted externally, in his unattainable glory and eternity. Here he has acted in himself and has gone on to suffer in himself."[21]

The problem I see here is that Moltmann, like other contemporary scholars who start from God *pro nobis*, is reading God from history without qualification. I will come back to this point later in my critical analysis of Moltmann's work, so it suffices to say that Moltmann has missed a central principle of Christian theology: God's economy reveals something about God in himself, but God in himself cannot be determined by the order of God's economy. A similar problem has been discussed when I reviewed the relationship between the *logos asarkos* and the *logos incarnandus* in the previous chapters. When we move from God for us to God in himself, we must clarify the additive element that belongs in the sphere of God for us—e.g., the assumption of the flesh in the case of the *logos incarnandus*.

Going further, Moltmann speaks about the actual separation between the Father and the Son on the cross. Moltmann declares that the cross is the "point when the Son is furthest divided from the Father, and the Father

---

19. Moltmann, *The Crucified God*, 227.
20. Moltmann, *The Crucified God*, 205.
21. Moltmann, *The Crucified God*, 205.

from the Son, in the accursed death on the cross, in the 'dark night' of that death."[22] For Moltmann, the Father abandoned the Son on the cross, and as a result, there was an actual, ontological split between the Father and the Son. He supports this thesis with his own interpretation of Romans 8:32 and Galatians 2:20, in which Paul states that Jesus was handed over to death. He writes, "According to this [saying of Paul] God gave up his own Son, abandoned him, cast him out and delivered him up to an accursed death."[23] The split between the Father and the Son is sharp, because it is all the more intensified by dual forsakenness. On the one hand, the Father forsakes the Son on the cross, and on the other hand, the Father forsakes himself.[24] Moltmann is being faithful to the trinitarian logic here, since if one person is forsaken, all persons in the Godhead must be forsaken as well. So, in order for this logic to work, we must also speak of the forsakenness of the Spirit.

However, Moltmann stops short of explaining the forsakenness of the Spirit. At this point, he is satisfied only with the idea that the Spirit suffers with the Son. He writes, "On Golgotha the Spirit suffers the suffering and death of the Son. The Spirit's suffering, unlike the Son's and the Father's, is not affected by a rupture in relationship, but by the Spirit's solidarity with the Son in his godforsakenness."[25] Thus, there is no "actual" godforsakenness in the Spirit. In my view, with his idea of godforsakenness, Moltmann is making his theology inconsistent. If there is godforsakenness in God, all three persons of the Godhead must undergo the ontological separation. We cannot exempt the Spirit from this event. To prevent a theological inconsistency, we must either import godforsakenness into the life of all three persons or remove it so that the Trinity is not involved with godforsakenness at all. I opt for the latter and I detail its dynamics in the next section.

One last issue is outstanding, the question of the death of God. Did God die on the cross? Moltmann explains the death of God dialectically. He writes, "God is dead and yet is not dead."[26] Once again, relying on Hegelian dialectic, Moltmann is trying to preserve the two poles of God without sacrificing one at the cost of the other. If he were to say that God is not dead,

---

22. Moltmann, *The Trinity and the Kingdom*, 82.
23. Moltmann, *The Crucified God*, 242.
24. So Moltmann frees himself from the error of patripassianism. For Moltmann, the Father's suffering is distinct from that of the Son.
25. Moltmann, *The Spirit of Life*, 64.
26. Moltmann, *The Crucified God*, 244.

then he would be splitting the two natures of God-man Jesus to spare the divine aspect of the Son from death, which is not acceptable. For him, "the divine being must encompass the human being and vice versa."[27] Likewise, if he were to say that God is dead, then he would be making God a mortal being, which is absurd. To avoid these two errors, he brings death and non-death of God together and dialectically combines them into a single conceptual matrix of godforsakenness. He writes,

> The Son suffers in his love being forsaken by the Father as he dies. The Father suffers in his love the grief of the death of the Son. In that case, whatever proceeds from the event between the Father and the Son must be understood as the spirit of the surrender of the Father and the Son, as the spirit which creates love for forsaken men, as the spirit which brings the dead alive.[28]

This means that God has taken up "death" to himself as "godforsakenness."

Moltmann is unafraid to say that God goes through a dialectical process of death and non-death. He writes, "The 'bifurcation' in God must contain the whole uproar of history within itself."[29] And the bifurcation consists of "all disaster, forsakenness by God, absolute death, the infinite curse of damnation and sinking into nothingness" as well as "eternal salvation, infinite joy, indestructible election and divine life."[30] What Moltmann has done is that the order of God's pathos follows the order of a dialectical process. God has two poles that are synthesized by their interactions. Just like human pathos, there is a negative and positive aspect of divine pathos. He says that God's glory is eternally lasting despite this duality, but nonetheless, after the event of the cross, God has been synthesized. He has both death and life and they became part of God's history. Consequently, our history is God's history and vice versa, though God's history is much fuller than ours.

Although Moltmann's explication of God's order of pathos is innovative and provides for this study a starting point to rethink about the nature of God's experiential and emotional dimensions, there are several areas that need to be qualified in order to make use of his theological proposal. The following section will evaluate three of those areas: Moltmann's dialectical approach, trinitarianism, and godforsakenness.

27. Moltmann, *The Crucified God*, 205.
28. Moltmann, *The Crucified God*, 245.
29. Moltmann, *The Crucified God*, 246.
30. Moltmann, *The Crucified God*, 246.

Moltmann's Dialectical Approach

First, we need to correct Moltmann's eschatological-dialectical approach, which makes God something else other than himself, thereby violating the principle of identity. The violation begins with Moltmann's depiction of the future as the mode of God's existence.[31] Because God's ontology is determined by the future, which is a real possibility to be unfolded through the ebb and flow of history, God has a dual polarity of already and not yet.[32] This means that, at least from our perspective, God is still in the process of becoming. For this reason, Moltmann states that "a new future for God, man and the world in their history together is being inaugurated."[33] God and the world are so interwoven that there is always a *novum* in God. What this *novum* does to God is that "the new possibilities in the world spring from the world as a possibility of the creator God."[34] In short, according to Moltmann, because the determinative mode of God's existence is his future, God is ahead of us already, and at the same time, a not-yet-being. How can God be ahead of us already but a not-yet-being? This is possible because of Moltmann's principle of dialectic. God is not yet complete because of his openness to the future, but at the same time, God's future is complete because of God's hope-fulfillment.

This is precisely why the principle of identity is violated. In Moltmann's claim of God's future ontology, we have lost the real, ontological identity of God. If God is a future possibility, God remains just that, a pure possibility. A pure possibility is always open for revision so there is no permanent or lasting identity of God. Although Moltmann guarantees that God will converge with the rest of the world under the single rubric of hope, because that is where God is leading us, God has to embrace many new things, such as the pain and suffering of this world in order for him to arrive there, and as a result, God has to become something new every day and every moment. Thus, Moltmann is undeterred to accept the changeability of God. He notes in this regard, "If God is not passively changeable by other things like other creatures, this does not mean that he is not free

---

31. Moltmann, *The Experiment Hope*, 50–51. He writes in this regard, "If we follow the biblical discourse about the 'God of hope,' we will have to give prominence to the future as the mode of God's existence with us."

32. Moltmann's book is suffused with this dialectic. For example, Moltmann writes, "God is dead and yet is not dead," "God is transcendent and yet immanent," and so on.

33. Moltmann, *The Crucified God*, 99.

34. Moltmann, *The Crucified God*, 219.

to change himself, or even free to allow himself to be changed by others of his own free will."[35] Moltmann ensures that the change in God that he mentions is not like the change that takes place in a man, but nonetheless, he accepts the fact that God changes, according to his free will. Hence, in Moltmann's theism, there is no principle of identity at work. God does not remain himself in his act of becoming. Rather, God becomes someone like us in his act with and for us.

Contra Moltmann, we must uphold the principle of identity at all cost because there is no change in God. If we work with the idea that God changes and becomes something new as he mingles with the things of this world, then we lose the thing-in-itselfness of God. As I have said before, the thing-in-itselfness of God safeguards theological realism, that God is not just phenomenal but a true being with his own independent identity, logic, and ontological status. Without this safeguard, God is easily turned into something that is to our liking. Moltmann thus may have not addressed the Feuerbachian criticism properly—i.e., God is really a projection of our self. The only way to avoid this criticism is to stay within the bounds of the principle of identity like Karl Barth. God must always remain who he is even in his act of becoming.

So, I suggest that, for the order of God's pathos, we must make a difference between God's thing-in-itselfness and God's phenomena. God's thing-in-itselfness is that which is unchangeable. God remains who he is always. However, God is free to add things onto his thing-in-itselfness, such as the experience of human life, without changing his spirit-essence. God can feel the pain and suffering in this world as he experiences the death on the cross. This is God's phenomena. Accordingly, God can experience the vast spectrum of human pathos without losing his thing-in-itselfness.[36] Furthermore, since the experience in this world is a tagged-on item, we can also speak of God's *novum* without violating his ontology. God experiences new things though he remains who he is. God can add new things to himself because he is the future of the world. However, regardless of how extensive the addendum may be, God remains who he is, because the only thing that changes is what God experiences, not God in himself.

35. Moltmann, *The Crucified God*, 229.

36. My distinction of God's thing-in-itself and phenomenon is not meant show that God is dialectical like Moltmann's theological program. Rather, it ensures the principle of identity. My claim is that God remains who he is even in his experience of the world. By contrast, Moltmann stresses that God changes as he experiences the "new" things in this world.

The question at this point that we may ask is that, why does God need an addendum? He does not. God is self-sufficient. However, he is undertaking the same historical process as we do for the sake of *koinonia* (e.g., fellowship), to borrow Moltmann's language. To redeem us, to restore the lost fellowship between God, man, and the world, God has come voluntarily to be with us and for us. Hence, the logic of grace all the more enhances the principle of identity. God came to this world so that he could redeem what was lost as he made himself available for us all. He came because the world needs transformation bottom up and top down, and such dramatic transformation can come about only if his unchanging essence revitalizes the changed and corrupted nature of this world.

Moltmann may contend that, if we assume that God is not changeable, it is doubtful that God is actually suffering like us. If this is true, God's experience may not be qualified as suffering at all. Moltmann has stretched his theology far and wide so that he wants to avoid this dilemma and claim boldly that God experiences everything that we experience. In my judgment, even if God remains who he is, God experiences everything that we experience and more. As we have seen in the previous chapter, God's order of communication proceeds from himself to the unthematic dimension of our existence. Hence, God and only God can penetrate deep into our being and experience the core of our existence. For us, this is not possible. We have limitations. Our experience of I and Thou can only extend to what is consciously recognizable.[37] God's experiential dimension is much broader and richer than ours because he reaches into deep things of this world (e.g., Job 12:12; Heb 4:12; 1 Cor 2:10). Moreover, he communicates not just consciously but spiritually as the Father-spirit, the Son-spirit, and the Holy Spirit. What this means is that God remains who he is, spirit-persons, as he shares his pathos with us, that is, the *koinonia* of the spirit (Phi 2:1). The *koinonia* of spirit does not entail change in God because God's spirit is changeless, and at the same time, "spirit" creates shareability because spirit is the mutuality that connects divine spirit-persons as well as God and man, as in the case of Jesus' hypostatic union and our union with God.

---

37. Buber, *I and Thou*, 43–44. To put this idea differently, our experiential spectrum may be broadened if we connect to God spiritually. Otherwise, we will remain only within the scope of our thematic dimension of experience.

Trinitarianism

Moving to the next topic, we come to Moltmann's trinitarian logic. According to Moltmann, there is a temporary separation between the Father and the Son as the Son is abandoned by the Father on the cross. After the separation incurred by the Father's delivering up the Son to the cross, the Spirit reunites the two with his power of resurrection. Thus, the passion narrative becomes the grammar for Moltmann's trinitarian language to speak about the separation-and-unity of God. In this way, Moltmann is able to highlight the critical point of Jesus' suffering on the cross. The critical point on the cross is none other than the death of the Son of God. It signifies for Moltmann the ultimate suffering that reveals the complete separation between the Father and the Son.

However, this is in violation of the trinitarian logic that we have been discussing in the previous chapters. The trinitarian logic is that God is one, and the same time, three distinct persons. Or more specifically, God is at once one and three. Pneumatologically, we note that God is at once one spirit and three spirit persons. If God is at once one in spirit, how is it that God can be separated into three distinct entities, one forsaking the other as though they are ontologically separated from each other? Such division in God can only be conceived if we treat the trinitarian relationship discretely. However, we can never treat God discretely, even if the three persons of the Godhead will be united as one in the Spirit after the separation is completed. This is precisely what Moltmann is arguing for. He takes this route because he wants to eschew the static ontology of God.

In Moltmann's view, the trinitarian relationship fluctuates.[38] It is not static. It changes from one state to another. For example, Moltmann's conception of the Trinity moves from the threeness of God to the oneness of God. So, the starting point for Moltmann's doctrine of God is the threeness of God which is revealed in and through the cross event. Because he begins with the threeness of God, Moltmann has the right to say that the Father and the Son can be divided without losing the integrity of the Trinity. What about the oneness of God? For Moltmann, the oneness of the Trinity is "to come" in the unitive power of the Spirit. In this way, Moltmann affirms the

---

38. Moltmann, *The Crucified God*, 265. He writes, "The relationships in the Trinity between Father and Son are not fixed in static terms once and for all but are a living history." Because the relationship between the Father and the Son progresses from the love to the pain of death and finally arriving at the hope of resurrection, the life of the Trinity also fluctuates.

oneness of God as well as his threeness. However, having just one (unitive) and three (distinctive) elements of the Trinity is not enough. We must also state that they are *at once* one and three. We should not separate the two categories and choose one over the other.

If we follow Moltmann, inevitably, we have to address the question of "which is first, the threeness of God or the oneness of God?" This is an old false dichotomy. If we start with the oneness of God, then we may fall into the error of modalism, and if start with the threeness of God, we may fall into the error of tritheism. Theology cannot start with either the oneness or the threeness of God. Either point of departure is a dead end. God is at once one and three. This is the fundamental logic of the Trinity. Pneumatologically, if we prefer threeness over oneness of God, we have to divide God's spirit into three parts, which is absurd, since God's spiritness cannot be divided or separated into discrete units. Spirit by definition is non-discrete. The threeness of God always presupposes the oneness of God and vice versa. For this reason, Moltmann's desire to start with the threeness of God to which the oneness will be completed in the process of the death and resurrection of Jesus Christ cannot do full justice to the at-once-one-and-three principle of God's trinitarian logic.

Granted that God experiences a sequence of events, from the forsakenness on the cross to the hope of resurrection soon after the crucifixion, such an order in the dimension of God's economy should not determine the order of God in himself. What Moltmann seems to operate is based on Rahner's order—e.g., the economic Trinity is the immanent Trinity, and vice versa.[39] He does this for two reasons. First, by unifying the two trinities, he may avoid the metaphysical speculation, such as the impassibility of God, which is assigned to the untouchable order of the immanent Trinity, and second, he may avoid the error of turning the Trinity into a quaternity. The quaternity of God could happen if we have two trinities, since one absolute person of the immanent Trinity and three relative persons in the economic Trinity could add up to four persons.

To address Moltmann's concern as well as all those who follow Rahner's rule, I do not see the need to conflate the two trinities in order to preserve the proper logic of the Trinity. Rather, to save the proper logic of the Trinity, we must find a way to circumvent the conflation of the two. Even if we keep the immanent Trinity, God's order of passibility and God's order of immutability can be reconciled. As a matter of fact, without the

39. Moltmann, *The Crucified God*, 240.

immanent Trinity, we cannot preserve the proper mode of God's passibility. I will detail this aspect in the following paragraph, so I limit the discussion here and say that the immanent Trinity helps clarify God's order of pathos instead of veiling its true content. Moreover, as I have shown already, the issue of quaternity in God can be resolved if we recognize that each person of the Godhead is always both absolute and relative.

Going back to Moltmann's trinitarian program, Moltmann's theological problem stems from his reading of God's ontology from God's economy. If we start from the economic Trinity and think that it is the controlling mechanism for God *in se*, we come to the immanent Trinity seeing the things of this world strewn in God's inner life. As I have mentioned already, when this confusion occurs, the things that have been tagged-on to God in the economic Trinity will be carried into the inner life of God indiscriminately, and as a result, God will be indistinguishable from the things of this world. Certainly, this is the error of Moltmann's dialectic. I do not see that Moltmann is attempting to preserve God's ontological order or the principle of identity. For Moltmann, God does *not* remain who he is in his act of becoming. For Moltmann, God is an event just like us—i.e., God has a history that is no different from us. Consequently, according to Moltmann, the negative elements of life such as suffering, pain, and agony that we go through belong to God, though God may not suffer like we do.

I cannot accept Moltmann's claim that suffering is intrinsic to God. Moltmann does not consider the suffering of God as a tagged-on item, but an aspect of God's essence, that is, God's love. For him, God's love has both positive and negative aspects.[40] The positive aspect of love is God's mercy and its negative aspect is suffering. Moltmann insists that God's suffering reveals God's true nature of love, because in his suffering God takes the love of God to another level far greater and higher than before. However, as Thomas Weinandy argues, the love of God does not need the service of suffering to make its greatest impact, because we can commit to the opposite—e.g., "a God who does not suffer is more loving, compassionate and merciful than a God who does."[41] In the Book of Revelation, we catch a glimpse of the divine utopia, which supports Weinandy's claim. In God's kingdom-to-come, there is no death, tears, or pain (Rev 21:4). If there is

---

40. Moltmann, *The Crucified God*, 245. He does this because he knows that God's suffering in itself cannot be attributed to God's essence. Since "love" is God's essence, he attaches suffering to love so that he can justify suffering as a part of God's essence.

41. Weinandy, *Does God Suffer?*, 159.

no death or pain in God's kingdom, then the suffering is not an inherent quality of God. I can only conclude that it is an addendum, which God has taken upon himself for the sake of our salvation. Suffering is in God but not of God.

Godforsakenness

Lastly, we come to Moltmann's most commanding and yet controversial idea about God's pathos—that is, godforsakenness. Because of godforsakenness taking place within the life of the Trinity, Moltmann is able to divide the oneness of the Godhead into three separate persons, each going through the pain of godforsakenness in his own unique way. For example, the Son of God suffers the death on the cross, the Father suffers the death of the Son, and the Spirit suffers along with the Father and the Son. However, as I have shown already, Moltmann's approach necessarily creates a division in God. Because Moltmann's idea of godforsakenness creates a division in God, it has been well contested by contemporary scholars, and as a representative case, I present David Coffey's argument here.

As one of the avid critics of Moltmann, Coffey contends that Jesus could not have been alienated, delivered up, or cursed ontologically.[42] According to Coffey, the alienation of God has been reserved only for those who are actually sinful, and so, in Coffey's view, it is wrong to speak about the "sinless" Jesus being forsaken by God. Upending Moltmann's idea, Coffey says that the cross is not a place of God's dereliction but a place where the love of God is manifested most powerfully through Jesus Christ as he pours out his life for us all on the cross.[43] Thus, rather than seeing the cross as God's rejection, abandonment, or alienation, Coffey views the cross as a sacrificial self-surrender of Jesus to his death for the sake of reconciliation. Translated to his mutual love theory, he says that there is a give-and-take love between the Father and the Son on the cross, and this give-and-take love represents the reconciling power of the Holy Spirit. For this reason, Coffey does not see the need to place a wedge between the Son and the Father as shown by Moltmann's abandonment theory. How can it be? Can the mutuality of the Trinity ever discontinue at some point in time? Coffey insists that there can never be a discontinuity of any kind in the divine life.

---

42. Moltmann, *The Crucified God*, 123–50.
43. Moltmann, *The Crucified God*, 149.

But then, how do we explain the cry of Jesus noted in Mark 15:34? Coffey writes in this regard, "But this alienation remained for him at the level of psychological and spiritual experience, not at the level of actual reality."[44] He makes an additional comment. "For him it was the supreme trial and test of his faith, hope, and love, a test that he passed triumphantly and that therefore brought the relationship of mutual love between the Father and himself to completion."[45] So, Coffey does not think that Jesus was *actually* cursed, delivered up, or forsaken; instead, Jesus went through a psychological trial that we go through when God is silent to our cry for help, as it is implied in Psalm 23, to which Jesus' cry refers in Mark 15.

Though I believe Coffey is right to reject Moltmann's idea of godforsakenness, I cannot accept his conclusion here. If Jesus went through a psychological motion and did not actually experience God's forsakenness on the cross, we cannot claim that Jesus' atoning work on the cross was successful. How can Jesus save the things that he did not embrace on the cross? If Jesus had not actually gone through the pain of death, suffering, abandonment, and curse, how can we say that the cross actually "paid" for our sin? Besides, the exegetical implication of ἐγκαταλείπω (forsaken) affirms that Jesus did not merely go through a psychological motion but the actual experience of forsakenness. New Testament scholar Richard Bauckham explains,

> To be forsaken by God means that he has allowed this to happen and does nothing to help. So it is somewhat misleading to say—of the psalmist or of Jesus echoing his words—that he *feels* forsaken by God as though this were an understandable mistake. What Jesus experience is the concrete fact that he has been left to suffer and die. God has, in this sense, abandoned him, not merely in psychological experience but in the form of the concrete situation that Jesus experiences.[46]

Even without Bauckham's exegetical support, theologically, we cannot accept Jesus merely experiencing the psychological dimension of God's forsakenness on the cross. Without a real experience, Jesus' sincere cry of pain could be demoted to mere stage acting.

So, we come back to Moltmann. He is right to assert that there is an actual godforsakenness on the cross. But I also agree with Coffey that there

---

44. Moltmann, *The Crucified God*, 149.
45. Moltmann, *The Crucified God*, 149.
46. Bauckham, *Jesus and the God of Israel*, 256.

is no ontological separation in the life of the Trinity. If this is the case, how can we reconcile the two? How did God experience a genuine forsakenness if there was no ontological separation of God? We need to approach these questions from a relational point of view. We need to recognize that God's forsakenness on the cross is a special type of relationality. It is based on the God-man relationship. It is not based on the God-God relationship. More clearly, godforsakenness can only be meaningful if it describes the relationship between God and man. Godforsakenness is meaningless between the Father, the Son, and the Holy Spirit. If we read the God-man relationship into the God-God relationship, once again, we violate the principle of identity. I cannot say enough that God remains who he is even in his forsakenness. In truth, on the cross, God forsakes man, not just any man, but sinful and cursed humanity, and Jesus, who had become sinful and cursed for us, is that humanity, going through this actual forsakenness on the cross. However, what God is forsaking is not God himself on the cross, or in a trinitarian language, the Father forsaking the Son. Rather, God is forsaking the sinful and cursed man on the cross. This has to be differentiated.

If we make this differentiation, are we splitting up Jesus into two mutually exclusive dimensions, one divine and the other human? As I have said before, Jesus' human nature and divine nature cannot be divided. They remain as one though distinct. We cannot even say that Jesus has a dual polarity, since his divinity and humanity are so thoroughly entangled that it is meaningless to find a point of distinction between the two. Despite this entanglement, formally speaking, Jesus is God-man. In him are these two natures that undergird his existence. In this respect, formally, we can speak about Jesus as a man experiencing godforsakenness, and at the same time, Jesus as God experiencing divine reconciliating love that nullifies godforsakenness. Jesus experienced these two antithetical qualities at once when he was on the cross. Hence, Jesus' experience on the cross encompasses all experiences, one in the sphere of man and the other in the sphere of God.

Likewise, we can speak about the death that Jesus experiences on the cross in the same manner. The death of Jesus is not a transaction that occurs between God and God but God and man. The death that Jesus is going through is not the death of God, which is a meaningless assertion since God by his nature is without death. Death is a death of man that God has embraced to himself. A sinful and cursed man has been carried into the life of God through the Son, since Jesus is both God and man, and as a result, death has been resisted, curse rejected, godforsakenness defied in Jesus by the power of the Spirit operating in the divine-human dimension of Jesus. So, neither Moltmann nor Coffey is right. It is wrong for Moltmann to assign to the Trinity godforsakenness, death, and division. There is no godforsakenness, death, or division in God the Trinity. Also, it is wrong for Coffey to deny the actual forsakenness of God on the cross. There was godforsakenness on the cross and it was a matter between God and man, not an internal trinitarian affair that involves the God-God relationship.

To conclude, I suggest rethinking Moltmann's order of God's pathos in light of God's logic of grace. God came to earth and voluntarily accepted the fate of man, his misery, pain, agony, and even death. He took this path because of grace, not because it was necessary for him to do so. Thus, the cross, although it can be a valuable hermeneutical lens for us to interpret the nature of God's pathos, is an addendum to God. It does not belong to God intrinsically. The event of the cross therefore is best understood in light of the God-man relationship rather than the God-God relationship (e.g., the intra trinitarian relationship), although the cross impacts God's trinitarian life through and through.

Based on God's logic of grace, we should be able to make sense of God's pathos. In my view, God's order of pathos moves from the positive pathos to the negative pathos, followed by the negative pathos to the positive pathos. What I mean by the positive pathos is that there is perfecting work of God's love along with all its positive cognates such as mercy, kindness, forgiveness, joy, and so on. This is the pathos of God in its "original" form—that is, prior to God taking upon himself the negative pathos, such as suffering and pain in this world. This is why it is vital to differentiate between the pre-temporal immanent Trinity and the economic Trinity. In the immanent Trinity, free from God's involvement with the world, there is no suffering, death, or pain.

By contrast, in the economic Trinity, God freely expresses his negative pathos as he intermingles with the "negative" order of this world. The broad panorama of God's work in history is inclusive of God's embrace of the negative pathos that is not a reflection of God's "true" pathos. Thus, the negative aspect of God's pathos is an addendum to God. It is what God has graciously embraced to bring about positive transformation. For this reason, in the post-Easter era, God's experience entails spiritual transformation. God comes and experiences the negative pathos with us so that he may transform death to life, suffering to joy, and misery to happiness. However, at the eschaton, God's order of pathos will make a full circle, returning to the positive aspect of God's original pathos, removing all negative pathos in this world.

In spite of such a positive view of God, we still have to cope with the issue of God's openness. Is God open to the future? Does God know the future exhaustively? Is there a limitation in God? Has God emptied himself and restrained his divine powers until the eschaton? Is God truly omnipotent? These questions hover over our head as we continue to unpack the order of God's pathos. In order to delve deeper into these issues, I review Clark Pinnock's open theism.

Clark Pinnock's Open Theism

To explain Pinnock's open theism, it is necessary to cover a wide range of theological topics. Open theism is a newly adopted form of Christian theism that has deconstructed classical theism in so many ways that no single theological theme, or even a few categories of theology, can cover the full spectrum of its shape and form. The proper way to tackle open theism is to narrow down and focus on its chief theological questions that have come up over the past few decades. What I need in this section then is to examine a set of theological questions that Pinnock's open theism has opened up for Christian theology, especially concerning the order of God's pathos. Thus, I review in this section a selected list of questions brought up by Pinnock. There are five. The list I have here is not exhaustive, but it highlights the issues that are associated with Pinnock's interest in clarifying God's order of pathos.

To add, I must inform that some of the topics covered here will overlap my evaluation of Moltmann's theology of God's pathos due to the similarities of interest between Pinnock and Moltmann. However, there are many areas that are different and even antithetical to Moltmann's work, so this review has an additional functionality, a study that compares the works of Moltmann and Pinnock.

Five Questions from Open Theism

1. Is God impassible? Pinnock's questioning of God's impassibility is motivated by his theological understanding of God as love. According to Pinnock, the early Christian thinkers who adhere to the doctrine of divine apathy contradicted themselves by contending that God is both loving and

impassible. According to Pinnock, this is wrong. God cannot be impassible because God is love. What we need to recognize here is that the theme of love becomes Pinnock's central argument. For Pinnock, love is God's pathos. For this reason, he conceives God as the "most moved mover." He writes, "Of course, the living God is not dead. He is the God of the Bible, the one who is genuinely related to the world, whose nature is the power of love and whose relationship with the world is that of a most moved, not unmoved, Mover."[47] In his other writing he comments, "God is moved by love to restrain the divine power, temporarily and voluntarily, out of respect for the integrity of creatures, even creatures whose activities fall short of God's purposes."[48] As we can see, Pinnock's statement directs our attention to the key implication of God's love, that is, God's ability to be moved like us, even to the extent that he restrains his own power to do so. I see no problem with Pinnock's identification of God's pathos as love, but I detect a clear and present danger associated with Pinnock's endorsement of the limitation of God underwritten by his concept of love.

Before we move on, let me briefly flesh out the details of Pinnock's conception of love. In his monograph, *Most Moved Mover*, he unpacks the meaning of "love" philosophically and calls this project the metaphysics of love. In a nutshell, Pinnock explains love in terms of process metaphysics. Like Moltmann, this is the only way for Pinnock to keep his distance from old Aristotelian ontology that portrays God as a static being. So, he discards the metaphysics of being, and in its place, he installs the metaphysics of becoming as his main philosophical framework. With this idea, Pinnock can run with his theological program and denote God as affecting everything and is affected by everything.

At this point, I cannot but ask Pinnock. Are we solving the theological dilemma by substituting one form of metaphysics with another form of metaphysics? Pinnock implicitly affirms it by saying that he is switching from static metaphysics to process metaphysics because the concept of becoming aligns with the Bible more closely than the concept of being.[49] I do not see how this is so. I have discussed about Pinnock's treatment of biblical hermeneutics elsewhere, so I limit my comment here and say that, if we press the biblical narratives about God, we can glean both metaphysical implications of the being and becoming of God. As a matter of fact, in relation

---

47. Pinnock, *Most Moved Mover*, 3.
48. Pinnock, "Constrained by Love," 150.
49. Pinnock, *Most Moved Mover*, 7–18.

to God who does not change (e.g., Mal 3:6; Num 23:19; Heb 6:17), the static metaphysics is more prominent in the Bible than the God of becoming.

As I have said before, process metaphysics, though it has a few theological values such as its emphasis on the relationality of things and the open nature of reality, cannot be the substantiating metaphysics for God. The only substantiating metaphysics of God is the principle of identity-in-distinction, that is, God remains himself even in his way of loving us. Process metaphysics violates this principle. Because God is conceived as the ground of becoming, which sums up all actual entities that come and go, God becomes an entity that cannot remain the same at any moment.[50] Although Pinnock is not accepting all aspects of process metaphysics, nonetheless he, like Moltmann, prefers God to be in the process of becoming more than he is unchanging. The fault I point out here is this: the process that God experiences has to be conceived as an addendum to God. It cannot be part of God or underwrite who God is. This does not mean that we should opt for a static God. God is not a static being. God's unchangeability does not entail God's immobility or impassibility. God can remain who he is in his act of love. This is the logic of God as the Psalmist declares that "his love endures forever" (Ps 100:5). God can embrace the trans-temporal events into his life, as he experiences the sequence of the Trinity in his own self. The logic of God is thus the logic of the Trinity. God is at once one and distinct. The oneness and distinction go hand in hand, without one violating the other. Because process metaphysics does not meet this requirement, it cannot underwrite Christian theism.

2. Is God omnipotent or vulnerable? Pinnock accepts the latter as his theological *modus operandi*. He contends that the theology of God's omnipotence is the most misconceived topic that has befuddled the minds of Christian scholars for centuries. The misconception he is talking about is the confusion between God's omnipotence and God's omni-causality; the former is about what God can do for us and the latter about God's all-controlling power. So, he revises the doctrine of God's omnipotence and states that God cannot be an all-controlling tyrant who has no feeling about what humans go through in the misery-stricken earthly life. Rather, God is self-limiting in such a way that he "risks the pain of rejection and loss."[51] In a simpler term, Pinnock's God does not sustain a complete control of the affairs of this world. Consequently, there are things that God cannot do

---

50. Dombrowski, *A History of the Concept of God*, 16–19.

51. Pinnock, "Constrained by Love," 151.

or cannot know. I will discuss more about God's limited knowledge of the future later, so I focus on the things that God cannot do here.

According to Pinnock, there are many things that God cannot do. For instance, God cannot break a promise. Once he has tied himself to a legal standing with us in a covenant relationship, God cannot do things that would violate the covenant.[52] I do not think this is a good example to show that there is a limitation in God. Actually, it defies Pinnock's argument. Because God is able to keep his promise and fulfills all covenantal agreements, we can say that God is omnipotent. God's word always comes true (Mark 13:31). It is what God does, not what he cannot do, that makes God who he is. Thus, if we say that God cannot break a promise, and therefore, God is impotent, we are making a logical fallacy. It is like saying that God creates a rock that is too heavy for him to lift. This is logically absurd since the statement already includes the limitation of what God cannot do. In order to make sense of Pinnock's claim, we have to translate the statement, "God cannot break a promise," to "God always keeps his promise," since logically God only wills what he can do.[53] So, we should not treat God's inability to break a promise as a negativity of God; rather, we should think of it as God's limitless power that underwrites his faithfulness.

There is an additional issue with Pinnock's contention of the traditional understanding of God's omnipotence. Pinnock like many other contemporary scholars is arguing God's self-limitation based on the theory of divine *kenosis* (in reference to Phil 2:5–11).[54] Broadly, there are two views associated with the theory of divine kenosis. The strong view of kenosis may state that God has emptied himself of divine power ontologically, whereas the weak view of kenosis may assert that God has emptied himself of divine power only temporally and functionally.

The strong view of kenosis does not work, according to David Brown. He says that "with 'emptied' as the main verb, the New Testament scholars argue that the kenosis consists simply in acquiring the form of a slave, with nothing removed that was essential to his nature prior to that point."[55] Essentially, Brown is pointing out the fact that the theory of divine kenosis

---

52. Pinnock, "Constrained by Love," 151.

53. Again, I can restate it this way. God cannot will what he cannot do. The double negative does not mean that God is "limited." Rather, it shows that God can only do what is logical to him. This shows the importance of recognizing God's own logical order.

54. A good review of the varying type of kenoticists is available in Oliver Crisp's work. See, Crisp, *Divinity and Humanity*, 118–53.

55. Brown, *Divine Humanity*, 9.

changes the logic of God. He is right. If we say that God has emptied himself in such a way that God is ontologically changed, then God is no longer who he is in himself. This clearly violates the logic of God. The basic logic of God is that God is who he is in himself, even in his act of kenosis. If we say that God is not who he is in himself because he has emptied himself, then we are talking about a God who has become someone else. At this point, I cannot affirm that we have a God at all. If we lose God's logic of he-is-who-he-is-in-himself, then we lose God altogether. God who cannot be himself is no God at all. God must be who he is, regardless of the experiences that he may undergo. Without this principle, I do not see how we can sustain the biblical order of God.

Appropriately, Pinnock does not follow the strong view of divine kenosis, but instead, he opts for a weak view of divine kenosis. He contends that although God empties himself, God remains who he is, though in a limited way. The limitation then is explained as God's self-constraint. What this means for Pinnock is that God is all-powerful, but despite his all-powerfulness, he decides not to exercise that power, saving it for later until he is finished with the work of redemption through the Son. Hence, Pinnock's kenosis theory only entails a temporary God's self-limitation, not an actual decanting of God's nature.

Although Pinnock has softened the tone of the kenotic theory, the problem remains. The problem I have with Pinnock's view is that it may fall under a form of adoptionism. Even if we say that God could empty himself, temporarily doing things as any human person would, we have to ask, Is Jesus really divine during the time of his self-restraint? In what ways is Jesus divine if his divinity is set aside for a moment? What I am after here is the kenoticists' incessant focus on the divine Logos acting only as a human, with little or no regard for the divine Logos acting as God. If God has emptied himself and his divine powers have been restrained, as claimed by Pinnock, then Jesus cannot be working fully as God. He works simply as a human. Because Jesus' divinity has been set aside, his divine power remains dormant, waiting to be actualized at a later time.

If Jesus' divinity is restrained, when will it be re-actualized? Perhaps, Pinnock has in mind that only when Jesus is resurrected by the power of the Holy Spirit can Jesus display his full divinity. Regardless to when Jesus regains his full divine power, if Jesus does not actualize his divinity always and everywhere, we fall into the same error of the ancient form of adoptionism. From the standpoint of adoptionism, Jesus becomes divine only at a certain point in time, during or after his ministry on earth. I cannot accept this theological program, for it violates the principle of identity. Jesus from his inception to death always remains God. At no point in time can he be not God, or his divinity be limited.

There is a way to avoid the adoptionistic insinuation of kenosis—e.g., via the theory of Extra Calvinisticum. Kilian McDonnell succinctly summarizes this theory.

> The Godhead of Christ fills all things, and although it is joined to the humanity and dwells in it, the Godhead is not bound to the humanity. One can predicate no dependence of the divinity on the humanity, not even in the smallest degree. The divinity has not "left heaven to hide itself in the prison of the body." The divinity, unmixed and undivided, does not limit itself to the humanity, but while dwelling there, remains also entirely outside of the humanity.[56]

The theory of Extra Calvinisticum highlights God's principle of identity, that God is always who he is even when he assumes the human flesh. In other words, Jesus is always divine even in his humanity, and for this reason, we cannot focus only on one aspect of Jesus, that is, his humanity. Jesus' divinity, perhaps, at times, did not manifest the way we anticipated, as an amazing display of power that throws people into an inexpressible awe; however, this does not mean that Jesus' divine power was inactive. The divine *modus operandi* should not be configured only based on God's awe-inspiring work. Isn't he involved with the mundane day-to-day sustenance of our life? In this respect, God's providential care and redemptive work are inseparably linked. With qualification, Pinnock could have done better had he accounted for the theory of Extra Calvinisticum. But if kenoticists are wrong, how should we interpret this verse: "[Jesus] emptied himself, taking the form of a servant, being made in the likeness of men" (Phil 2:7)?

In my view, the entire pericope of Philippians 2:1–11 revolves around the theme of Jesus' exaltation-humility duality. Paul is exhorting the church to remain humble, not doing things out of "selfish ambition or conceit, but in humility" (Phil 2:3), and he points out that this is precisely what Jesus did for us (Phil 2:5–11). So, the "emptying" here in the proper context means Jesus' humility. Jesus humbled himself in such a way that, being equal to God (Phil 2:6), he took the "form of a slave, being born in human likeness" (Phil 2:7). Paul perhaps took these verses out of the existing hymn

---

56. McDonnell, *John Calvin*, 221.

or poetry that summarizes Jesus' self-sacrifice.[57] Regardless, the point that Paul is making in this pericope is that Jesus humbled himself and we must do likewise. We must also remember that, in spite of Jesus' humbleness, "Jesus is Lord" (Phil 2:11). Thus, the principle of identity is applied here, that is, Jesus is always the Lord even in his humbleness. More clearly, from John's perspective, Jesus' glory is manifested even through his humiliating experience of the cross (e.g., John 12:23 and 13:31). It is theologically one-sided to say that because of Jesus' humility his divine power is set aside. We could well say the opposite that Jesus' humility is a display of his divine power.

3. Does God have a single or dual polarity? Pinnock chooses the latter. For him, God has a dual polarity—e.g., the unchangeable and changeable aspects of God. Before talking about God's changeability, Pinnock wants to make himself clear that God's essence is immutable. He explains, "The Trinity is unchangeably what it is from everlasting to everlasting—and nothing can change that."[58] However, at the same time, Pinnock asserts that "God changes in his response to events in history."[59] So, for Pinnock, God has two poles. On the one hand, there is an absolute transcendent pole in which God is untouched, unaffected, and unchanged. This immutable aspect of God is kept within the boundary of God's noumena. Therefore, God's transcendence is always beyond this world. It cannot co-operate or interact with the things of this world. What is mixed with this world is the other pole of God, that is, God's immanence. In Pinnock's theological program, God is not only transcendent, but more importantly, immanent. Unlike God's transcendent pole, Pinnock's God is active in his immanent pole—God feels and experiences the things of this world like any other personal agents residing on this earth. This is where it matters most to God according to Pinnock.

There are several problems with this theological claim. I mention two. The first problem concerning Pinnock's conception of God's dual polarity is his undue attention given to God's immanence. His theological pendulum swings to the far left that God's transcendence is a mere subsidiary pole that is disconnected and servient to God's immanence. He justifies this move by stating that in the today's climate "we understand the world as an interconnected ecosystem, a dynamic and developing whole, which has

---

57. Brown, "Ernst Lohmeyer's Kyrios Jesus," 21.
58. Pinnock, "Systematic Theology," 117.
59. Pinnock, "Systematic Theology," 117.

made this idea of God's immanence even more meaningful," and "easier for us to imagine God the Spirit everywhere working as creativity in the whole cosmic situation."[60] Pinnock is certainly unapologetic about his theological approach, moving from the scientific and philosophical climate of the day and reading God's economy back into Godself so that God is fitted into the Procrustean bed of today's scientific, philosophical worldview. The theological hazard that I want to indicate here is the modern turn facing away from God's transcendence and constructing theology primarily on God's immanence. The corrective to the previous theological bias toward God's transcendence should not give us the freedom to apportion more weight to God's immanence; rather, our effort must be to find a way to hold this intricate balance that may not overextend one category at the expense of the other.[61] I suggest as previously explained that the balance can only be achieved by recognizing the at-once-one-and-distinct principle as the key operating logic of God.

On a positive note, Pinnock is judicious about the way he connects God and the world. He comments, "Plainly God is not at the moment all in all—this has yet to happen when the kingdom comes (1 Cor 15:28)."[62] So, Pinnock eschews a panentheistic overtone that may blur the distinction between God and the world. For Pinnock, God is immanent in the world, and yet, he remains ontologically distinct from the world.[63] Also, to emphasize this asymmetrical relationship between God and the world, he notes that the world does not exist necessarily for God. Such a clear statement that is missing in Moltmann's writings help diffuse Pinnock from his critic's tirade against overly emphasized immanentism.

Nonetheless, Pinnock's excessive attention given to God's immanence undermines God's transcendence. For this reason, he is especially silent on how God's essence is correlated to God's economy. This is the second troubling aspect of Pinnock's dual polarity. Because God's aseity and God for us are distinguished without making any connection between the two, it seems that Pinnock's theological system is operating on two mutually distinguishable God, one as an absolute God who transcends the things of this

---

60. Pinnock, "Systematic Theology," 112.

61. This is well attested by Grenz and Olson. For more details, see, Grenz and Olson, *20th-Century Theology*, 11–23. Grenz and Olson present the cycle of tipping the scale between the immanence and transcendence of God that never ends.

62. Pinnock, "Systematic Theology," 114.

63. Pinnock, *Most Moved Mover*, xii.

world unaffected and unchanged, and the other as a relative God who is immanent in this world being affected and changed unlike the absolute pole of God. With such a clean break, I do not know how Pinnock can correlate the two. If he cannot, then we would end up with two Gods, one absolute and the other relative, which is unacceptable to any Christian theological agenda. I do not think that this is Pinnock's intention, but nonetheless, Pinnock has left an unbridgeable gap between God *in se* and God *pro nobis*.

The difficulties associated with the disconnected polarity of God can be teased out further with its cognate issue, the problem of God's simplicity and complexity.[64] Is God simple or complex? To put the matter in the right context, let us consider God's attributes. God has many attributes—e.g., God is holy, loving, just, good, and so on. If we say that these attributes are different aspects of God, then we are affirming the complexity of God. God is not made up of one attribute but many different attributes that are distinguishable from one another. By contrast, if we say that, despite these different attributes, God is essentially one, and therefore, God's attributes are of one qualia of God, whatever it may be (e.g., God's infiniteness). In this case, God's different attributes are consolidated into a simple property of his infiniteness so that God's simplicity is affirmed.

As Steven J. Duby's insists, the bulk of Christian scholarship sides with harmonists, and the doctrine of divine simplicity is considered orthodox in the past and in today's Evangelical circles.[65] However, Pinnock is taking a different stance. He is accentuating divine complexity more so than divine simplicity. Even though he acknowledges that God is simple in essence, Pinnock pays more attention to God's complex dealing with the world he created. For him, God is complex because he has restrained himself from the God of simplicity and freed himself to be differentiated and varied just like us. Pinnock's defiance to the program of divine simplicity, in my opinion, aggravates the divine simplicity-complexity controversy. Although he has done a great service to Christian theology by blowing the clarion to wake us up from our ignorance to the complexity of God,[66] because he has marginalized the doctrine of divine simplicity, his theology cannot be taken seriously.

---

64. For a historical analysis, see Christopher Hughes's *On a Complex Theory of a Simple God* and Everett Ferguson's *Doctrine of God and Christ in the Early Church*.

65. E.g., Duby, *Divine Simplicity*, 34–54.

66. For instance, Pinnock's work could be a good counterargument against Alvin Plantinga. See Plantinga, *Does God Have a Nature?*, 1–126. Plantinga flat out rejects the idea of God having "complex" properties.

We must keep them both while avoiding the concept of divine dual polarity. As I have pointed out already, we cannot have two polarities in God that are mutually exclusive. So, in order to avoid this fallacy, we need to move beyond the either-or mindset and say that God is always at once simple and complex. This is God's trinitarian ontology. If God's essence is trinitarian, which I believe it is, then God's attributes are also at once simple and complex. If we understand this trinitarian logic as God's logic, belonging only to God's life, which is wholly different from our logic, we can accept the fact God can be at once loving, holy, just, and good, without blurring their distinction. In other words, God's holiness, love, justice, and goodness identify one another, although they have their own distinguishable characteristics. For this reason, in today's divine simplicity-complexity discussion, the doctrine of the Trinity needs to be qualified even more as the key motif of this theological discourse.

4. Is God social? For Pinnock, God is indeed social. He writes, "Trinity means that shared life is basic nature of God. God is perfect sociality, mutuality, reciprocity and peace."[67] He adds, "Social Trinity means that there are three Persons who are subjects of the divine experiences . . . God is constituted by three subjects, each of whom is distinct from the others and is the subject of its own experiences in the unity of one divine life."[68] In his other writing, he emphasizes the threeness of God. "These [three persons of the Trinity] are three distinct ways of God's being present in the world; three ways that are grounded in God's eternal being."[69] As we can see here, Pinnock is essentially endorsing social trinitarianism.

In today's theological ethos, social trinitarianism is in high demand. As Kevin Giles notes, it is undoubtedly one of the favorite theological lenses through which Christian scholars view God and the world. The reason behind the resurgence of social trinitarianism is very complex. It has taken Giles several published works to trace its roots and delineate the basic contours of social trinitarianism that color today's theological landscape, so I will not attempt to do the same here.[70] In brief, social trinitarianism reappropriates the relational logic used by the early Christian thinkers vis-à-vis

---

67. Pinnock, *Flame of Love*, 31.

68. Pinnock, *Flame of Love*, 34.

69. Pinnock, *Most Moved Mover*, 28.

70. For more details, see Kevil Giles' work such as *The Rise and Fall of the Complementarian Doctrine of the Trinity*, *Eternal Generation of the Son*, and *The Trinity and Subordinationism*.

the social language of modern philosophy. Due to its claim of orthodox heritage rooted in the patristic trinitarian thought,[71] social trinitarians enjoy unimpeded explorations in the world of community-oriented theology and its method. Being a trinitarian, Pinnock takes a ride on the bandwagon of social trinitarianism, and he does not hide his affiliation with the large crowd of social trinitarians. Pinnock, I believe intentionally, follows this crowd to revamp his doctrine of God, even though he is aware of many troubling aspects of social trinitarianism such as subordinationism and tritheism.

Due to these troubling aspects of social trinitarianism, there is an on-going debate that is creating a sizeable rift in the Evangelical camp. The rift has spread to even the social trinitarian camp itself. Largely, it has divided into two sides. On the one side are egalitarians and on the other complementarians. Egalitarians tend to accentuate mutuality, reciprocity, and equality amongst three individuated subjects of the Trinity, whereas complementarians highlight the functional and subordinated role of the individuated persons of the Trinity. Egalitarians are spearheaded by well-known scholars such as Jürgen Moltmann, Stanley Grenz, Millard Erickson, Miroslav Volf, Leonardo Boff, and Elizabeth Johnson. The major proponents of complementarians, though it seems they are less popular amongst the Evangelicals, are Bruce Ware and Wayne Grudem. Situated in this theological ethos, Pinnock has pitched his tent near the egalitarian camp, though he has taken up some of the positions from the complementarian camp as well.[72]

Because of Pinnock's meddling with social trinitarianism, I see several difficulties associated with his theological program. I mention two. First, Pinnock is focusing more on the individuated personalities of the Godhead than their unity. The key motivating factor for social trinitarians is the identification of individual roles of each person in the Godhead. Pinnock writes in this regard, "God is constituted by three subjects, each of whom is distinct from the others and is the subject of its own experiences in the

---

71. Rightly so, Lewis Ayres does not see any relationship between modern social programs and the trinitarian language of the patristics. Ayres, *Nicaea and Its Legacy*, 409.

72. Steven Studebaker sees a hint of subordinationism in Pinnock's work. He explains, "Although the intent is otherwise, however, conceiving the primary work of the Spirit in terms of empowerment extends a subordination of the Spirit in christological thinking and in the doctrine of grace." Studebaker, "Integrating Pneumatology and Christology," 5–20.

unity of one divine life."⁷³ This statement echoes the social trinitarians who argue that each divine person possesses his own will, feeling, and energy of operation. Without such well-distinguished individual qualities, it is difficult for social trinitarians to talk about the sociality of God. Pinnock is doing the same thing. He is trying to recover the individuated experience of each person all the while unifying them as a social network of divine experience. At this point, we may ask: Does God have one will, feeling, and energy of operation or three wills, feelings, and energies of operation?

We cannot create three different wills, feelings, and operations in God. If we do, we are treading in the water of tritheism. There is only one will, feeling, and operation in God. Although I am not comfortable with Barth's language of "three modes of being" with one absolute subjectivity, I agree with his theological simplicity that affirms God's one mind, will, and energy of operation.⁷⁴ Indeed, the single personal attribute makes more sense if we follow the logic of the Trinity, that is, God is at once one and three, than three differentiated qualia. Let me unpack its significance in terms of the doctrine of appropriation.

From the perspective of divine appropriation, we can say that the redemptive work (e.g., the energy of operation) applies to all three persons. The logic of the Trinity is constituted always by the principle of identity. The principle of identity ensures that whatever is predicated on one person must be predicated on all three persons both absolutely and relatively. Thus, according to the principle of identity to which God adheres, each person is equally operating as the redeemer of the world. However, there is a distinction that comes with the principle of identity. The distinction is already included in the logic of the Trinity along with its unity. Thus, according to the principle of distinction, there is a unique quality of the redemptive work assigned to each person. For instance, the Father is the sender of the redeemer, the Son is the redeemer who carries the burden of the cross, and the Spirit is poured out upon all flesh to continue with the legacy of Jesus' redemptive work. What I want to point out here is that, as we recognize the distinction in the way God operates, we must also recognize the oneness of such operation. The three persons of the Godhead—the Father, the Son, and the Holy Spirit—at no point in time or out of time can be wholly differentiated as three individuated subjects. We are dealing with one subject, that is, God's subjectivity, which is distinguished into three persons, who

---

73. Pinnock, *Flame of Love*, 35.
74. McCormack, "The Doctrine of the Trinity after Barth," 100.

appropriate the single subjectivity in a unique qualifying way according to the logic of the Trinity.

The second issue I want to cover is Pinnock's socialism underwriting God's ontology. For Pinnock, God's sociality is God's Trinity, and vice versa. He asserts that "the Trinity is a society of persons united by a common divinity."[75] He goes on and says that "God's nature is internally complex and consists of a fellowship of three."[76] This sounds good, if we want to read from the Trinity human social life as equal and mutually reciprocating. However, the divine trinitarian relationship is never socially driven. It is driven by the logic of at-once-one-and-three. Here, we must understand that our sociality is never at-once-one-and-many. We are always differentiated one in the many. We are individuated subjects who have different views and agendas. We can come together under a unifying theme, perhaps, for a short while, forming a community, but always, we end up going our own ways as separate individuals. In our world, there is no such thing as pure social equilibrium. So, we cannot define God with the concept of sociality. Nor can we say that God is communitarian like us. What underwrites God's relational ontology is not the idea of sociality but the logic of the Trinity.

God is relational because the Father presupposes and anticipated the Son and the Spirit from eternity to eternity. There is no point in time in which the Father does not presuppose or anticipate the Son or the Spirit. It is the same for the Son and the Spirit. Of course, despite this ontological communicability, there is incommunicability between the three persons. The incommunicability that I am thinking of is the fatherhood that the Son or the Spirit cannot be. Likewise, the sonship belongs only to the Son and the spirithood the Holy Spirit. The unique quality of the fatherhood or the sonship cannot be erased, even if we say that they are united in the spirithood of the third person. For this reason, we must recognize that there is an order in God, or what I deem a unique sequential logic of God. The Father is the firstness of God. The Son is the secondness of God. And the Spirit is the thirdness of God. This sequence cannot be undone or re-sequenced.

Moreover, granted that this divine eternal sequence could be easily translated as the self-subordination, in which the Son and the Spirit become the second and the third in the order of God respectively, we need to understand that there is no such thing as ontological subordination in God. The divine sequence is God's own way of making himself distinct, not

---

75. Pinnock, *Flame of Love*, 35.

76. Pinnock, *Flame of Love*, 35.

a way to introduce a hierarchy in God. As Torrance has said, the language of "father" must be treated analogically.[77] It cannot strictly read off as the head of the household to which the rest of the family members must follow. At the same time, we cannot erase the priority that the term "father" implies. Though the fatherhood is from the language of God's economy, it nonetheless reveals God's firstness in the order of his being.

At this point, I want to make myself clear that I am not dismissing the importance of the communitarian relationship that God desires. God wants to relate himself to us and he garners the mutual relationship with and among us. Although I do not agree with those who contend that the world is a necessary component of God's life because God has willed in himself to create the world,[78] I accept the fact that the world is an object of God's love. It is not because God's creation necessitates God's outreach but because God has freely decided to involve us in his life. Thus, as the Bible testifies, God is the God of love (e.g., 1 John 4:8). From the very start of creation he has reached out to us in love, and ever since, he has been caring and overseeing the affairs of the world.

The point I am trying to make is that the communitarian life of God is a direct reflection of God's self-transcending love. Accordingly, God wants us to maintain a communitarian life in love, developing a healthy relationship between God and humanity, and amongst ourselves (Mark 12:30–31). His demand does not come from any social agenda, but from his logic of grace. God out of his self-giving love wants to develop a sharing relationship with us, and we should do the same. This is why God is moved by his pathos to be with us, and Jesus and the Holy Spirit, even now, reveal God's pathos so that we can truly participate in God's order of love. It seems that Pinnock may have confused communitarianism with the logic of love. The two are certainly related but nonetheless not the same. The latter is of God's essence and the former a philosophical ideal that we impose upon ourselves.

5. Can God know the future? With this question, Pinnock along with the newly forged guild of open theists wrought havoc in the Evangelical

---

77. Although we should treat the language of "father" analogically, we cannot replace it with other "metaphor," such as "Spirit-Sophia" or "God as Mother." We must consider the language of "father" the primary language because it is a "revealed" metaphor. We should not indiscriminately substitute a revealed metaphor with our own concepts, taking advantage of metaphorical flexibility.

78. This is a citation from McCormack's 2011 Kantzer Lectures, "God Who Gracely Elects."

theological camp. Traditionally, no one has doubted or questioned God's exhaustive foreknowledge. As a matter of fact, as Romans 8:29 clearly states, Christians had been satisfied with the idea that God foreknows and predestines those who are to be confirmed to the image of the Son. Following the revolutionary new perspectives on Pauline writings, however, Pinnock dismisses this received view and claims that the biblical verses pertaining to the foreknowledge of God were never given as a means to solidify a doctrinal creed for the Christian audience.

Pinnock is not the only one to argue this way. For instance, N.T. Wright claims that Paul's mention of predestination and foreknowledge has to do with Paul's way of connecting the dots between the election of Israel predicated upon the acceptance and keeping of the covenantal relationship with God and the election of all those who are in Christ—it concerns more of the present faith decision than what God has already determined at some point in eternity.[79] Such a new perspective on Paul frees Pinnock and his open theist colleagues to move away from a deterministic reading that we have inherited since Augustine and adhere to a more flexible and open view of God. As a result, Pinnock has embraced the Arminian-Wesleyan teachings and made himself a partner to free will libertarianism.

As a free will libertarian, Pinnock emphasizes that we are able to make choices because there is a buffet of things that we can choose from. Where did all these options come from? For Pinnock, it came from God. God is the source of all our possibilities, which implies that God also makes choices.[80] Pinnock's argument makes sense only if God's knowledge is open and not exhaustive. If God is not open but deterministic, God does not need to operate based on reviewing the vast spectrum of possibilities out there. This is what Bruce McCormack claims. McCormack countering free will libertarianism states that God's will and knowledge are immediate.[81] There is no gap between them. What this mean is that God carries out what he knows and God knows what he is carrying out. For McCormack, there is no "possibilities" in God. I believe, to some extent, he is right. If we were to introduce "possibilities" to God, we would put God under the matrix of

---

79. Wright, *Justification*, 67.

80. Pinnock, "Constraint by Love," 153.

81. This is a citation from McCormack's 2011 Kantzer Lectures, "God Who Gracely Elects." McCormack addresses this issue in-depth in his treatment of "The Being of God as Gift and Grace."

probability. In other words, if God has to choose from mere possibilities, God needs to operate on the best possible scenario at all times.

The optimized work of God may sound good to us, for God seems to be doing what is best for us, but actually it is deleterious to God's order. If God is working with an infinite number of possibilities, calculating his statistics to see which outcome is the most rewarding for us all, we have a God of chance. A God of chance is not exactly a God who is all-powerful. If he needs to resort to a probable action, always risking a chance of failure, even if he succeeds most of the time, God has to abdicate his throne. This is not a God we expect to find in the Bible, or in the teachings of our early Christian thinkers. The God of the Bible is always dependable and faithful, fulfilling his promises and knowing the exact outcome of every event. Surely, as the Calvinist camp would agree, the plenitude of scriptural testimonies about God's sure knowledge of the future ensures us that there is a sense of determinism pertaining to God's plan and action.

However, unlike McCormack, I believe that God makes "real" choices. Although his choice does not depend on an infinite number of possibilities, nonetheless, he makes choices because there are options for him to choose from. For instance, in the Book of Genesis, there is a statement that reveals that God knows good and evil (Gen 3:22). The implication of this statement is that God knows himself as well as the things that do not belong to God. Because God has knowledge of not only himself but also the things that do not belong to him, God makes a choice, at least, for the sake of sorting out the good from the evil. Moreover, once God makes a decision, he stays on it, and for this reason, his plan always comes to pass (Matt 24:35).

To reiterate, from a broad perspective, God's knowledge entails two options—e.g., good and evil.[82] Thus, contra McCormack, there is a gap between God's knowledge and God's will, for God does not always do what he knows; regardless of God's knowledge of evil, God can only be good. This does not mean that what God knows is irrelevant to God. God knows evil so that he can counter it with that which is good—e.g., God himself. That is to say, God's knowledge of evil is also an act that accords with God's nature, that is, grace. By the logic of grace, God moves out of his own sphere and counters the evil for the sake of transforming the world into something that which is good, conforming to the image of Christ.

---

82. This does not mean that God does not know the "infinite" number of possibilities that exist between these two options. Because of God's at-once (or eschatological) principle, all possibilities in this world can be narrowed down to these two options.

With this in mind, let us go back to Pinnock. Pinnock is right to say that not only is God free but also we are free. However, as McCormack warns, we must make sure that our liberty and God's freedom are not the same. We operate based on possibilities but God on the logic of surety. Nevertheless, we must account for free actions of free agents that accompany God's deterministic plans. How to reconcile the two? Pinnock's way is obvious. He removes God's foreknowledge and makes God's operation entirely indeterministic. In this way, Pinnock is able to say that God is free to make decisions without determining ahead what the future may be, and we are free because we are living in an open, indeterminate world.

Countering this view, compatibilists may say that God's free will and determinism can coexist.[83] We do not need to dismiss determinism for the sake of preserving free will. How can they coexist? Compatibilists have put forth many different theories,[84] but to simplify their argument, let me give an example. We know that the winter is coming soon after the fall. With it comes snow and road hazards. This is determined. There is no change. However, despite the pre-set cycle of seasonal activities, we do things freely, enjoying "new" snow every year and going through "unforeseen" road hazards that come with winter. So, there is a truth to compatibilism. Determinism and free will could coexist.

However, when it comes to God's foreknowledge, compatibilists are not at their best. Philosophically, they have good standing theories, but theologically, it is not precise. The key issue that I have with them is their inability to address the contingency factor in God. If we keep the idea of "free will," we must address God's contingency since God, though he may be deterministic, is working in conjunction with a free willing agent who is unpredictable. I could reframe this issue with the following questions. How does God elect? Does he ground his election on our free will or his own determined will? If we say the former is true, then God's election is contingent upon our free choice. We are saved not by God but our action. If we say the latter, we are back to determinism. In dealing with God, from a compatibilist perspective, it is impossible to take a middle position. At best, like Arminians, theological compatibilist could say that God knows what we are going to choose, and he determines his plan accordingly. Still,

---

83. Fischer, "Compatibilism," 44–84.

84. For a list of different theories, see Justin D. Coates and Michael McKenna's "Compatibilism" in Stanford Encyclopedia of Philosophy.

this idea would make God a contingent being who is dependent upon our choice. So, we fall back to the problem of libertarianism.

As for me, I am optimistic about finding an alternative solution that could eschew the errors of libertarianism and determinism, if we understand the order of God properly. What we need is to recognize that God is both deterministic and indeterministic. Without the introduction of God's duality, we cannot reconcile free will with determinism. To note, this duality is not like Moltmann's or Pinnock's order that creates a dual pole in God, because the principle of duality I propose is underwritten by the principle of identity, and vice versa. By this I mean that indeterminism in God is not an antithetical category of God's determinism, but rather a complementary category that supports God's determinism. As an illustration, let us consider the biblical concept of the book of life.

The book of life has been mentioned in several places in the Bible, but I focus primarily on two major aspects of the book of life in reference to God's election working in not only the past but also the future affecting the present.[85] The first aspect is the names written in the book of life that can be "blotted out" (e.g., Exod 32:33; Ps 69:28). The second aspect has to do with two types of the book of life. The one is plainly called the "book of life" (e.g., Luke 10:20) and the other the "Lamb's book of life" (e.g., Rev 21:27). These two books are eschatological. They are already but not yet. It is not yet since the book of life can be "blotted out," and it is already because the names recorded in heaven are fixed (e.g., Rev 3:5). Putting these two thoughts together, we can say that God is making adjustments to the book of life that has been already set in eternity. So, paradoxically, God is adding and deleting names written in the book of life. From what we have gathered thus far, we may say that the addition of the names transpires new life being born every day; thus, there is the existential divine self-communication taking place coming into the present from the future. Also, the deletion of the names transpires death of those who reject his invitation to his kingdom (Matt 22). But how can God add or delete if the book of life is already pre-determined?

Here, we need to pay attention to the Lamb's book of life, which is never altered. There is no mention of change. In fact, the Lamb's book of life is set from the foundation of the world (Rev 13:8). This aspect contrasts

---

85. A brief justification of relating the book of life and God's election is given by John Piper. For more details, see Piper, "Late Night Meditations on the Book of Life," lines 1–42.

well with the alterable book of life. It seems that God is working with two books, one alterable and another unalterable. So, from this analysis, we glean two aspects of God's work of election, one that is determined and the other in the process of being finalized. What I did not mention is that the book of life and the Lamb's book of life are not two separate books but one and the same book. We cannot say that God has two distinct books of life, because neither God's kingdom nor eternal life is more than one. Furthermore, there is a sequential logic involved with these two books, as the particularity of the Lamb's book of life is prior to the generality of the book of life, for the former is already and the latter is not yet. Logically, the book of "not yet" can never determine the book of "already"; rather, the reverse is true.

So, the order of God's election has two aspects that are inseparably linked. Let me unpack this further from a pneumatological perspective. On the one hand, God's election is universal. It is because the book of life is related to the Spirit of life. The universal work of the Spirit giving life is well attested in the Bible (e.g., Gen 1:2, 2:7; Job 33:14; Ps 33:6, 104:30; John 6:63; 1 Pet 3:18). Thus, God's election is for all as his Spirit is "over all and through all and in all" (Eph 4:6). Making a theological connection, we may label "the book of life" as the Spirit's book of life.

On the other hand, God's election is particular, for only those who are in Christ have a new life. This is well attested by Paul's declaration. "And if the Spirit of him who raised Jesus from the dead is living in you, he who raised Christ from the dead will also give life to your mortal bodies because of his Spirit who lives in you" (Rom 8:11). Or more specifically, Paul notes again that "the law of the Spirit of life in Christ Jesus has made me free from the law of sin and death" (Rom 8:2). So theologically, we can speak of the Lamb's book of life as the Spirit's book of life in Christ. Thus, the universal aspect of God's election is signified by the Spirit's book of life, and the particular aspect of God's election by the Spirit's book of life *in Christ*. What this means is that God's future is determined, and at the same time, open. It is determined because all those names that are in the Spirit's book of life in Christ have been set in stone—they will be saved for certain—although from our perspective, it remains veiled. At the same time, God's future is not yet determined, for God is not finished with the Spirit's book of life. It is working in progress, for God is continually creating life even in the future. Translated to our world, God's future in the form of the Spirit of creation and the Spirit of redemption is impacting our world as more lives, more invitations, and more outreach of the Spirit are given to the world. So, the work of election must be discussed in light of God's pneumatological-eschatological operation, that is, the principle of already but not yet in Christ. Because of the eschatological logic, the Spirit's work of creation and redemption extends from the future (and the past) to the present. If the Spirit is the Spirit of creation and redemption in the past and the present, he must be the same way in the future as well. His work of creation and redemption should not end but continue until the eschaton and beyond. This is why the future is open. God's creative and redemptive activity continues in the future, which is affecting us today. Consequently, the world is full of possibilities.

We are not out of the woods yet. If God is adding and deleting names in the book of life as we accept his offer of grace, is his salvific work contingent upon human free will? Understanding the order of God properly, I must re-emphasize that God's work of redemption is never dependent upon humanity or anything else in creation.[86] More specifically, God's salvation is not contingent upon human free will. As we have seen, salvation is granted only to those who are in the Spirit's book of life in Christ.

This means that God's work of salvation is christological and spiritual through and through. More clearly, God's election is processed through what the Spirit in Christ will do, that is, his affirmation of life for all those who are written in the Spirit's book of life in Christ. God does not look at our merits to determine our salvation (Luke 13:27). Had it been so, God's election could not have come about before the foundation of the earth, or in the future, or in eternity. The salvation is of the Spirit of life in Christ. It is not of us. For this reason, salvation does not depend upon human free will. It depends upon the work of the Father, the Son, and the Spirit. Then what is the role of our free will?

Our free will can only accept or reject the offer of grace. When we accept the offer, we are affirmed by the Spirit of life in Christ and have life to the fullest, and only in this respect are we made righteous before God and enjoy his salvation. Our free will does not enact or effectuate salvation. Again, salvation is of the Spirit and Christ sent by the Father. We move our free will only to enjoy what has been prepared for us by the Spirit and the Son sent by the Father.

---

86. God does not change his path because of what we say or do. Rather, God can make new paths for us all the while keeping the old path. A good illustration is the crossing of the Red Sea narrative (Exod 13:17—14:29).

Therefore, we can conclude that neither libertarianism, determinism, nor compatibilism can explain God's electing process. God's order of election is plainly christological, pneumatological, and eschatological. It is already determined and yet open to God's future activities. Without taking into account the duality of God's determinism and indeterminism, God's order of election cannot be fully understood.

In the final analysis, we cannot say that God does not have exhaustive foreknowledge. This logic is absurd, since God creates future, not vice versa. God is already always. There is no indeterminism in God's order of being. The "not yet" aspect of God that we are talking about is the logic of his grace. Because of his grace, God has opened up his shop in the future, continuing his unflagging effort to give more opportunities for us so that we can have not only life in this world but also life in Christ in eternity. His work continues into the future but there will be a time when the book will be shut, and the final tally be made. Until then, God embraces the not yet component of life, and because of it, he operates with the order of already-but-not-yet for us.

Concluding Remarks

In an attempt to clarify and finalize the order of God, I have critically reviewed God's order of pathos proposed by Moltmann and Pinnock, respectively. I had to confront each of these scholars due to the fact that they have marginalized God's order of pathos. Granted that both Moltmann and Pinnock gave their best to preserve the key components of Christian faith such as the doctrine of the Trinity, due to their incessant effort to disclaim and revise classical theism vis-à-vis social programs and "new" metaphysics of process, God's order has been reduced to the order of worldly affection. It is one thing to ignite a spark of interest for the order of God's pathos, but it is quite another to subsume God's pathos under the matrix of the world's process. God's order of pathos, as with all his orders, must start from himself. Starting with God's own order eschews the modern tendency to read God from the ways of this world. Of course, there is no way of getting around the reading of God from what is taking place in the world. However, in spite of it, we must recognize that God's order is never dependent upon the order of creation. God is who he is even when he decides to feel for and with us.

What does it mean to be "God is who he is" even when he displays his affection toward us? It means that God's order of ontology and God's order of pathos are the same. In other words, God's feeling is of God's essence. Thus, unlike Moltmann, God's love is purely positive. It makes no sense to introduce the negative dimension of pathos to God in himself. If suffering belongs to God's life intrinsically, then suffering either must be something positive or something that God cannot overcome. The former would do no justice to those who are suffering in extreme conditions. Surely, at times, suffering can be utilized by God to bring about renewal, but in and of itself, suffering must be treated negatively. Likewise, the latter would do no justice to God's order of being. He may be vulnerable for us, but he is not vulnerable against the power of darkness that brings suffering upon the world. God must be able to diffuse suffering, but if suffering is inherent in God, we are left with God who is not only incompetent but also impotent against evil and suffering. For this reason and many others, I had to deviate from Moltmann and Pinnock and opt for a renewed version of God's order of pathos that accounts for the principle of identity and duality underwritten by the logic of the Trinity.

Despite all the theological difficulties brought up by Moltmann and Pinnock, they make an important contribution to Christian theology. They have boldly explored the unknown territory of God's pathos and found the treasure trove of theological data that may service the Christian community for centuries to come. In an age of hopelessness, Moltmann found hope in God. In an age of indifference, Pinnock found loving care in God. In an age of *theologia gloriae*, Moltmann found *theologia crucis*. In an age of theological determinism, Pinnock found an open theism. Although the way they have fleshed out some of theological categories conflicted with my understanding of God's pathos, nonetheless they provide for this project valuable resources to rethink about the pathos of God.

Epilogue

Since I began with the discussion of order, it is appropriate to end with the same discussion, but nuanced differently. Rather than recapping what I had written, as a way forward, I offer a "new" theological order for the twenty-first-century audience. What I have in mind is calling theology a science, or in short, theological science. Because God can be configured in light of his own order, like a natural science that seeks to define a specific order of nature, theology in its own right should operate like a science. Undoubtedly, there are scholars who are skeptical of either calling theology a science or doing theology scientifically, for a good reason.[1] I will come back to this point later, but the burden is on me to lay out the specific scientific criteria of theology that justify theology's alignment with other scientific disciplines. For now, I return to the discussion of God's order.

We had talked about the need to account for the order of God, not because God must abide by our logic, but because God has his own logic that is strikingly different from ours, and at the same time, strangely coincides with certain aspects of the natural and human order. In my previous published work, I used the threefold analogy to describe this relationship—e.g., ontological analogy, personal analogy, and transcendental analogy.[2] The threefold analogy brings us back to the asymmetrical-symmetrical relationship between God and creation, the order of similarity in difference and difference in similarity. In dealing with God's order, we cannot avoid the fact that there are things we cannot know due to not only God's overwhelming greatness but also our own limitation that stems from depravity and ignorance. This fact automatically makes the differentiation between God and man necessary. Because of this infinite qualitative difference, we

---

1. E.g., Clayton, *Adventures in the Spirit*, 34.
2. Yom, *Number, Word, and Spirit*, 138–152.

cannot make the jump from the world to God. However, by God's grace, despite God's logic of "without us," God has come in the likeness of us, revealing himself through the natural processes and human history. Being in the world, God communicates in the language that we can understand, and for this reason, we are now able to approach God with confidence. The similarity thus has been established by God's logic of grace. So, we need both similarity and difference to understand God.

Having said this, I must admit that God's order of self-revelation, though toned down for us vis-à-vis the threefold analogy, is still filled with theological riddles and puzzles that baffle even the great minds of today. We may say that many of the riddles and puzzles are man-made rather than divinely incurred. Regardless, we need to burn midnight oil more than ever to figure out God's order and its implications that impact the whole spectrum of our thinking. Even with a few laws that I have laid out in this book, such as the principle of identity, the principle of duality, the order of sequence, and the logic of the Trinity, they are not the end but a mere provisional means to an end. They do not address all the questions and solve all theological problems that plague our generation. In spite of it, we must be persistent and continue with the intellectual journey so that we can draw ever closer to the precise ordering of God. In this respect, theology is a science.

My point here is that the scientific status of theology is not given but earned. Allow me to illustrate this point by sharing what I learned from the Barth-Scholz debate. There was a clash between Karl Barth, who was the defending champion of theology, and Heinrich Scholz, the philosopher of science who interpreted science (as well as theology) from a logical positivistic point of view. There was no winner in this debate in my view, because both parties did not try to make the conversation productive. On the one hand, Barth refused to hear Scholz's criticism and claimed that theology does not need to adhere to the demands from other scientific disciplines, whatever that may be, because it has its own logic. Barth was essentially opting for a ghetto theology. He privatized theology in such a way that he exempted theology from the critical examination of natural sciences. Barth had a good reason. Natural sciences, like logical positivism, dismissed the faith component of theology such as the belief in the biblical miracles, and Barth could not go along with it. On the other hand, Scholz was frustrated with Barth since he was calling theology a science. For Scholz, in order for theology to qualify as a science, it had to follow the scientific criteria of the day. Scholz had in mind the criteria of logical positivism, which adhered to a strict form of empirical verification. The debate was not successful, I would say, because the two scholars were speaking in two different languages.

Did we solve this problem already? I do not think so. Reading Andrew Moore's article recently, I found out that we are still debating over the same issue, trying to ascertain the scientific nature of theology.[3] As I have said in my other writings, the underlying issue is not theology ignoring the demands of natural sciences but the differences of worldview. Normally, when the conversation breaks down between theologians and scientists, the conflicting philosophical worldview is behind it. Scientists hold to a different worldview than theologians. As in the case of Scholz, he was talking to Barth from a logical positivist perspective. Scholz read science from a unique perspective and developed the scientific criteria out of strict empiricism, whereas Barth read science from a revelatory theological perspective. Barth's theological worldview, which includes divinely inspired miracles, and Scholz's logical positivism, which does not include miracles, had no common denominator that could translate each other's language.

Having said this, I sense that there is another problem that lurks behind the obvious differences in the way we view the world. Scholz touched upon it but never made an explicit statement about it. Interpreting Scholz's argument, I feel that theology must earn its scientific standing rather than just claim its status. Barth claimed that theology is a "received" work rather than a "constructive" enterprise that must adhere to the logic of human rationality, and for this reason, Scholz could not accept theology as a scientific discipline. In order for any theory to be accepted by a scientific community, according to Scholz, it ought to go through the rigors of fact-checking, and when the theory has gone through substantial corrections and revisions, it is accepted or rejected for the future use. Simply put, in Scholz's criticism against Barth, I see that if theology is to be called a science, it must earn its status rather than simply stating the fact that it is so.

Well, Scholz was right that theology needs to show its scientific criteria but he also misunderstood Barth. Barth had no intention of stating that theology is just a passive activity in which we do nothing but "receive" the theological claims without going through fact-checking. As George Hunsinger has shown, Barth was serious about critically appraising the work

---

3. Moore, "Theological Realism," 79–99. For my critical analysis of Moore's claim, see Yom, *The World of Open Systems*, 70–118.

of each theological proposition.[4] Barth scrutinized every theological claim and tested its viability against the coherent set of theological criteria he developed. What Scholz missed is that Barth was talking about contextuality when he asked for theology to work out the details of its own logic.

The idea of contextuality cannot be taken lightly. Here is why. For example, I play a game of soccer. Soccer has its own rules. It prohibits the player from using his or her hands, except for the goalie, who can use the hands only within its goal tending area that is clearly marked off from the rest of the field. However, when I go to the gym and play a game of basketball, the rule changes. I am no longer required to use the feet; rather, I must use my hands. Although some of the rules may overlap between soccer and basketball such as the criteria for scoring and fouling, the fundamental rule is different. For this reason, when we move from soccer to basketball, we cannot be doing the same thing. This is what Barth wants Scholz to see. Scholz asserted that Barth needs to play the game of soccer like everyone else. He disallowed him from playing his own game of basketball. However, Barth says that like soccer, basketball is a sport, though it has its own rules that are different from soccer. Soccer should not be the standard upon which we decide what sports are all about. So, the implication of Barth's claim is clear. Theology did earn its scientific status because it is playing its own game like science, though grounded on its own logic. It was wrong for Scholz to ask Barth to change the rules of theology to be like science. Had Barth done so, he would no longer be playing the game of theology, but the game of Scholzian science, which is not Barth's game.

Having said this, I also see Barth's fault of not providing the specifics of theological criteria that clearly outline the scientific status of theology. If theology is playing a game like science, what are its rules? What makes it unique, and at the same time, overlap with other sciences, if any? Barth did not work on this detail and left it to his readers, like Thomas Torrance and George Hunsinger, to figure them out for him. Thankfully, throughout Barth's writing, he left behind many traces of his rational criteria for theology. We just need to look for them and comb through his writings.

To make the matter more complicated, the understanding of science has changed since the debate. It is difficult to ascertain one common set of scientific criteria nowadays.[5] It is because there is not just one theory but

---

4. Hunsinger, *How to Read Karl Barth*, 49–54.

5. Clayton, "Philosophy of Science," 95–104. Clayton provides a short reflection on the nature of the past and the present scientific theories and practices. In the end,

multiple theories that explain what science is all about. After all, we are living in a postmodern world. No one single paradigm dictates the criteria of science. Besides, logical positivism is now passé, except for a few who still cling to it.[6] In today's philosophical ethos, it is safe to say that there is nothing "positivistic" about science anymore. Does this mean that there are no specific scientific criteria that we can work with? I am more optimistic than the current ethos of the philosophy of science. Being old schooled, I rely more on working scientists rather than metaphysicians who evaluate the trend based on a mere philosophical hunch. Meeting many working scientists in the field of engineering, chemistry, biology, and physics, I realize that working scientists hold to a conspicuous scientific worldview that guides their scientific activities. It may not be the same across the board, but nonetheless, it is the most respected rational criteria for science as far as I know. It is critical realism.[7] I have already worked out the details of critical realism in my previous writing, so I will not duplicate the work here but mention its key implications.

Critical realism, as the term suggests, has two aspects: the critical aspect and the realist aspect. At first sight, it may be easily mistaken that we have put together two antithetical components—i.e., what is of the mind and what is not of the mind. What is of the mind is the critical aspect of science that not only interprets the world around us through our own intellectual grid called "experience" but also constructs the world by adding our own creative work. By contrast, what is not of the mind is the realist aspect of science. It assumes that the world we interpret exists independent of the mind. More importantly, the world not only guides our observations but also shapes our frame of mind. Despite the difference between the critical and realist aspect of science, critical realism combines these two aspects into one single rubric of science that highlights the give-and-take transaction between the thing in itself and our experience of it. So, the ultimate

---

Clayton ends with six conclusive ideas of what science is all about: (1) science is not foundationalist; (2) science is not relative; (3) scientific rationality is fallible; (4) scientific facts are not the final truth; (5) science fundamentally explains the world; (6) theology and science work to *"make sense of one's total experience."*

6. For example, see Bas C. van Fraassen's *The Scientific Image*.

7. I am not alone in this fight for critical realism. Many theologians also adopt to this standard—e.g., Thomas F. Torrance, Alister McGrath, Janet Soskice, Wolfhart Pannenberg, John Polkinghorne, and Arthur Peacocke, to name a few. Of course, critical realism may be nuanced differently from one scholar to another, but nonetheless, due to their pragmatic approach to science, they are all respectable realists.

criterion of science is its critical examination of reality that demands not only the rigors of our systematic investigation of the thing in itself and the data we gleaned from studying it, but also "seeing" what the reality is revealing itself to us.

With the risk of oversimplification, I may sum up the complex nature of science in this way. From a critical realist perspective, science relies on the examination of the nature of things, which prescribes to the scientists the order and law it formulates. Hence, scientists bring together theory and data from making observations of the reality in question. In this scientific exercise, although theories, models, and laws are configured by the rational agent, the thing in itself is the guiding object that clarifies and even modifies the pre-existing concepts and ideas of reality. Thus, working scientists are, in a sense, dependent on the reality for resolving discrepancies, fallacies, and problems they created or inherited from the past. They look for an agreement between theory and data based on what the thing reveals itself to be. Though our interpretation of reality is always provisional since there is no one single theory that is able to explain the totality of reality, scientists are optimistic about finding "truths" about it because their work is guided by the thing itself.

What does critical realism have to do with theology? Well, in theology, critical realism is a dominant frame of reference for understanding God, humanity, and the world.[8] Despite the fact that theology performs its scientific work differently than natural sciences because of the inclusion of the God-factor, like any other science, it is underwritten by the critical investigation of "the things out there." It attempts to solve problems by studying what God the ultimate reality is revealing itself to us. Because God's self-revelation is the theological guide, theologians scrutinize their own theories, models, and claims critically and realistically. For this reason, the efforts in this book had been centered on revealing the true form of God's reality, or more specifically, the order of God.

I must conclude then that theology must engage the order of God, his logic, and ontological status, from which all other theological claims flow. It is because theology should be undergirded by God's own being and act. However, the current trajectory of Christian theology is that it is slowly deviating from doing theology critically and realistically—e.g., Christians are refusing to do theology scientifically. We must change this trend and pursue God on his own terms. We have been reading God on our own

---

8. McGrath, *Scientific Theology*, 195.

terms for too long. For this reason, theology has been excessively polarized. It is being stamped out from the mold of political, denominational, and traditional agendas. Of course, theology inevitably crosses the path with our political, denomination, and traditional creeds and policies, but it does not negate the need to pursue God's order on God's own terms. Theology in this respect needs renewal. It needs to be freed from the shackles of traditionalism and recover the proper theological parameters imposed by God himself. As A. W. Tozer has shown many years ago, the pursuit of God can only be done when we embark on a spiritual journey fixated on the very essence of God. Fixating on the very essence of God entails "deep calling unto deep."[9] In other words, it demands a spiritual communication between spirit and Spirit. Without it, we lose the true aim of theology, that is, our exploration of God who remains himself even in his act of revelation.

---

9. Tozer, *Pursuit of God*, 18.

Bibliography

Abraham, William J. *Crossing the Threshold of Divine Revelation*. Grand Rapids: Eerdmans, 2006.
Adams, Nicolas. "Rahner's Reception in Protestant Theology." In *The Cambridge Companion to Karl Rahner*, edited by Declan Marmion and Mary E. Hines, 217–26. New York: Cambridge University Press, 2005.
Anselm. "On the Fall of the Devil." In *Anselm of Canterbury: The Major Works*, edited by Brian Davis and G. R. Evans, 193–232. Oxford: Oxford University Press, 1998.
Aquinas, Thomas. *The Summa Theologica*. New York: Benziger Bros, 1948.
Augustine. *Concerning the City of God against the Pagans*. Translated by Gerald Walsh. New York: The Catholic University of America Press, 2008.
———. *The City of God*. Translated by Marcus Dods. Peabody: Hendrickson, 2009.
Ayres, Lewis. *Nicaea and Its Legacy: An Approach to Fourth-Century Trinitarian Theology*. New York: Oxford University Press, 2004.
Balthasar, Hans Urs. *The Theology of Karl Barth*. San Francisco: Ignatius, 1992.
Barth, Karl. *Church Dogmatics*. Edited by G.W. Bromiley and T.F. Torrance. London: T&T Clark, 1957.
———. "Lessing" in *Protestant Theology in the 19th Century*. Edited by John Bowden. London: SCM, 2000.
Bauckham, Richard. *Jesus and the God of Israel: "God Crucified" and Other Essays on the New Testament's Christology of Divine Identity*. Milton Keynes: Paternoster, 2008.
Berry, Christopher J. "The Kantian Revolution." In *Hume, Hegel and Human Nature*, 43–53. Springer, Dordrecht, 1982.
Bracken, Joseph A. *Society and Spirit: A Trinitarian Cosmology*. Toronto: Associated University Press, 1991.
Brown, Colin. "Ernst Lohmeyer's Kyrios Jesus." In *Where Christology Began: Essays on Philippians 2*, edited by Ralph P. Martin and Brian J. Dodd, 6–42. Louisville: Westminster John Knox, 1998.
Brown, David. *Divine Humanity: Kenosis Explored and Defended*. London: SCM, 2011.
Brueggemann, Walter. *Theology of the Old Testament: Testimony, Dispute, Advocacy*. Minneapolis: Fortress, 1997.
Brunner, Emil. *The Christian Doctrine of God: Dogmatics*. Translated by Olive Wyon. Philadelphia: Westminster, 1950.
Buber, Martin. *I and Thou*. New York: Bloomsbury Academics, 2013.
Bulgakov, Sergius. *Comforter*. Translated by Boris Jakim. Grand Rapids: Eerdmans, 2004.
Bultmann, Rudolph. *New Testament and Mythology*. Edited by Schubert M. Ogden. Minneapolis: Fortress, 1989.

Burhenn, Herbert. "Pannenberg's Argument for the Historicity of the Resurrection." *JAAR* 40 (1972) 368–79.
Calvin, John. *Institutes of the Christian Religion*. Translated by Henry Beveridge. Grand Rapids: Eerdmans, 2013.
Castelo, Daniel. *Apathetic God: Exploring the Contemporary Relevance of Divine Impassibility*. Eugene: Wipf and Stock, 2009.
Clayton, Philip. *Adventures in the Spirit: God, World, Divine Action*. Minneapolis: Fortress, 2008.
———. "Philosophy of Science: What One Needs to Know." *Zygon* 32 (1997) 95–104.
———. *The Problem of God in Modern Thought*. Grand Rapids: Eerdmans, 2000.
Cobb, John B. *God and the World*. Eugene: Wipf and Stock, 1998.
Coffey, David. *Deus Trinitas: The Doctrine of the Triune God*. New York: Oxford University Press, 1999.
———. "The Holy Spirit as the Mutual Love of the Father and the Son." *TS* 51 (1990) 193–229.
———. "The Spirit of Christ as Entelechy." *PT* 13 (2001) 363–98.
———. "The Theandric Nature of Christ." *TS* 60 (1999) 405–31.
———. "The Whole Rahner on the Supernatural Existential." *TS* 65 (2004) 95–118.
Coolman, Boyd Taylor. *The Theology of Hugh of St. Victor: An Interpretation*. New York: Cambridge University Press, 2010.
Cooper, John. *Panentheism—The Other God of the Philosophers: From Plato to Present*. Grand Rapids: Baker, 2006.
Cortez, Marc. *Embodied Souls, Ensouled Bodies: An Exercise in Christological Anthropology*. New York: T&T Clark, 2008.
Creel, Richard. *The Divine Impassibility: An Essay in Philosophical Theology*. Eugene: Wipf and Stock, 1986.
Crisp, Oliver D. *Divinity and Humanity: Incarnation Reconsidered*. New York: Cambridge University Press, 2007.
Cross, Terry L. *Dialectic in Karl Barth's Doctrine of God*. New York: Peter Lang, 2001.
Davis, Stephen T. *Logic and the Nature of God*. Grand Rapids: Eerdmans, 1983.
De Lubac, Henri. "A Way toward the Determination of the Relation of Nation and Grace." *PT* 11 (1999) 381–94.
Diller, Kevin. *Theology's Epistemological Dilemma: How Karl Barth and Alvin Plantinga Provide a Unified Response*. Downers Grove: Intervarsity, 2014.
Dillistone, Frederick William. *C. H. Dodd, Interpreter of the New Testament*. Grand Rapids: Eerdmans, 1977.
Dodd, C. H. *The Parables of the Kingdom*. New York: Charles Scribner, 1961.
Dombrowski, Daniel A. *A History of the Concept of God: A Process Approach*. Albany, State University of New York, 2016.
Duby, Steven J. *Divine Simplicity: A Dogmatic Account*. New York: T&T Clark, 2016.
Feinberg, John S. *No One Like Him: The Doctrine of God*. Wheaton: Crossway Books, 2001.
Ferguson, Everett. *Doctrine of God and Christ in the Early Church*. New York: Grand, 1993.
Fischer, John Martin. "Compatibilism." In *Four Views on Free Will*, edited by Ernest Sosa, 44–84. Malden: Blackwell, 2007.
Gavrilyuk, Paul. *The Suffering of the Impassible God: The Dialectic of Patristic Thought*. Oxford: Oxford University Press, 2004.

Giles, Kevin. *The Eternal Generation of the Son: Maintaining Orthodoxy in Trinitarian Theology.* Downers Grove: Intervarsity Press, 2012.

———. *The Rise and Fall of the Complementarian Doctrine of the Trinity.* Eugene: Cascade, 2017.

———. *The Trinity and Subordinationism: The Doctrine of God and the Contemporary Gender Debate.* Downers Grove: Intervarsity Press, 2002.

Grenz, Stanley J. and John R. Franke. *Beyond Foundationalism: Shaping Theology in a Postmodern Context.* Louisville: Westminster John Knox, 2001.

Grenz, Stanley J. and Roger E. Olson. *20th-Century Theology: God and the World in a Transitional Age.* Downers Grove: InterVarsity, 1992.

Grenz, Stanley J. *Theology for the Community of God.* Grand Rapids: Eerdmans, 1994.

Griffin, David Ray. *A Process Christology.* Philadelphia: Westminster, 1973.

Habets, Myk. "Prolegomenon: On Starting with the Spirit." In *Third Article Theology: A Pneumatological Dogmatics,* edited by Myk Habets, 1–20. Minneapolis: Fortress, 2016.

Hall, Basil. *John Calvin: Humanist and Theologian.* London: Historical Association, 1967.

Hallman, J. M. "The Seed of Fire: Divine Suffering in the Christology of Cyril of Alexandria and Nestorius of Constantinople." *JECS* 5 (1997) 369–91.

Hart, David Bentley. "No Shadow of Turning: On Divine Impassibility." *Pro Ecclesia* 11 (2002) 184–206.

Hector, Kevin W. "God's Triunity and Self-Determination: A Conversation with Karl Barth, Bruce McCormack and Paul Molnar." *IJST* 7 (2005) 246–61.

Heschel, Abraham J. *The Prophets.* New York: HarperCollins, 1962.

Hughes, Christopher. *On a Complex Theory of a Simple God: An Investigation in Aquinas' Philosophical Theology.* Ithaca: Cornell University Press, 1989.

Hunsinger, George. "Barth on What It Means to Be Human." In *Karl Barth and the Making of Evangelical Theology: A Fifty-Year Perspective,* edited by Clifford B. Anderson and Bruce L. McCormack, 139–56. Grand Rapids: Eerdmans, 2015.

———. *How to Read Karl Barth: The Shape of His Theology.* New York: Oxford University Press, 1991.

Jaegar, Werner. *Padeia: The Ideals of Greek Culture.* Translated by Gilbert Highet. New York: Oxford University Press, 1965.

Johnson, Eric L. "Should the God of Historic Christianity Be Replaced? In *God Under Fire: Modern Scholarship Reinvents God,* edited by Eric L. Johnson, 11–41. Grand Rapids: Zondervan, 2002.

Johnson, H. Wayne. "John 4:19–24: Exegetical Implications for Worship and Place." Presented at the Annual Meeting of the Evangelical Theological Society, Baltimore, 2013.

Kant, Immanuel. *Critique of Pure Reason.* Translated by J.M.D. Meiklejohn. London: Colonial Press, 1900.

Karkkainen, Veli-Matti. *The Doctrine of God: A Global Introduction.* Grand Rapids: Baker, 2004.

Kelly, J. N. D. *A Commentary on the Epistles of Peter and Jude.* London: Adam & Charles Black, 1969.

Kilby, Karen. *Karl Rahner: Theology and Philosophy.* New York: Routledge, 2004.

Kim, Kirsteen. *The Holy Spirit in the World: A Global Conversation.* Orbis: Maryknoll, 2007.

LaCugna, Catherine. *God for Us: The Trinity and Christian Life*. New York: HarperCollins, 1991.
Loder, James Edwin, and W. Jim Neidhardt. *The Knight's Move: The Relational Logic of the Spirit in Theology and Science*. Colorado Springs: Helmers & Howard, 1992.
Macchia, Frank. *Baptized in the Spirit: A Global Pentecostal Theology*. Grand Rapids: Zondervan, 2006.
Matera, Frank. "New Testament Theology: History, Method, and Identity." *The Catholic Biblical Quarterly* 67 (2005) 1–21.
Mays, William J. *Whitehead's Philosophy of Science and Metaphysics: An Introduction to His Thought*. The Hague: Martinus Niihoff, 1977.
McCormack, Bruce L. "The Actuality of God: Karl Barth in Conversation with Open Theism." In *Engaging the Doctrine of God*, edited by Bruce McCormack, 185–244. Grand Rapids: Baker, 2008.
———. "The Doctrine of the Trinity after Barth: An attempt to Reconstruct Barth's Doctrine in Light of His Later Christology." In *Trinitarian Theology after Barth*, edited by Myk Habets and Phillip Tolliday, 87–120. Cambridge: James Clarke & Co., 2012.
———. "God Who Gracely Elects." Kantzer Lecture at Carl F. Henry Center for Theological Understanding, Trinity Evangelical Divinity School, Deerfield, 2011.
———. "Seek God Where He May Be Found: A Response to Edwin Chr. van Driel." *SJT* 60 (2007) 62–79.
McDonnell, Kilian. *John Calvin, the Church, and the Eucharist*. Princeton: Princeton University Press, 1967. 221.
McGrath, Alister E. *Christian Theology: An Introduction*. Malden: Blackwell, 2007.
———. *The Order of Things: Explorations in Scientific Theology*. Malden: Blackwell, 2006.
———. *Scientific Theology: Nature*. Grand Rapids: Eerdmans, 2001.
———. *Scientific Theology: Reality*. New York: T&T Clark, 2006.
Meeks, Douglas. *Origins of the Theology of Hope*. Minneapolis: Fortress, 1974.
Michaels, J. Ramsey. *The Gospel of John*. Grand Rapids: Eerdmans, 2010.
Miller, Ed L. "Salvation-History: Pannenberg's Critique of Cullmann." *The Iliff Review* 37 (1980) 21–25.
Molnar, Paul D. "Can the Electing God be God without Us? Some Implications of Bruce McCormack's Understanding of Barth's Doctrine of Election for the Doctrine of the Trinity." *NZSTR* 49 (2007) 199–222.
Moltmann, Jürgen. *The Crucified God*. London: SCM, 1974.
———. *The Experiment Hope*. Eugene: Wipf and Stock, 1975.
———. *In the End—The Beginning: The Life of Hope*. Translated by Margaret Kohl. Minneapolis: Fortress, 2004.
———. *The Spirit of Life: A Universal Affirmation*. Minneapolis: Fortress, 2001.
———. "Theology as Eschatology." In *The Future of Hope: Theology as Eschatology*, edited by Frederick Herzog, 1–25. New York: Herder and Herder, 1970.
———. *The Trinity and the Kingdom: The Doctrine of God*. Minneapolis: Fortress, 1993.
Moore, Andrew. "Theological Realism and the Observability of God." *IJST* 2 (2000) 79–99.
Nash, Ronald H. *The Concept of God: An Exploration of Contemporary Difficulties with the Attributes of God*. Grand Rapids: Zondervan, 1983.
Neville, Robert Cummings. "Naturalism and Supernaturalism in American Theology." *AJTP* 26 (2005) 77–84.
Nietzsche, Friedrich. *The Will to Power*. New York: Barnes and Nobles, 2006.

Nix, Echol, Jr. *Ernst Troeltsch and Comparative Theology.* New York: Peter Lang, 2010.
Olson, Roger E. "Was Karl Barth a Universalist? A New Look at an Old Question." *Patheos* http://www.patheos.com/blogs/rogereolson0133/was-karl-barth-a-universalist-a-new-look-at-an-old-question.
Pannenberg, Wolfhart. *The Historicity of Nature: Essays on Science and Theology.* Edited by Niels Henrik Gregersen. West Conshohocken: Templeton Foundation, 2008.
———. *An Introduction to Systematic Theology.* Grand Rapids: Eerdmans, 1991.
———. *Jesus—God and Man.* Translated by Lewis L. Wilkins and Duane A. Priebe. Philadelphia: Westminster, 1977.
———. "Salvation-History." *The Iliff Review* 37 (1980) 21–25.
———. *Systematic Theology.* Translated by Geoffrey W. Bromiley. London: T&T Clark, 1991.
———. *What Is Man?: Contemporary Anthropology in Theological Perspective.* Minneapolis: Fortress, 1970.
Peters, Ted. *God—The World's Future: Systematic Theology for a New Era.* Minneapolis: Fortress, 2015.
Pinnock, Clark H. "Constrained by Love: Divine Self-Restraint according to Open Theism." *PRS* 34 (2007) 149–60.
———. *Flame of Love: A Theology of the Holy Spirit.* Downers Grove: Intervarsity, 1996.
———. *Most Moved Mover: A Theology of God's Openness.* Grand Rapids: Baker, 2001.
———. "Systematic Theology." In *The Openness of God: A Biblical Challenge to the Traditional Understanding of God,* 101–25. Downers Grove: Intervarsity, 1994.
Piper, John. "Late Night Meditations on the Book of Life." *Founder and Teacher of desiringGod.org* (October 2017). https://www.desiringgod.org/articles/late-night-meditations-on-the-book-of-life.
Plantinga, Alvin. *Does God Have a Nature?.* Milwaukee: Marquette University Press, 1980.
Poythress, Vern S. *Logic: A God-Centered Approach to the Foundation of Western Thought.* Wheaton: Crossway, 2013.
Rahner, Karl. *Foundations of Christian Faith: An Introduction to the Idea of Christianity.* New York: Crossroad, 1982.
———. *Theological Investigations.* New York: Crossroad, 1991.
Ricoeur, Paul. *Fallible Man: Philosophy of the Will.* Translated by Charles Kelbley. Chicago: Henry Regnery, 1965.
Rowe, C. Kavin. *Early Narrative Christology: The Lord in the Gospel of Luke.* New York: Walter de Gruyter, 2006.
Sartre, Jean-Paul. "Bad Faith." In *Jean-Paul Sartre: Basic Writings,* edited by Stephen Priest, 206–20. London: Routledge, 2001.
Shults, F. LeRon. *Reforming the Doctrine of God.* Grand Rapids: Eerdmans, 2005.
Spinoza, Baruch. *Theological-Political Treatise.* Translated by Michael Silverstone. New York: Cambridge University Press, 2007.
Stone, Jerome A. *Religious Naturalism Today: The Rebirth of a Forgotten Alternative.* Albany: State University of New York Press, 2008.
Studebaker, Steven M. "Integrating Pneumatology and Christology: A Trinitarian Modification of Clark H. Pinnock's Spirit Christology." *Pneuma* 28 (2006) 5–20.
Teilhard de Chardin, Pierre. *Activation of Energy.* Translated by Rene Hague. New York: Harcourt, 1976.
Thiessen, Henry C. *Lectures in Systematic Theology.* Grand Rapids: Eerdmans, 2003.
Tillich, Paul. *The Courage to Be.* New Haven: Yale University Press, 2000.

Titus, Eric J. "The Perfection of God in the Theology of Karl Barth: A Consideration of the Formal Structure." *Kairos* 4 (2010) 203–22.
Torrance, Thomas F. *The Christian Doctrine of God: One Being Three Persons*. New York: T&T Clark, 1996.
———. *Divine and Contingent Order*. Edinburgh: T&T Clark, 1981.
———. *The Ground and Grammar of Theology*. New York: T&T Clark, 2001.
———. "Karl Barth," *SJT* 22 (1969) 1–9.
———. *Karl Barth, Biblical, and Evangelical Theologian*. Edinburgh: T&T Clark, 1990.
———. *Theological Science*. Oxford: Oxford University Press, 1969.
———. *Theology in Reconstruction*. Eugene: Wipf and Stock, 1996.
Tozer, A.W. *Pursuit of God*. Sudbury: Wyatt North, 2013.
Van Fraassen, Bas C. *The Scientific Image*. Oxford: Clarendon, 1980.
Ward, Graham. "Barth, Hegel and the Possibility for Christian Apologetics." In *Conversing with Barth*, edited by John C. McDowell and Mike Higton, 53–67. Aldershot: Ashgate, 2004.
Ward, Keith. *The Christian Idea of God: A Philosophical Foundation for Faith*. Cambridge: Cambridge University Press, 2017.
Warfield, Benjamin B. *Revelation and Inspiration*. Grand Rapids: Baker, 1991.
Wax, Trevin. "The Justification Debate: A Primer." *Christianity Today* 6 (2009). http://www.christianitytoday.com/ct009/june9.34.html.
Weinandy, Thomas. *Does God Suffer?*. Notre Dame: University of Notre Dame Press, 2000.
Weinstein, Galina. *Einstein's Pathway to the Special Theory of Relativity*. Newcastle upon Tyne: Cambridge Scholars, 2015.
Welker, Michael. *God the Spirit*. Translated by John F. Hoffmeyer. Eugene: Wipf and Stock, 1994.
Whitehead, Alfred North. *Process and Reality*. Edited by David Ray Griffin and Donald W. Sherburne. New York: Free Press, 1978.
Wright, N.T. *Justification: God's Plan and Paul's Vision*. Downers Grove: Intervarsity, 2009.
Yom, Aaron. *Number, Word, and Spirit: Rethinking T. F. Torrance's Theological Science from a Pneumatological Perspective*. New York: Peter Lang, 2018.
———. *The World of Open Systems: Re-appropriating Four Foundational Themes of Christian Theology from an Interdisciplinary Perspective*. Austin: Sentia, 2018.

Index

abandonment theory, 131
absolute spirit, 60, 76, 106-7
actualism, 44, 47, 59, 62
actus primus, 96
adoptionism, 56, 63, 139
aitia, 65
analogia fidei, 45
Anselm, 108
anthropological equation, 9
Aquinas, 92-93, 97
Arminianism, 103
Augustine, 1, 33, 69, 72, 102-3, 149

Balthasar, Hans Urs von, 43, 45
baptismal formula, 1, 52
Barth, Karl, 5-35, 39-60, 62, 70-71, 74, 77, 80, 82-83, 88, 90-91, 126, 146, 158-160
Bauckham, Richard, 132
biblical theology, 70, 91
Boff, Leonardo, 145
Bracken, Joseph, 34-35
Brown, David, 138, 141
Bulgakov, Sergius, 59-60, 63-69, 75

Calvin, 14, 25, 103, 106, 140
Cappadocian Fathers, 1
Castelo, Daniel, 116, 120
Catholic theology, 82-84
Christian theism, 135, 137
christocentrism, 9
Christology, 8, 10, 12, 28, 36, 52, 77, 93, 116, 145
classical theism, 117-8, 135, 155
Clayton, Philip, 42, 157, 160-1
Cobb, John, 34

Coffey, David, 5, 26-42, 58-62, 64, 66, 69-76, 82-99, 104-6, 108, 113-4, 131-2, 134
cognitive constructivism, 71
coherentism, 49
compatibilism, 151, 155
complementarianism, 145
complexification, 29, 32, 34
Copernican Revolution, 2
Cortez, Marc, 8
Creel, Richard, 117
critical realism, 16-17, 161-2
Cullman, Oscar, 18

Deism, 112
descending Christology, 59, 98, 101, 105
de-spiritualization, 107-10, 115
determinism, 37, 103, 150-2, 155-6
dialectical theology, 52, 120-1
doctrine of appropriation, 74, 146
dual telos, 99
dualism, 18, 72-4, 79, 114
Duby, Steven, 143
duplex ordo, 85, 88

economic Trinity, 37, 51, 54, 56-57, 61, 67-68, 70-79, 91, 129, 130, 134
egalitarians, 145
emanation, 66, 68, 77
empirical determination, 15
Enlightenment, 3, 114
epistemological order, 64, 113
Erickson, Millard, 145
eschatology, 120
Evangelical theology, 82, 84

Index

Feuerbach, Ludwig, 12
fideist, 21, 49, 50
finitum capax infiniti, 83, 93
finitum non capax infiniti, 83
formal logic, 16
foundationalism, 47–48
Franke, John, 48

general history, 18–19
geocentricism, 2
Giles, Kevin, 66, 144
glorification, 38
godforsakenness, 121–4, 131–4
Grenz, Stanley, 3, 5, 23, 32–33, 48, 82, 84, 98–107, 110, 113, 118, 120, 142, 145
Griffin, David, 34
Grudem, Wayne, 145

Habets, Myk, 59
hamartiology, 98, 101, 105
Hegelian idealism, 12
Heideggerian existentialism, 12
heliocentric model, 2
Hellenic philosophy, 1, 117
hierarchism, 57, 63, 65, 88
Holder, Rodney, 10
hominization, 29, 36
homoousion, 52, 61–64, 68
Hugh of St. Victor, 2
Hunsinger, George, 9, 11, 21–22, 44–46, 49, 160
hypostatic union, 29–30, 54, 62, 91–97, 127

imago Dei, 83
immanent Trinity, 37, 51, 54–56, 61, 67–68, 70–73, 75, 77–78, 81, 91, 129, 130, 134
immutability, 116, 129
impassibility, 116–117, 122, 129, 135, 137
Incarnation of Christ, 30
indeterminism, 152, 155
infralapsarianism, 37
intellectua fidei, 47
intellectualism, 20
irrationalism, 21, 50

isolationism, 21

Jenson, Robert, 50
Johnson, Elizabeth, 60, 117, 145
justification, 5, 36–38, 48, 83, 93, 111, 152

Kant, 2, 9, 43, 72
Kelly, J. N. D., 27
kenosis, 138–9, 140
Kirsteen, Kim, 112
koinonia, 127

LaCugna, Catherine, 78
Laplace, Pierre-Simon, 3
laws of nature, 3, 6
liberalism, 11–12
libertarianism, 149, 152, 155
logical positivism, 158–61
logos asarkos, 52–54, 62, 66, 68, 122
Logos Christology, 93
logos incarnandus, 53–54, 62, 66, 68, 79, 122
Lonergan, Bernard, 70
Lubac, Henry de, 84–88

Marxist, 119
material causality, 105, 109, 114
McCormack, Bruce, 50–59, 61, 71, 146, 148–51
McDonnell, Kilian, 140
McGrath, Alister, 4, 14, 16, 74, 161–2
metaphysics, 9, 122, 136–7, 155
modernism, 2–3, 11
Molnar, Paul, 57–59, 61, 71
Moltmann, Jürgen, 5, 13, 23, 78, 118–37, 142, 145, 152, 155–6
monergism, 108–9
Monophysitism, 94
mutual love theory, 69, 75, 131
mutuality of God, 75–76

natural analogy, 4, 15, 22, 35–36, 40–42
natural science, 15, 17–18, 157
natural theology, 7–8, 12–15, 22, 33, 40, 49, 83
naturalism, 12, 17, 39

Neoplatonic philosophy, 65
Nestorian, 94
Neville, Robert, 13
Nicene Creed, 52, 62
Niebuhr, Reinhold, 101
Nietzsche, Friedrich, 25
nouvelle theologie, 85, 88

objectivism, 44
objectivist realism, 44, 48, 71
occasionalism, 90
Olson, Roger, 3, 19, 23, 118, 120, 142
Omega Point, 29
omni-causality, 137
omnipotence, 26, 137-8
ontological order, 43-79
ontology, 5, 34, 56, 63, 68, 78, 81, 93, 113, 118-9, 122, 125-6, 128, 130, 136, 144, 147, 155
open theism, 37, 118, 135, 156
order of duality, 114
ordo salutis, 36, 108-9

Pannenberg, Wolfhart, 13, 18-24, 48-50, 100
pantheism, 6
particularism, 8-13, 22, 44-47, 50, 58-60, 83
passibility, 5, 116-118, 129-30
pathos, 116
patristic theology, 72-73
personalism, 39, 44
Peters, Ted, 22-23
phenomenology, 9, 12
Pinnock, Clark, 5, 118, 135-152, 155-6
Platonism, 1
pneumatological logic, 77
pneumatology, 59, 61, 64, 68-69, 77, 121
postmodern theology, 4
postmodernism, 22
predestination, 36-37, 149
prelapsarian state, 111
principle of analogy, 6-7, 35, 38
principle of duality, 30, 37, 40, 42, 52, 55, 58, 73-74, 77, 88, 94-95, 114, 152, 158

principle of identity, 33-34, 40, 42-43, 50-63, 67, 73-75, 95, 118, 125-7, 130, 133, 137, 140-1, 146, 152, 156, 158
process metaphysics, 136-7
Pseudo-Dionysius, 93
Putnam, Hilary, 42

radial energy, 28-29
Rahner, Karl, 5, 13, 28-31, 72-73, 82-96, 104-105, 108, 113, 129
rationalism, 11, 44-45, 47, 50, 58-59
realism, 159
Reformation, 83, 103

salvation history, 10, 18-22
sanctification, 38, 91-92, 97, 112
Sartre, Jean-Paul, 114
Schaeder, Erich, 20
scientia generalis, 17
scientia specialis, 17
scientific reductionism, 12
scientism, 17
self-transcendence, 24
semi-Pelagianism, 103-4
sensus divinitatis, 14
social trinitarianism, 144-5
Spinoza, Baruch, 3, 6, 116
spiritual entelechy, 28-29, 32
spiritual order, 59
spiritualism, 11
staurocentric trinitarianism, 118
Stones, Jerome, 24
subordinationism, 56, 65, 145
supernatural causality, 6
supernatural elevation, 87, 90, 92, 95-97, 104, 112, 114
supernatural end, 30, 85-90, 92
supernatural existential, 83-91, 94-99, 105, 108-9, 113-4
supralapsarianism, 37
synergism, 108-9

theandric nature of Christ, 62, 91-97
theologia archetypa, 81
theologia crucis, 156
theologia ectypa, 81
theologia gloriae, 156

theologia perennes, 81
theory of emergence, 28
theory of evolution, 12, 27
theory of relativity, 15–16
Thiessen, Henry, 60
thing-in-itselfness, 43, 126
threshold crossings, 32
Tillich, Paul, 25
Torrance, Thomas, 4, 14–18, 21, 46, 52, 62–63, 70, 79, 148, 160–1
total depravity, 25, 84, 90, 98, 101–5, 113
transcendence, 4, 11, 14, 24–27, 29, 31–33, 36–40, 76, 82, 85–86, 97, 106, 111, 119–21, 141–2
transcendentalism, 11
trinitarian logic, 61–62, 123, 128–9, 144

trinitarian ontology, 5–6, 31, 82, 91, 95–100, 102, 104–110, 113–114, 127
trinitarianism, 124, 144–5
tritheism, 63, 129, 145–6

universalism, 19, 89–90
utopianism, 119

Volf, Miroslav, 145

Ware, Bruce, 145
Warfield, B. B., 40–41
Weinandy, Thomas, 130
Welker, Michael, 78, 107, 113
Whitehead, Alfred North, 34–36, 79
Wright, N. T., 111, 149

www.ingramcontent.com/pod-product-compliance
Lightning Source LLC
Chambersburg PA
CBHW071454150426
43191CB00008B/1344